THE LIBRARY The Library is operate
owned subsidiary cor

University of Ulster at Magee

Due Back (subject to recall)

- 9 APR 2008		
= 9 APR 2008		
0 1 OCT 2012		

Fines will apply to items returned after due date

100500301

ANTHONY SHAY

❦ Choreographic Politics

State Folk Dance Companies, Representation, and Power

WESLEYAN UNIVERSITY PRESS
MIDDLETOWN, CONNECTICUT

Published by Wesleyan University Press, Middletown, CT 06459

© 2002 by Anthony Shay

All rights reserved

Printed in the United States of America

5 4 3 2 1

Library of Congress Cataloging-in-Publication Data

Shay, Anthony, 1936–
  Choreographic politics : state folk dance companies, representation, and power / Anthony Shay.
    p. cm.
Includes bibliographical references (p.   ) and index.
  ISBN 0-8195-6520-2 (cloth : alk. paper) — ISBN 0-8195-6521-0 (pbk. : alk. paper)
  1. Dance—Government policy. 2. Dance companies—Government policy. 3. Folk dancing—Government policy. I. Title.
  GV1588.45 .S5 2002
  793.3'1—dc21   2001008180

For all of the men and women dancers, musicians, and choreographers of folk dance ensembles around the world who have made my life a joyful dance, and especially for Nena and Misa Sokcic who, for more than thirty years, have shared their passionate love of Croatian folklore with me

Contents

	Preface	ix
	Acknowledgments	xv
	Introduction: Ethnicity and Nationalism	1
1	Parallel Traditions: State Folk Dance Ensembles and Folk Dance in the Field	13
2	Anatomy of a Dance Company	38
3	The Moiseyev Dance Company: Ancestor of the Genre	57
4	Ballet Folklorico: Viva Mexico!	82
5	LADO, Ensemble of Folk Dances and Songs of Croatia: Proper Peasants	108
6	Egypt: Bazaar of Dance	126
7	Greece: Dora Stratou Greek Dances Theatre, A Living Museum	163
8	Turkish State Folk Dance Ensemble: The Last of the Great Ensembles	193
9	Conclusion: The Power of Representation	224
	Notes	233
	Bibliography	251
	Index	263

Preface

At the outset of this study, I must, in this period of scholarship in which self-reflexivity is much the fashion, confess that I am a folk dance ensemble junkie. Everyone has a circle of friends who shake their heads in wonder at one among them who is what I call an "old movie junkie." That individual is the one who watches endless reruns of *Gone with the Wind*, *The Wizard of Oz*, *Sunset Boulevard*, or *The Women* and can quote or sing chapter, line, and verse from the entire film, often with the original inflection and stress. That individual has spent many happy hours watching and studying old celluloid masterpieces, and with each revisit of the old masterpiece he or she finds a new nuance of dialogue or a detail of decor or gesture never before noticed.

In the field of folk dance company watching, I am that individual. I have spent over forty years and thousands of happy hours watching performances and rehearsals, viewing reruns of films and tapes, and pouring over souvenir programs that I have lovingly collected of folk dance ensembles from all over the world. I grew up in a primarily Latino suburb of South Central Los Angeles and later on a remote ranch in Central Oregon, where I never dreamed of the rich life of dance that awaited me. In 1954, when I was seventeen years old, my family was forced to return to Los Angeles because of a disastrous fall in agricultural prices. I spent the rest of that decade running from classes at Los Angeles City College and UCLA to community halls and playgrounds to participate in a wide variety of folk dance activities. I attended Greek picnics sponsored by Saint Sophia's Greek Orthodox Cathedral; I spent time in grubby Greek nightclubs on Hollywood Boulevard dancing with Greek sailors who knew no English and watching belly dancers. Dressed in a dashing Huszar costume, I was the only non-Hungarian member of the Pearly Bouquet Hungarian Dance Company (of the Hungarian community center) directed by Laszlo Tabanyi, a former character actor of the pre–World War II Hungarian film industry. I danced the *dabka* while attending *haflas* (parties) at the local Syrian Orthodox church that showed old Egyptian films, featuring such famous belly dance luminaries as Samiya Gamal and Tahia Carioca, and I spent happy hours at the Fez cabaret listening to Arabic music and watching more belly dancing. I also spent many happy hours with fellow students from Latin America in mambo parties at Virginia's nightclub and enjoyed folk dance evenings at the Serbian church, learning Turkish folk dances from Turkish students and Iranian dances from Iranian students. I danced Russian, Ukrainian, Hungarian, and Greek dances with the Gandy Dancers, a then prominent group of local folk dance enthusiasts. As a dancer in many amateur companies, culminating in my own experiences as a dancer in professional folk ensembles as well as numerous marching bands, I was hooked on what historian William H. McNeill characterized as "'muscular bonding,' that is, the human emotional response to moving rhythmically together in dance and drill" (1995, vi). It is a deeply emotional response that is difficult to convey to one who has never experienced it.

In 1956, Tanec of Macedonia and KOLO of Serbia, the first of the Eastern European national state dance ensembles to tour America, arrived on our shores. I danced the choreographies of Serbia and Croatia learned from KOLO, the Serbian state folk dance ensemble, with the Yosemite Workshop, a group of local dancers, who, like myself, fell in love with the spectacle of that company during the 1956 tour. As one Yosemite member put it, speaking of the choreographies we had learned from the dancers of KOLO, "if the third girl from the left sneezed, the third girl from the left in our group also sneezed." We spent hours reproducing, in loving detail, the costumes we had seen in the KOLO performances, or we bought them from Narodna Radinost, a Belgrade-based concern that sold Serbian costumes. We threw ourselves into teach-yourself Serbo-Croatian grammars. We gave a joint concert with Sokoli, a San Francisco-based company of like-minded folk dancers, accompanied by the Hajduks, a local *tamburica* orchestra of South Slavic background.

My life was changed forever. In 1958 the Iranian Students Association of America invited me to attend its annual convention in Minneapolis. There I prepared and participated in a performance of folk songs and dances for the Shah of Iran and Ali Amini, the Iranian ambassador to the United States. Three months later I was in Iran, a student at the University of Tehran, beginning my first steps in my lifelong love of fieldwork, choreographing and performing traditional dance arranged for performance venues.

Whenever possible I spent days and months in Zagreb, Belgrade, Budapest, Sofia, Samarqand, Bukhara, Mexico City, Tashkent, Tehran,

Cairo, Istanbul, Ankara, Athens, Brussels, Moscow, St. Petersburg, Baku, Paris, London, and Vancouver, as well as several cities in the United States to see performances, attend workshops and rehearsals, visit and study museum collections of folk life and costumes, and amass a library of books, programs, and memorabilia. Sometimes these state dance companies gave obscure performances in odd corners of the world that I luckily happened to find out about. For example, Bakhor, the Uzbek state folk ensemble, gave one unadvertised performance in San Francisco in 1985 for the American-Soviet Friendship Society that I managed to catch, and the Georgian State Folk Company performed in our hotel in Moscow in 1989. On one memorable evening in the summer of 1971, LADO (the Croatian state folk dance ensemble), Tanec (the Macedonian State Folk Ensemble), and KOLO (the Serbian state folk ensemble) all performed in the small Slovenian resort of Koper in what was for me a once-in-a-lifetime opportunity to see all three companies in one program and make comparisons.

I was spurred on in my decision to undertake this study when I discovered that most of these major ensembles, which have dominated the world stages for more than five decades, received scant, if any, mention in the *International Encyclopedia of Dance*. This major scholarly undertaking covered two decades of hard work by scores of dance scholars. The massive six–volume work contains a single article on Igor Moiseyev, with little to no mention of the other companies or their founding directors. One might look in vain for mention of Zvonko Ljevakovic, perhaps Croatia's most famous choreographer. Amalia Hernandez, arguably the most famous Mexican choreographer in the world and whose career has spanned a half-century, can be found, with some diligence, under "Mexico," subheading "Dance Companies," sub-subheading "Folklore Ballets." Two short paragraphs chronicle and sum up Hernandez's contributions to Mexican dance. These influential volumes contain considerable coverage of "in the field" dance in most areas of the world—an editorial nod to world dance and the Rest. But the professional state ensembles and their voluminous creative work have been largely ignored in favor of a narrow and detailed focus on Western theater dance forms and Western dance forms in other parts of the world, or "authentic" dance in the field. The bulk of the entries address in admirable detail both major ballet soloists, companies, and choreographers and obscure modern dance companies and choreographers whose works have been seen by a few aficionados in lofts in New York, London, and Berlin. This intense scholarly focus on Western dance traditions stands in stark contrast to the lack of attention given to national folk dance companies, which were viewed by millions of enthusiastic audience members around the world throughout the second half of the twentieth century.

To some extent, I blame myself for these lacunae. I incorrectly assumed, while I was writing my contributions to the *International Encyclopedia of Dance* on dance in the field in various parts of the Middle East, that the editors must surely have approached more knowledgeable experts to write articles on these various national companies. This study is an attempt to begin addressing this scholarly gap.

Since this book focuses on the primary topic of representation, and due to the sheer volume of national companies that can provide examples, I had to carefully select from among them six of the state folk ensembles to illustrate the theoretical points concerning representation that I make in this study. I chose to analyze in some detail those companies with which I was most familiar and had seen multiple times over a period of several decades, observing the development of new work that often signaled political, social, and economic changes in their respective nation-states. Moiseyev and Ballet Folklorico, for example, have toured the United States at least ten times during the past thirty years. I also saw these companies in their home cities and other locations such as World's Fairs in Brussels and Seattle. Each time they appeared I attended their performances, often more than once, night after night when that was financially possible. Since I did not own an automobile in my earliest years of viewing these ensembles in the 1950s and 1960s, I spent many nights walking the long distance home from these performances after the buses I depended on ceased to run.

An exception to this practice of choosing companies with whom I had more or less intense familiarity is the national company of Turkey. I decided to approach one company about which I knew nothing to test the assumptions that I present in this study. I had been to Turkey before the founding of the national company and had seen a great deal of enthusiastic, professional-level amateur dance activity in Istanbul in 1968 and again in 1976. The opportunity to approach a company that I had never seen and could view with fresh eyes and insights was a very tantalizing prospect. I was not disappointed with this decision, for what I observed in Ankara fit into the overall pattern of this work. When I entered the rehearsal hall at the Ataturk Cultural Center in Ankara, and the dancers and musicians began to rehearse, a feeling of nostalgia and being in my own milieu of forty-five years of folk dance, a wondrous sense of having come home, swept over me. It was as if my whole life came together in that single instant.

After my return from Iran in 1960, I directed two major local professional folk dance companies, performing and creating choreographies and stagings. I received inspiration from both numerous forays in the field and examples provided for me by such artistic geniuses as Professor Zvonko Ljevakovic, the founding artistic director of LADO. Thus, I do not occupy the position of a distanced, objective participant-observer of the positivist persuasion seated in a tent at night jotting notes about distant natives. As is the case with many dance ethnologists, I was drawn into the area of scholarly research through my embodied and passionate commitment to artistic and social participation in traditional folk dance. While rejecting claims to objectivity, I feel strongly that those years of participation have provided me with a unique lens through which I may view the representational strategies of these ensembles. That embodied experience of staged performances has sharpened my observational and analytical ability to see past the spectacle of performance, the glamour of the costumes, and the dazzle of the footlights. This enables me to provide a unique analytical picture of the performances of these ensembles—viewed through a trained angle of observation, informed by the practice of performing—and allow the reader to see the multilayered representations that make the performances of these ensembles so fascinating and compelling.

Acknowledgments

This study would not have been possible without the help and input of many people. For many years I have thought of how I might repay the many artists from whom it has been my pleasure to learn, so this study stands as a tribute to their artistry and generosity. I hope that it fulfills, in some small part, the trust and friendship they have so kindly given me. I must begin by thanking the many dancers, choreographers, and staff members of the many state folk ensembles with whom I have interacted over the past forty years. I have spent many pleasurable hours with hundreds of individuals, many of whom I count as cherished friends, throughout the many years that I have observed these companies. Many of them have given me gifts of books, recordings, programs, teaching, and above all, time. Many of these individuals from the older generation are now elderly, retired, or deceased, but the memory of their many talents informs this study.

From Mexico, the renowned choreographer Amalia Hernandez many years ago (1961) "loaned" me several dancers to show me how to dance the dances from her *Veracruz* choreography. Tomas Quiroja and Gabriel Loyo not only taught to me the steps and figures from *Veracruz*, but they also talked extensively and enthusiastically about their experiences in Ballet Folklorico de Mexico and what it was like to work with Hernandez. This encounter led to a series of journeys to Mexico City to watch the venerable company in the Bellas Artes, Ballet Folklorico's home theater, where I studied Amalia Hernandez' work in detail. More recently I must thank Mr. Julio Solorzano-Foppa, impresario and spokesperson for the company, who generously shared crucial details of the company's operations. Long-time friend and colleague Gema Sandoval, artistic director and choreographer of Floricanto Danza/USA provided insights into the folklorico movement in California, in which she participated from its inception, and kindly read and commented on early drafts of that chapter. Serena Tripi generously facilitated my most recent contacts and interviews with Ballet Folklorico. The office of Friedson Enterprises, Ballet Folklorico's representative in the United States, kindly provided photographs, slides, and other materials.

In Croatia, many members of LADO have been unstinting in their sharing of information about the ensemble's operations, giving interviews, teaching, and hosting me for more than thirty years. Nevenka (Nena) and Mihovel (Misa) Sokcic, Bozo and Andela Potocnik, Vlado and Ana Kelin, Ljubomir and Mira Tunukovic, and Ivica Dabac have been friends, hosts, and supporters for the long years in which I showed an interest in their artistry. Misa and Nena Sokcic, especially, spent many long hours in the field finding sets of costumes for me and even sacrificed on a financial level to ensure that the costumes reached me in the United States because of—as Misa wrote in a letter to me dated October 15, 1999—my "love and interpretation of Croatian folklore." Dr. Stjepan Sremac, former managing director of the company and an outstanding folklorist, also provided hours of conversation about the mechanics of running the company and the philosophical issues of staging folklore during the 1992 LADO tour of North America. The late Professor Zvonko Ljevakovic graciously allowed me to attend weeks of classes and rehearsals with LADO in 1968 and many subsequent years. All of the members of LADO throughout the years have been unstinting in their sharing, especially during the weeks I traveled with them on their 1992 North American tour, which was made particularly stressful for them because of the war with Serbia. The late Ivanka Bakrac, a curator with the Ethnographic Museum in Zagreb, gave me many private interviews, tirelessly answering my endless questions concerning the proper wearing of the costumes, giving tours of the museum and its remarkable costume collection, and providing a number of valuable publications. Emil Cossetto, composer and arranger, gave me a personal signed copy of his masterpiece, *Ladarke*, with permission to perform it. Bozo Potocnik, former musical director of LADO, kindly gave me several of his coveted arrangements of folk songs with permission to perform them.

In Tashkent, the late Mukarram Turganbaeva, founding director of the Bakhor Folk Dance Ensemble of Uzbekistan, talked to me at length and graciously permitted me to film the Bakhor ensemble in six intensive days of interviews, rehearsals, and workshops, and she also provided tours of the company's wardrobe and backstage workings in 1976. In 1987 and 1989, the company again hosted members of my company and gave me access to files, programs, and publicity materials as well as permission to attend rehearsals and performances. The Uzbek Friendship Society arranged for me to have master classes in Samarqand and in Tashkent with the legendary Galiia Izmaelova. They also arranged for an inspiring meeting with the late Tamara Khanom, perhaps the most famous Uzbek dance artist in history, who also granted an interview. I also thank the staff and students of the *koreografski instituti* (conservatories for dance) in Tashkent and Baku for spending long hours in interviews and for sharing class time with me.

In Bulgaria, in 1968, Philip Koutev gave me the run of his rehearsals and, as he ushered me into his rehearsal chamber in which forty-four of the finest voices in Bulgaria were assembled, asked, "What would you like us to sing for you?" "Everything," I breathed, and as they sang I thought surely there is a heaven. The late Iliya Rizov, former principal dancer with the ensemble, stayed at my home in 1970 and gave me many long interviews about life in the Bulgarian State Ensemble of Folk Dances and Songs (known in America as the Philip Koutev Ensemble).

For his insights on the history and inner workings of Bayanihan, the Philippine national ensemble, and other Filipino dance companies, I thank my colleague and friend, Patrick Alcedo.

From Iran, I am grateful to Farzaneh Kaboli, former soloist with the Mahalli Dancers, for a lengthy interview. Mohammad (Saidabadi) Nejad and Hayedeh Changizian also supplied information about the inner workings and history of the company. Jamal, my partner and co-artistic director of the AVAZ International Dance Theatre, not only reviewed the Iranian portion of the study, but as always, gave helpful insights and sage advice throughout the process of writing this study.

I wish to express my deep gratitude to a pioneer in the field of Egyptian oriental dance, Jamila Salimpour, who through the years has sent me countless videos of Egyptian dance and introduced me to her wide acquaintance. Shareen el Safy, editor of *Habibi Magazine,* shared her extensive knowledge of the *danse orientale* in Cairo with me and gave me valuable advice. Tambra provided me with an introduction to Mahmoud Reda, the founding artistic director of the Reda Troupe.

In Egypt, Mahmoud Reda, the pioneer in choreographing Egyptian dance for the stage, generously gave me his time and shared his experiences and insights. Abdul Rahman Al-Shafie gave several interviews and arranged for me to attend rehearsals of the Musicians of the Nile ensemble, which he directs. Both gentlemen provided me with photographs. Morocco (Carolina Varga Dinicu) provided valuable historical information, friendship, videotapes, and newspaper articles, and led me through the intricacies of the Egyptian dance world as well as the twisted pathways of the Cairo bazaar.

Acknowledgments

In Greece, Dr. Alkis Raftis, president of the Dora Stratou Greek Dances Theatre, the national company of Greece, spent valuable hours and days in interviews and discussions that were always challenging and enlightening. His store of knowledge of Greek history, folklore, and ethnography are truly awe-inspiring; his friendship and generosity were some of the unforeseen bonuses of this project. He kindly read drafts of and offered suggestions for the chapters on Egypt and Greece. His staff put up with my presence for days on end while I perused the ensemble's extensive library collections, and Adiamanta Angelis and other staff members patiently accepted my intruding presence in the Dora Stratou offices for several weeks. Over the years, my dear friend Vilma Matchette, who passed away recently, and whose deep friendship and long conversations on folk dance and costumes I will sorely miss, shared her knowledge of the inner workings of the Greek immigrant community, which I drew on for the development of that section of Chapter 7. She also gave me a valuable collection of old dance programs. I also thank Athan Karras for his insights into both the Dora Stratou Greek Dances Theatre, with which he danced, and the Greek immigrant and folk dance communities in which he has taught extensively.

In Turkey, Mustafa Turan, the artistic director of the Republic of Turkey State Folk Dance Ensemble (Turk Devlet Halk Danslari Toplagantu) and recipient of the prestigious title of State Artist, provided interviews, printed materials, and videos, and arranged for me to attend rehearsals and performances of the ensemble in Ankara. He kindly kept his patience in check and even encouraged me while conducting our discussions in my halting Turkish. Dr. Kaan and Pam Edis, friends for more than forty years, allowed me to engage them in hours of discussion and hosted me in Istanbul, introducing me to many individuals who voiced their opinions on the topic of the national dance ensemble.

Here in the United States, I am grateful to my colleagues in the dance field for selecting me as one of the recipients in the first round of the James Irvine Foundation Dance Fellows, a singular honor and one that permitted me the opportunity to travel extensively. The Social Sciences Research Council awarded me a fellowship to undertake important aspects of this study in the Middle East in Turkey and Egypt. The International Research and Exchanges Board (IREX) provided funding to travel to Zagreb. I thank my friends, colleagues, and mentors Dale Eickelman, Jennifer Fisher, Paul Gelles, Robert Georges, Sally Ann Ness, and Nancy Lee Ruyter for their continuous support. Jennifer Fisher encouraged me to expand and develop a lecture for her class into this book. Barbara Sellers-Young made this book a richer document through her generous suggestions. Jim La Vita donated stimulating discussions about folk dance. My gratitude to Wesleyan editor-in-chief Suzanna Tamminen for guiding the book to its finish. I wish to also thank my editor, Yvonne Ramsey, for the meticulous attention to detail that she gave this book.

Finally, I thank all of the dancers and musicians who have performed in my own companies during the past forty years. I am particularly grateful to the years of friendship and the courage that Penny Kamin Baker, Mario Casillas, and Sherwin and Bonita Edelberg have given me when the chips were down. I also thank the members of my board who have served for many years and have generously contributed to my artistry: Ahmad and Pary Azad, Boualem Bousseloub, Sherwin and Bonita Edelberg, Norm Toback, and Conrad and Patricia Von Bibra. Of course my mother, Margaret (Peggy) Shay, and my sisters, Kathleen Walters and Penny Graves, lend me constant support. Because of all of these hundreds of individuals I have learned firsthand the day-to-day intricacies of how dance companies function and run.

Any errors are, of course, my very own.

Choreographic Politics

Introduction: Ethnicity and Nationalism

One evening in 1995 when the insurrection of hungry peasants in the Mexican state of Chiapas was front-page news and images of desperate masked rebels filled the television screens, I sat and watched a performance of the Ballet Folklorico de Mexico. The world-renowned national folk dance company of Mexico performed a dance in which a female octet danced liltingly around the stage wearing lacy black dresses covered with bright embroidered flowers and accompanied by a waltz-like melody from a huge marimba played by four men. I realized with a sense of shock that this lighthearted choreography was the popular Mexican state dance company's very different representation of Chiapas being shown before an enthusiastic audience of thousands at the Universal Amphitheatre in Southern California. The vast disparity between the CNN video clips of soldiers breaking down doors and randomly shooting at anyone moving in the villages of Chiapas and the breezy, carefree, romantically lit choreography occurring on the stage vividly called into question the role of state-sponsored folk dance companies and the politics of representation that they choreographically convey. The official program notes underscored my impression of unreality: "Chiapas. A land of fantasy where we dream of places that grow in tropical jungles; places where the dwellers are happy people who abound in musical inspiration and develop beautiful folk dances. . . . Their costumes are inspired by the tropical flowers, and they reflect the golden sands of the coast, and the majesty of the wooded mountains" (Ballet Folklorico de Mexico 1995a). These companies, and their spectacle and color, serve as unforgettable representative images of the nation-states they represent, and I wondered how many other viewers watching the panorama of colorful historical and regional dances of Mexico unfold before their eyes shared my thoughts. In the politics of representation, these state-sponsored dance companies serve up colorful dance programs representing an often highly essentialist portrait of their respective nation-states.

Thus, these state-sponsored professional dance ensembles represent "The Mexico" or "The Philippines" or "The Soviet Union" that the audience experiences. These cultural representations are in fact multilayered political and ethnographic statements designed to form positive images of their respective nation-states. They form and present elaborate and often highly spectacularized public relations statements, often of great subtlety and sophistication. As social scientist Gillian Bottomley observed about folk dance and representation: "Representation itself implies a kind of power, the power to define, to describe, to act on behalf of someone else. Describing particular forms of dance as 'folk dance' for example carries certain historical and political connotations" (1987, 1). These dance ensembles thus have the power to represent an entire nation.

That performance of Ballet Folklorico de Mexico crystallized the need to undertake this study, since over the years I have watched hundreds of such performances by dozens of state-sponsored dance companies the world over. Examples abound. Bayanihan, the national company of the Philippines, through its elegant and unforgettable choreographic depiction of Muslim life, belies the political strife and turmoil of the southern islands as Muslim Filipinos (Moros) seek to secede from the central government. Charming Tatar dances by the Moiseyev Dance Company shut out and glossed over, choreographically, the brutal reality of that ethnic group's shameful expulsion from its homeland during the Stalin period. The time has come to arrange these viewings into a coherent pattern, one that can be read as a social and political document in which dance plays a role in the intricate minuet of international politics and diplomacy, creating colorful, exciting images that reach and charm millions via stage and electronic media. These choreographically spectacular images sometimes remain the predominant impression viewers retain of the particular nation-state represented—a stage full of happy young dancers forms a more palatable memory than the scenes of carnage projected by the nightly news.

The performance of the lighthearted dance from Chiapas brought forth other images: genocide in Bosnia, Kosovo, and Croatia compellingly recited and analyzed on CNN by Christine Amanpour; the banning of dance performances, and even a ban on mentioning the word "dance" (raqs), in Khomeini's Iran and Taliban-dominated Afghanistan; the era of the heavy hand of Marcos in the Philippines; shady politics and racial contestation in Mexico; and the fallout of cultural and ethnic politics of Central Asia in the post-Soviet era. For fifty years the makings and portrayals of all of these events, and many others, were cast into relief or, alternatively, masked by choreographies from dozens of dance companies, their dancers wearing colorful quaint costumes and sporting friendly smiles.

These companies almost all claim to be ambassadors of peace and friendship. "And finally, more than being ambassadors of goodwill, Bayanihan dancers have brought joy into the hearts of millions in a world and age wracked by conflict and anxiety" (Bayanihan 1987, 94). For the past fifty years these state-sponsored professional folk dance companies have dominated concert stages around the world. In many ways the end of the Cold War brought to an end what I call the "Golden Era" of these companies. The present period, at the end of the twentieth century, seems an appropriate time to analyze their role and the meaning of their performances in the context of political propaganda strategies that characterized that period.

One might inquire, What has dance to do with political and social representation? Some individuals might question the notion that dance is political, and yet I will analyze how these state-sponsored folk and traditional dance companies accrued valued symbolic and cultural capital for their respective nation-states. Political representations of power through dance performances do not constitute a new concept. As Herzfeld observes, and I concur: "Visual and musical iconicities have been especially effective in rallying entire populations" (1997, 27). Rumanian dance scholar Anca Giurchescu adds,

> State cultural management supported and encouraged the selection of folklore products, separated from their original contexts, "enriched" and "raised to a superior artistic level"; these then became the transmitters of new political and cultural messages through staged performances.... Folklore has always been employed in politics to symbolize the nation-state, to awaken and rally people's national consciousness. (1999, 43)

The effect of creating powerful emotional responses does not simply occur in the home country, but also resonates with diaspora populations. The response of the Mexican-American population to the first U.S. performances of the Ballet Folklorico in the 1960s was so electrifying and politically transforming for that population's self-image that it spawned dozens of folklorico companies. Groups of Mexican-American activists lobbied for the formation of school programs—in grade schools through the university level—to teach Mexican folk dance throughout California and the Southwest. These Chicano activists were not interested in an anthropological interpretation of folk dance. They wanted the dances that were created by Amalia Hernandez for the Ballet Folklorico and the spectacle and pride they represented. This response alone deserves a full-length study.

Historically, the Baroque court of Louis XIV consciously adopted dance performances crowned by the potent image of Louis XIV himself dancing the role of Apollo, the Sun God, to create a political message of power.[1] During the Il-Khanid and Safavid periods (1370–1722) artists painted Persian miniatures and regularly used dance scenes to illustrate the court in relaxed splendor and might. More recent historical examples show how Nazi Germany mobilized the spectacle of thousands of folk dancers in vast stadiums, valorizing the Volk, who in turn symbolically embodied the German State. The former Soviet Union (USSR) utilized the technical prowess of dancers and athletes, as well as mass performances of folk dance with thousands of participants, to suggest the immense power of a state capable of producing world-famous performers of awe-inspiring athleticism and the support of its ethnic rainbow masses.[2] In the 1950s the impact of the one hundred Moiseyev dancers, performing never-before-seen synchronized choreographic feats with the power and ease of circus acrobats, created an electrifying impact on audiences worldwide that is difficult to imagine for those not present or unaware of this phenomenon when this group first burst upon the world.

This study will undertake the project that Jane C. Desmond identified as a current concern of dance research: "to foreground theoretical concerns which do focus on the ideological underpinnings of aesthetic practices" (1997b, 1). As she correctly observes,

> So ubiquitous, so "naturalized" as to be nearly unnoticed as a symbolic system, movement is a primary not secondary social "text"—complex, polysemous, already always meaningful, yet continuously changing. Its articulation signals group affiliation and group differences, whether consciously performed or not. Movement serves as a marker for the production of gender, racial, ethnic, class, and national identities. (1997a, 31)

The performances of these ensembles meet at the intersection of art and popular culture; the materials of folklore and popular culture are abstracted for the stage through the choreographic staging strategies of what is called "high art" in the West. This study will look at and analyze how national dance companies create images of representation of ethnicity, gender, religion, and class through the use of choreographic strategies.

* * *

Although I do not wish to dwell at length on the crucial but wide-ranging topics of ethnicity and nationalism, it is important to define these concepts since they will arise frequently in the following pages.[3] These two concepts are closely related to the subject of the nation-state, and some of the most telling aspects of the nation-state's political policies can often be found in an analysis of the content of the repertoire for any given official state folk ensemble. The terms "ethnicity" and "nationalism" are intertwined in the popular mind. Indeed, nationalists frequently forge their patriotic and sometimes chauvinistic positions and claims by the use of elements of ethnicity such as language, religion, and traditional music and dance as representing the common origins of the majority population on the stage of nationalist discourse.

The concept of ethnicity, if not the actual term, is most likely prehistoric. Names of many tribes, most of which are only a memory, appear in the ancient records of Mesopotamia, China, and Egypt, as well as in the Bible. The Romans and Greeks marked the "Other" in the copious descriptions of the many tribes and ethnic groups that inhabited the edges of the ancient world. They revealed their prejudices of the Other in their unflattering writings that described the differences between "us" and "them" in such areas as language, religious practices, cultural cuisine, clothing, and other customs. However, use of the term "ethnicity" to characterize this phenomenon of describing the Other is relatively recent. According to John Hutchinson and Anthony C. Smith, the term "ethnicity" first appeared in the English Language in the 1950s (1996, 4). Simply put, "At the core of ethnicity is a consciousness of belonging to a group with whom one's humanity is inextricably intertwined" (Nash 1989, 115).

In terms of this study, ethnicity is most commonly made visual by its presence or absence through the depiction of what I call "rainbow ethnicity" in the repertoires of the various state dance companies under discussion. The opposite is also true. The state ensembles of Turkey, Greece, and Croatia currently show only the single ethnic identity of the majority population. Minority groups are neither recognized by the government nor included in the repertoire of their respective folk dance companies. Ethnic identity is both generally self-ascribed and recognized by outsiders. Not all nations welcome the presence of state folk dance companies *because* of ethnic tensions. For example, in China "the folk forms were heavily marked with ethnic associations, and the government wanted to play down ethnic associations while celebrating the nation as a whole" (Desmond 1997a, 45).

Nationalism is a more recent phenomenon than ethnicity and, according to many historians and political scientists, largely dates from the French Revolution in Western Europe and subsequently spread throughout the world as the nation-state became the primary unit of political governance. To be more precise, nationalism, in Paul Gilbert's terms, is "not so much a system of beliefs as a set of practices, through which national loyalty is cultivated and nations sustained" (1998, 6). Thus, while Iranians one thousand years ago expressed their ethnic identity in Persian literature, this expression did not necessarily take the form of modern nationalist patriotism.

Nationalism, which often expresses patriotism or chauvinism, can be seen in the repertoires of various state dance companies. Igor Moiseyev features a rousing vision of the partisans in World War II. Ballet Folklorico de Mexico furnishes vivid examples of patriotism in its Revolutionary Suite, in which rifle-toting male and female dancers assume heroic poses, and at the end of the finale of the *Fiesta in Jalisco*, when the dancers shout "Viva, Mexico" to the wildly enthusiastic cheers of audience members for whom these images and words resonate. Another striking example is furnished by a videocassette of KOLO, the Serbian state folk dance ensemble, in which the images of Serbian Orthodox saints are juxtaposed with long still shots of dancers, with suitably solemn expressions, in traditional Serbian peasant costume symbolically demonstrating a holy "Young Serbia."[4]

Thus, while nationalism is of recent origin, ethnicity seems to always have been with us. Because the core of ethnic identity is not readily available in overtly written texts, dance companies become useful vehicles for the expression of ethnicity and nationalism through the symbolic substitution of movement. The dances, music, and costumes found in dance companies constitute symbols or what Nash (1989, 15) terms as "surface markers," which in fact represent and stand for the core elements of ethnic identity such as language, religion, and common origins and history.

The value of utilizing folk dance for the representation of an entire nation emanates from the common public view that these dances emerge from some primordial source of the nation's purest and most authentic values, and that folk dances, music, and costumes are timeless and date from some prehistoric period.[5] The music, dance, and costumes represent each ethnic group's common and authentic origins. "Nationalists had produced, among other things, a more effectively aestheticized politics, a politics which could often appear as prepolitical or apolitical precisely in its aesthetic forms—national mythology and folklore, poetry and plays, folk music and grand symphonies, the very identification with the national language" (Calhoun 1995, 232). Thus, the very choice of traditional dance, arguably the most visually spectacular form of performance expression, showing an innocent youth engaged in wholesome folk activity, actually achieves the highly political choice of depicting and representing the nation, in its essentialist entirety, in this "nonpolitical," "innocent," and "naturalized" cultural fashion. Bosnian ethnomusicologist Ankica Petrovic astutely observed an additional point, that "Traditional music by its very innocence tempts tyrants to use and distort it for political purposes" (1997, 59). Of this latter folklore, Russian ethnomusicologists Izaly Zemtsovsky and Alma Kunanbaeva commented: "The 'amateur artistic activity' that the regime so prominently supported consisted, for the most part, of an imagined folklore, one fabricated by socialism for its own purposes" (1997, 6).

Like many nonverbal forms of performance, dance is polysemic—that is, filled with multiple meanings—and for this reason, as popular culture scholar Dominic Strinati reminds us, its meaning is "open to a number of different interpretations" (1995, 208). Anca Giurchescu, Romanian dance scholar, further clarifies in which ways dance, in particular, is polysemic:

> The capacity of dance for symbolic transformation, which assures its endurance in time, lies in its polysemous character. The polysemy of dance arises at the point where the conceptual, the social and the artistic levels of meaning interact. If we admit that people may combine or choose between these semiotic levels then, from a semantic perspective, dancing may be seen as an "open creation." This trait explains the use and abuse of dance as symbol for political and ideological goals. (1992, 15)

I have found that traditional dance forms a unique lens through which one may enter a world of embodied representation. Dance performances of state folk dance ensembles often create and perpetuate devastatingly accurate portraits of national prejudices, class strife, and ethnic and religious tensions, expressing a reality often avoided in the verbal discourse of strident nationalism and chauvinism. Political verities can be choreographed and packaged for foreign and domestic consumption, and thus the state folk dance ensemble—representing, in the most essentialistic fashion, the true and authentic national spirit—merits a closer look, beyond the spectacle, the footlights, the choreographic athleticism, and the striking costumes. "Cultural producers consciously or unconsciously (usually the latter) instill meanings into cultural products which are then decoded or interpreted by audiences in relatively diverse and independent ways which are none the less, in the final analysis, in keeping with some general dominant ideology" (Strinati 1995, 127). This study searches for the multiple meanings in the decoding and deconstruction of those colorful performances.

In some cases those politics and nationalist viewpoints were, and are, blatantly displayed through dance performances. In one of the most striking examples of ethnic denigration, the Serbian state ensemble, KOLO, has staged at least two Gypsy suites that depict the Gypsies as childlike, irresponsible, sexually lax individuals who dance, sing, fight, and fornicate the night away. The over-the-top visual and choreographic clichés of obviously non-Gypsy women in off-the-shoulder blouses shaking their breasts and showing their bare legs contrasts strikingly with the rest of the repertoire, in which the KOLO dancers wear long stockings and traditional folk costumes that cover them modestly. In this way KOLO misrepresents Gypsy society, which would never permit such an openly sexual display; the dancers perform with abandon in costumes bearing large, unsubtle patches, denoting the not inaccurate state of poverty in which many Gypsies are forced to live in Serbia. The men pull knives on one another and, at the end of the number, carry the willing women into the darkness for a night of carefree and unbridled passionate lovemaking. All of the visual clichés—the campfire, the gypsy wagon, the false mustaches—are present. Thus the choreography performed by the KOLO ensemble parades a spectrum of stereotypical, essentialistic traits—laziness, sexual abandon, irresponsibility, and childlike behavior—as seen through the lens of unfriendly, non-Gypsy eyes. These choreographies represent a form of portraying the "Other" by utilizing images that bring to mind similar blatant racist portrayals of African Americans in turn-of-the-century minstrel shows in the United States.[6] This stereotyped depiction of the Gypsies, a chillingly accurate visualization of public attitudes toward Gypsies throughout much of Eastern Europe, dramatically contrasts with the opening of the same video showing several Serbian religious icons superimposed with long face-shots of individual dancers in costumes of Serbian villagers, posed with noble expressions, embodying and representing the Serbian state ("KOLO" 1987). This video also portrays, in a highly orientalist (Said 1978), Grand Guignol style, the dances of the Muslim population of the Sandzak district. The women wear costumes straight out of the Broadway musical *Kismet,* with see-through gauze veils never seen in the clothing of the Balkans but immediately recognizable to viewers of dozens of Hollywood film depictions of *A Thousand and One Nights*. Thus, the Slavic Muslims and the Gypsies constitute the Other by which the Serbian nation is defined. Such portrayals of the Other, carried to their illogical extreme, contribute to the dehumanizing process that results in the types of genocide and ethnic cleansing that occurred in Bosnia, Kosovo, and Croatia, the televised scenes of which horrified viewers in the early 1990s.

Other companies portray cultural difference in a more subtle fashion. Bayanihan represents its Muslim minority by displaying aristocratic, distant Muslim royal hauteur: the unapproachable, dangerous, and implacable autocratic stance assumed by the prince wielding a large scimitar, the princess alluring, disdainful, and cold. In contrast, the audience can enjoy the warm-hearted, happy-go-lucky young peasants of *Rural Suite,* portraying a bucolic romp by boys and girls somewhere in the Tagalog-speaking "Philippine countryside" having what I call "fun in the village."

The "fun in the village" motif is a common denominator for many of the choreographies of state folk ensembles, and even more so among amateur companies. Taking a cue from Moiseyev's "innocent" depiction of village boys and girls acting like pre-adolescents on a school yard, the village that the audience views becomes a metaphor for the happy bucolic life of endless bountiful harvests and prosperity under whichever benevolent regime supports the ensemble. This "fun in the village" type of choreography, with high jinks among the peasant boys and finger-wagging by the simpering girls, became almost de rigueur in many Soviet bloc dance companies, upon political command from above. As Laszlo Madcz noted for Hungary, "Elegant presentation of the original dances and a cheerful, optimistic tone became obligatory" (1983, 62). This simplistic and romantic depiction of village life where even work is a game—a hangover from nineteenth-century images of peasants—stands in stark contrast to the grim reality of village life in Eastern Europe and the Middle East.

Other companies, reflecting state priorities and prejudices, elect not to represent specific groups at all. Their very omission from the rainbow of ethnicity constitutes a choreographic strategy. For example, reflecting the still-smoldering resentment of Bulgarians toward the historical Ottoman occupation, no Turkish dances are included in the repertoire of the Bulgarian State Ensemble of Songs and Dances (known in the West as the Philip Koutev Ensemble, after the name of the founding artistic director). Even though the Turkish minority numbers over one million, there is no place for representing Turks or Gypsies in an official Bulgarian state company.[7] (See Silverman 1997; Rice 1997.)

In the late 1940s and throughout the 1950s (and later in countries such as Turkey, Iran, and Egypt), the world saw the birth, growth, and development of the professional state folk dance ensemble in many countries around the world. The first wave of these companies appeared after World War II. All of the nation-states and several regional areas as well in areas under Soviet control had founded state-sponsored performing companies by the early 1950s. What became a worldwide phenomenon, with the notable exception of the capitalistic Western powers and Japan, began, in my opinion, in response to the phenomenal success of the State Academic Ensemble of Folk Dances of the Peoples of the USSR, known in the West as the Moiseyev Dance Company, under the artistic direction of its founder, Igor Moiseyev. This ensemble was begun in 1937 just prior to the onset of World War II, but its major impact began with the political reformation of the world a decade later in the aftermath of the war. The USSR's direct political domination of Eastern Europe, and popularity and influence in other regions of the world, led to widespread emulation of Soviet models of different types of institutions, including the formation of state-sponsored dance companies. The second wave of companies began in other areas of the world such as Greece, the Philippines, and Mexico in the 1950s. A third wave of companies, such as those of Turkey and Iran, began in the 1960s and 1970s. In the late 1950s and 1960s many individuals (and I was among them) in the United States and Western Europe founded private companies in emulation of the spectacle and success of these extremely popular state dance ensembles.[8]

Such companies, their repertoires, and the ways in which they are characterized in movement and in print raise important issues of representation on a wide variety of levels—political, historical, ethnic, economic, gender, and aesthetic, among others. State ensembles constitute the highly visible intersection of ethnic and nationalist representation and political interests through valorizing folklorized and idealized visions of village and tribal societies filtered through the national capital city and the elite populations residing there. Performances of these companies over the past five decades raise questions of who is represented—and perhaps, even move importantly, who is *not* represented, as the lack of Turkish dances in the performances of the Bulgarian state ensemble demonstrates—in the repertoires of these state-sponsored companies.

In addition, the question of *how* these different ethnicities are represented arises. For example, within the now-defunct Iranian State Ensemble, known in the West as the Mahalli Dancers, the Persian

Introduction: Ethnicity and Nationalism   11

dances are described in the concert program as "graceful," while those of the Kurds are "primitive and full of energy" (Mahalli Dancers of Iran 1976).[9] Since Iran is a multi-ethnic nation, with the politically dominant Persian-speakers numbering about one-half of the population, the Mahalli Dancers constituted a visual representation of the political, social, and ethnic views of that dominant group. Under these circumstances such textual and choreographic characterizations of the different ethnic groups represented in their repertoire take on multiple meanings, including the political and cultural centrality of the dominant group in relation to the margin.

In a similar vein, ethnomusicologist Ricardo Trimillos questions the Chinese State Folk Ensemble's depiction of minority groups within the Chinese state:

> In the same sentence, Lu [principal of the Beijing Dance Academy] refers to "our own folk dances"; his very formulation is politically problematic. It raises the question, whose dances are they? The majority of dances so labeled are attributed to minority groups in China, including the Yao, Dai, Tibetans, and Koreans. Conservatory presentations of these minority dances as choreographed and performed by Han Chinese are disturbingly inauthentic, suffering from terminal cuteness. Protests from carriers of these traditions are ignored, the most benign of possible reactions to criticism. This situation raises issues of cultural entitlement, ownership, and exploitation—all concerns of politics. (1995, 25)

This political and cultural layering represents the concept of rings and layers of marginalization presented in Tsing's (1993) study in postcolonial Indonesia. In this model one finds that a particular ethnic group such as the dominant Persian-speaking population, who were themselves earlier marginalized by colonial powers of the former USSR, Great Britain, and the United States, now dominates the nation-state of Iran. To some extent the dominant ethnic group (Persian, Javanese, Tagalog-speakers, Mestizos of Mexico, Serbs, Russians, Hindi-speakers) replace the colonial project of hegemony by further marginalizing an array of ethnic groups in the newly reformed, postcolonial state. This layered marginalization is not, of course, unique to Iran, but obtains in many postcolonial areas as well as the former Yugoslav, Czechoslovak, and Soviet states, among others.

On the other hand LADO, the Croatian state ensemble, marked its fortieth anniversary with a presentation of the moving 1989 premiere of *Na Baniji bubanj bije* (In Banija the great drum beats). This choreography consisted of a suite of dances depicting the lives and cultural differences between Serbs and Croats in the villages of the region of Banija, which was to be engulfed by war between them within two years. This work presaged the deep tensions and differences between these two ethnic groups through the highly effective dance suite created by Croatian dance scholar Dr. Ivan Ivancan. (Since the war between Serbia and Croatia, this choreography is no longer a part of the repertoire.)

To date, no scholarly inquiry, using anthropological theoretical and methodological approaches, has been conducted concerning the establishment, maintenance, and representations of these large-scale dance companies. With the collapse of the former USSR and Yugoslavia, and major changes in other former Soviet-controlled areas, some of these companies are beginning to wane or metamorphose while others thrive and continue to succeed in performing as if nothing had changed politically.[10]

With the historical perspective of the past fifty years, now is the time to assess the impact of these companies and the various messages they conveyed, and to some degree still convey. In the post-Cold War era, what will be the role of such ensembles as some new states, such as Uzbekistan and Turkmenia, face severe economic, political, and social change? In older states such as Rumania and Poland, now rid of Soviet rule and severely strapped for currency, how will post-Soviet governments assess the value of such representation? Will the new governments undertake the enormous costs of their maintenance? How have the representational choreographic strategies changed in light of new ethnic, nationalistic, and political realities?

In this introductory section I have put forth several concepts and elements that should be profitably examined before any meaningful analysis of these ensembles and their choreographic output can be properly addressed. These include issues of authenticity and representation, as well as the variety of social and technical restrictions and limitations—political, financial, artistic—faced by the artistic directors of these companies. The theoretical and methodological model established here thus forms the basis of study for professional and semiprofessional state folk dance ensembles as well as the numerous amateur performing and exhibition groups that emulate the state dance companies.

1

Parallel Traditions: State Folk Dance Ensembles and Folk Dance in the Field

All of these folk dance ensembles claim that specific individuals, most often the founding artistic directors and/or choreographers, conduct prodigious amounts of field research in order to present the most authentic choreographic products possible. Claims of authenticity loom large in the program notes, newspaper stories, and other publications that these companies generate. Nevertheless, because these professional companies clearly present an often highly stylized, carefully choreographed and staged genre of dance that differs from dances found among nonprofessional populations of villagers and tribal people, most dance researchers have shunned serious analyses of these companies as "unauthentic," "slick," and "theatrical." It is not unusual to find the researcher of traditional dance situating his or herself as the "protector" of the national heritage, what Theresa Buckland calls the "Keeper of the Truth" (1999a, 196). For example, Greek dance scholar Marica Rombos-Levides states:

> The treasures, carefully handed over to us by previous generations must be treated not only with respect but with theoretical restlessness and questioning. The responsibility of moulding a public is immense, especially when the object is traditional culture, which is not the product of an individual but of an ethnic collectivity. Demand for high quality performances of traditional dance increases year by year, and we must safeguard traditional culture from becoming a theatrical object expressing the artistic priorities of individuals. (1992, 104)

As dance ethnographers Georgiana Gore and Maria Koutsouba state, "Any representation of traditional dance outside its customary context is no more than 'imitation' and may be seen as an artificial and adulterated version of the 'original'" (1992, 30).

This scholarly avoidance has created a crucial lacuna in dance research literature. Consequently, few studies that address the topic of ethnic/traditional/folk dance analyze or even mention that these highly visible and influential dance companies, which are seen by millions of enthusiastic viewers, exist.[1] This is unfortunate in view of the fact that the repertoires of some of these companies, in a cyclical fashion, have influenced the way in which dance is performed "in the field."

Essentialization and Particularization

A wide gap, indicated on a chart that I will introduce later, exists among the various state folk dance ensembles regarding the degree of authentic elements that each company utilizes for its presentations. An effective concept for evaluating the utilization of authentic elements in folk dance ensemble performances is "essentialization" and "particularization," which I borrow from Urban and Sherzer (1991) but use in a different context. "Essentialization" refers to the phenomenon of using uniformly produced costumes in matching colors, generalized orchestral tonal quality to cover the purported musical output of an entire country, and a series of steps, movements, and choreographic strategies to represent an essentialized nation. The choreographic strategies of Igor Moiseyev illustrate the concept of essentialization. He was interested in displaying the essential qualities of "Soviet Man" in broad choreographic strokes. The same steps and figures found in the Russian dances are also found in Ukrainian or Byelorussian dances. The same theater orchestra is used for dances from Uzbekistan, Moldavia, and Lithuania or to represent the various districts of Poland and Bulgaria.

"Particularization," on the other hand, represents the use of as many minute and authentic details of movement, costuming, and music as possible in order to emphasize how distinct and particular the various regions, no matter how small, of a specific country can be. Zvonko Ljevakovic, the founding director and choreographer of LADO, exemplified this approach. He attempted to draw the distinctions among small districts of Croatia by incorporating distinctive musical styles, choreographic elements, and clothing. For example, through the use of a variety of costumes gathered in the field and worn by the company performers, Ljevakovic was able to display the sartorial diversity of social classes (married, unmarried, widowed, etc.) and modalities of each clothing type—festive, everyday, and work clothes. This contrasts strikingly with the essentialized Moiseyev costumes that resemble uniforms in three of four basic colors but are otherwise identical in cut, length, "embroidery" and decoration, and other structural aspects. Musically, Ljevakovic utilized particular vocal styles and specific instruments within a single evening, and his choreographies showed minute detailing of styling in movements and steps, in order to call the viewer's attention to an entire spectrum of differentiation that he felt characterized Croatian folklore. He also participated, along with others, in making the musical arrangements.

In the chapters that follow, I examine the choreographic and other presentational elements of each ensemble in terms of essentialization and particularization. Regarding authenticity, many of the choreographic creations of several of these state ensembles have not descended from traditional folk dance but from the dance form that in classical ballet is known as "character dance," which Arkin and Smith characterize as "folk-derived" (1997, 12). In nineteenth-century character dance, Arkin and Smith observe, "anecdotal evidence suggests that folk dances were 'balleticized'" (ibid., 54). I would go a step further and point out that the steps and movements of character dance often have no connection with dance in the field, and yet ballet character dance characterizes the bulk of choreographic output of such twentieth-century folk dance companies as the Moiseyev Dance Company, the Reda Troupe of Egypt, and the Mazowse company of Poland. Such a dance form might be considered what Hobsbawm and Ranger (1983) term an "invented tradition."

By contrast, other companies such as LADO (the Croatian state ensemble) and the Dora Stratou Greek Dances Theatre are truly devoted to the inclusion of authentic elements of traditional life—indigenous musical instruments and vocal styles, costumes, dance steps and movements, and customs and ritual. Thus, the degree of authentic elements utilized by each company varies widely. Unfortunately, scholars have produced little material in English about the choreographic creations of the various state dance ensembles, preventing an analytical comparison.[2]

In order to analyze these elements, which one may subsume under the issue of authenticity, we must first look at the relationship of the choreographies and dancing found in state dance ensembles and the dancing found in village and tribal groups, as well as urban areas. Many dance ethnologists have addressed dancing in the field in great detail. This analysis and comparison, as well as the connections between these the presentations of professional state dance ensembles and what I call the dancing "in the field," form an important and largely uninvestigated area of dance research. This research is especially crucial now since the changing political and cultural situation in Eastern Europe and the former Soviet Union challenges the existence and meaning of these companies and their relationship to traditional dance.

The study and analysis of the repertoires, staging, and choreographic strategies of national state ensembles requires a discussion of dance "in the field," since all of the national companies claim connections with these field dance genres. These professional, semiprofessional, and often highly proficient amateur folk dance ensembles utilize varying degrees of choreographic and cultural elements that their researchers found, or professed to find, in the field for purposes of establishing claims of authenticity—a leitmotif that appears in all discussions of these ensembles. Other ensembles, such as the Moiseyev Dance Company, in spite of claims to authenticity create works from nontraditional sources such as character dance, with little or no actual utilization of the folk traditions upon which they claim to base their work. Nahachewsky claims that in some social environments these two traditions are developed in isolation from one another (1992, 74). Al-Faruqi (1987) points out that the "folk" dance of the Reda Troupe—which according to Saleh (1979) utilized USSR folk dance advisors in stagings—is European, not Egyptian.

Just as important, through the politicization of folk and traditional dancing in many parts of the world, dancing in the field also often exhibits a wide variety of staging and presentational techniques, some of which approach the theatricalization of presentations seen within the repertoires of some national dance companies. While authenticity of presentation does form a topic of discussion in some studies of ethnic dance, I have found no systematic discussion of the wide scope of degrees of elaboration and theatrical elements that people "in the field" utilize for their own presentations.[3] Nor has there been an investigation into the reasons behind the development of such elaborations of performance. Many studies of traditional dance forms are framed as if the traditions in the villages and tribal areas in the field have been unaffected by the presence of professional national folk dance companies. In this age of widespread availability of electronic media, broadcasts of appearances of national companies can be seen in even the remotest villages. Amalia Hernandez is one of many artistic directors of a state ensemble to relate seeing her own inventive elements in traditional dance performances.

> With only a small trace of irony, Hernandez describes being invited to judge a contest of traditional dancing in culturally conservative Veracruz. Watching the competition, Hernandez discovered that the participants

were openly incorporating steps she had invented for her classic Ballet Folklorico *Veracruz* suite. "I didn't say a thing," she recalls with a big smile. "The tradition is like a river of style that goes on." (Segal 1997, 67)

But it is a river that will now forever flow with the personal influences of Amalia Hernandez marking its passage in many regions throughout Mexico and the southwestern United States.

Parallel Traditions

As the above example demonstrates, choreographic and staging elements of the performances of the prestigious national companies are often emulated by rural groups desirous of professionalizing their performances, or merely because they are struck by the novelty of the national company's treatment of their dances. To many individuals, some of the state ensembles are considered an important resource for authenticity. Many Croatians, villager and town-dweller alike, conceive of LADO as being the keeper of the flame of older layers of dance. The dancers from LADO are regularly hired by different villagers to arrange their dances in the "old style." This exchange between the field and the professional dance ensemble creates a dynamic cycle that encompasses the appropriation of cultural and choreographic elements from field to stage and a return to the field of presentational elements.

A productive way in which the study and comparison of these two types of performances—those for stage and those found in the field—might be best characterized is "parallel traditions." These parallel traditions can often approach one another in the use of "authentic" elements found in the choreographic output of the professional companies as well as in the degree of theatricalization found in "traditional" performances. While these parallel traditions maintain obvious ties to one another, if only through the claims of such ties with the field that companies such as Ballet Folklorico and Moiseyev stress, they actually form separate genres. These genres differ from one another in important ways, such as the mode of transmission of the dances, use of improvisation, and the degree of separation from the represented traditions exhibited by professional folk dance performers. In many field traditions (for example, Mexico, Eastern Europe, and many areas of the Middle East) the dances are characterized by a high degree of improvisation while the staged performances are standardized and set. To some degree, an interaction between the two genres takes place through various forms of contact such as research projects in the field or joint participation in folk festivals. Interaction can include the conscious appropriation of images and staging techniques appropriated by villagers to make their presentations "more attractive," or "more interesting," as well as the acquisition of steps and figures from the field by choreographers from the performing companies. By utilizing the concept of parallel traditions, the dance researcher is not required to make invidious comparisons of authenticity and theatricality; rather, she or he may view the two types of dance as related but separate genres. Giurchescu underscores this point:

> It may be argued from a theoretical point of view, that vernacular folklore and staged folklore, exist in indivisible and unbroken continuity. However, considering the practice of symbol transformation and manipulation, it is necessary to formally segregate the socio-cultural processes of folklore from selected products (dances, music, costumes, etc.) which are performed in the framework of a spectacle (called folklorism or "fakelore"). (1992, 21)

Folklorism, or *folklorization,* is a process described by ethnomusicologist Thomas Turino as "the relocation of native customs (typically music and dance, but other art forms as well) from their original contexts to new urban contexts, usually under the direct sponsorship of the state" (qtd. in Urban and Sherzer 1991, 10–11). The process of folklorization, such as the choreographic elements developed and created in the repertoires of the Moiseyev and other companies, places much of what occurs on the stage in the context of an "invented tradition," in Hobsbawm and Ranger's (1983) terms.

Within these two general categories there also exist many micro-parallel traditions. For example, when a group of villagers journeys to a nearby town or capital city to show their dances, they may make minor alterations or none at all. Perhaps a young people's dance club will show the dances of the grandparents' generation that no longer constitute a living tradition but are certainly closer to that tradition than the dances of a professional folk ensemble. Each researcher may place these dance activities on a different level. The model presented here can be utilized as a basis for such decisions.

Past Studies

Two studies, the first by Joann Kealiinohomoku and a later one by Andriy Nahachewsky, have raised important questions for creating

State Folk Dance Ensembles and Folk Dance in the Field

analytical categories for the study of folk and traditional dance, both theatrical and in the field. Both authors have pointed out that Felix Hoerburger (1968) used the phrase "folk dance in its first existence" to distinguish dance in the field or in its "original" existence from "folk dance in its second existence" to cover what he termed "revival" dancing. These categories were appropriated by Joann Kealiinohomoku (1972) in a seminal article that raised a number of important questions regarding "folk dance" as a concept and a field of study. She utilized Hoerburger's terms to characterize the differences between "first existence," indicating folk dances in the field, and "second existence," meaning (among other phenomena such as theatricalized performances) the massive recreational folk dance movement that involved well over a million participants in the United States in the period 1950–1975.[4] Kealiinohomoku's article addressed one of the most crucial differences between "first existence" and "second existence" dancing: the manner of transmission. In "first existence" dance environments, those individuals who grow up in a society in which dancing constitutes part of the living tradition learn dances primarily in a one-on-one situation similar to the way in which games and language are acquired—that is, generally, but not always, in informal situations in trial-and-error fashion. Such a situation, therefore, constitutes a branch of folklore studies. The dance repertoire that such individuals acquired usually consisted of a body of choreographic and movement material and styles that was in vogue at the time in the region in which they lived, or was learned by immigrant groups from older generations.

By contrast, the typical professional folk dancer in a state dance company is, with some exceptions, an urban-born individual who has learned her or his repertoire in much the same way as the folk dance hobbyist from the United States, Japan, or the Netherlands, rather than from an individual in the field in his own district of the same nation-state.[5] These professional dancers learn their repertoire from a teacher in a conscious fashion in studio/classroom environments. Their "native" form, if they have one, is often classical ballet or some form of social dance.[6] The professional dancer from the state ensemble acquires a wide variety of styles and forms, so even if a specific dancer comes from the field, he or she acquires all of the other styles featured in the company repertoire in the same manner as urban-born colleagues.

Another difference between dancers in a professional state-sponsored ensemble and dancers from the field is the purpose of the performance. In the field, no matter how theatricalized the presentational strategies employed by the performers, representation of the village or region in a show of local pride or to attract tourists often forms a common goal of public dance presentations in venues outside of the normative social and ritual contexts and occasions of dance performance. By contrast, the performers of the state folk ensemble are generally paid as individuals to dance. Members of groups from the field who perform in presentational settings generally, but not always, perform for the benefit of the represented groups rather than for individual gain.[7]

Kealiinohomoku characterized the state folk dance ensemble as

> A government-sponsored organization of gifted dancers under the direction of a well-known choreographer. The latter coordinates and theatricalizes first existence dance into slick and attractive show pieces, in order to present a variety of forms that represent different regions of the country. (1972, 392)

In many cases, the first existence dances are not even referred to by the choreographer. For example, Igor Moiseyev's *Bulba*, purportedly from Belarus, is in fact, as indicated by one of his biographers, an original choreography created without reference to any specific dance in the field (Chudnovskii 1959). Moiseyev made clear that he was "against the literal transplantation of the folk dance to the stage . . . and that there are some character dances . . . [that] have become an improved version of the folk dances from which they stem" (Chudnovskii 1959, 28).

In another approach to this topic, dance scholar Andriy Nahachewsky proposed "presentational" and "participatory" as categories to distinguish, in a general way, folk dance in presentational and field contexts. He has suggested, however, that rather than considering these as separate categories, they may be conceptualized as a continuum: "Some readers may imagine that these categories are distinct in practice, creating a dichotomy or division in dance phenomena. Indeed, this is far from true. These two conceptual categories are idealizations, opposite poles on a theoretical continuum" (Nahachewsky 1995, 1).

I would agree that when people in the field prepare a performance of a dance for presentation that is native to them as a social dance form, Nahachewsky's concept is useful for analyzing the choreographic differences in such performances.[8] In many ways, in some instances such as I am describing for state dance ensembles, semiprofessional companies, and amateur performances, the "presentational"

State Folk Dance Ensembles and Folk Dance in the Field 21

and "participatory" categories form two separate genres. For example, the dancers in the state ensembles often do not know the "participatory" dance tradition upon which a specific choreography is based. They are often likely to participate in contemporary urban social and vernacular dances as their "native" tradition, and they have often received their basic formal training in classical ballet, which companies such as Moiseyev require.

For purposes of illustration, I propose a visual model of two continua representing the two genres: the field and the stage (see chart). In this model I show how Igor Moiseyev—who, as one Mazo (1998, ix) states, "uses some steps based on folk dances"—represents the character dance, the "essentialistic" end of the spectrum, in contrast to the choreographic output of LADO and the Dora Stratou Greek Dances Theatre, which are deeply committed to the extensive use of authentic, "particularized" elements. Above the line I have placed various professional groups, with those companies that have the least use of authentic elements at the top, while below the line are groups of traditional performers that demonstrate varying degrees of formal choreography and staging techniques common to performing companies. The groups nearest the line utilize the most theatrical elements also common to professional dance companies. Utilizing this model, the researcher may find that a village group whose performances she or he classifies as "in the field" may be placed below the line. By contrast, the investigator may choose to place a specific performance of that same group above the line if the group's presentations in festivals are theatricalized to any significant degree, and in this way utilize Nahachewsky's concept as well. In Eastern Europe, some village groups offered arranged selections from other areas in their district, or even the nation-state, sometimes taught to them by a professional dancer from the national dance ensemble. I would classify such performances as above the line. (Numbers following certain groups are from the JVC video collection; see videocassettes listing in the bibliography.)

Any scholar wishing to conduct research in this area may use Table 1 or a similar chart for mapping the use and comparison of authentic and theatricalized elements. This list is not exhaustive, but suggestive.

Representation

Representation manifests itself in many ways in state dance company performances, the two major vehicles being visual and textual. In the

TABLE 1. Continuum: The Field and the Stage

— Moiseyev, Reda (Egypt), Mazowse (Poland)
   — Bulgarian State Folk Ensemble (Philip Koutev)
     — Ballet Folklorico, Bayanihan (Philippines)
       — KOLO (Serbian State Ensemble)
         — Mahalli Dancers (Iran
           — Georgian State Folk Company
             — LADO (Croatian state ensemble)
               — Dora Stratou Greek Dances Theatre

                — Don Cossacks Chorus
         Kamensk Folk Song Group, JVC 23, not the
           professional group of that same name)
           — Timonia (Kursk Folk song group, JVC 23-19)
     — Groups from Poland (Folk Dances of Poland, entire tape)
   — Village Dances of Yugoslavia (film made in 1948, most
        groups have little or no arrangement to the dances)
   — Villagers from Torbat Jam and Bojnurd, Khorasan, Iran
— Villagers from Liamtsa (JVC 23-1/4)

analysis of each of the state dance companies that follows, I will peel away several layers of representation as manifest in choreography, costuming, and other elements of production, as well as provide a close reading of the company biographies, histories, mission statements, program notes, and publicity releases. Representation in the repertoire of the state-sponsored national dance ensemble casts an allure for many individuals in a nation-state and on many levels, both aesthetic and political. It represents, among other things, inclusion, participation, and belonging. In establishing national icons and symbols, Eley and Suny note: "A special case of this activity is the almost universal attempt to collect and adapt to new purposes the customary practices of common people, like folk songs and dance" (1996, 8).

Political issues, sometimes unseen in a government-sponsored festival context, for example, may also be taken into account for analyzing multiple facets of representation. Turkish dance scholar Arzu Ozturkmen points out that "the idea of folklore provided the emerging nation-states, and their devoted intelligentsia in particular, with ample opportunities to mobilize their subject populations toward the construction of a national identity" (1992, 83). In the United States, formerly all-white advertisements have given way to ethnic inclusiveness. This change from the middle years of the twentieth century to the present in which white models now share beer, cigarettes, headache remedies, laxatives, and fashionable attire with people of color has come about not through altruism or high moral ideals, but rather because it is good business.

Cultural theorist Peggy Phelan observes: "It is assumed that disenfranchised communities who see their members within the representational field will feel greater pride in being part of such a community *and* those who are not in such a community will increase their understanding of the diversity and strength of such communities" (1993, 7). The allure of representation and inclusion is certainly reinforced by reports of different ethnic groups seeking inclusion in the repertoires of state and regional dance companies. Having one's own dance company to represent each recognized ethnic unit became a political goal, a symbol of recognition, in the former Soviet Union.[9] Mary Grace Swift gives an account of how the Don Cossacks, who had been at loggerheads with the Soviet government since the aftermath of the 1917 Russian Revolution, as a mark of recognition and inclusion were allowed to wear their native clothing and "given official sanction to form their own song and dance groups" (1968, 105–06).

Phelan's observation is particularly relevant to this study: "While there is a deeply ethical appeal in the desire for a more inclusive representational landscape and certainly underrepresented communities can be empowered by an enhanced visibility, the terms of this visibility often enervate the putative power of these identities" (1993, 7). This perceptive point, well illustrated by the choreographies of the people of Chiapas in the repertoire of Ballet Folklorico and the Gypsies of North Serbia in the KOLO Ensemble's programs, demonstrate the inherent dangers of how a specific ethnic group or social unit is represented—a point that I will emphasize several times in the following chapters in addressing the specific representational strategies of each company. As Phelan emphasizes, "Gaining visibility for the politically under-represented without scrutinizing the power of who is required to display what to whom is an impoverished political agenda" (ibid., 26). As Phelan wryly reminds us about the illusory chimera of power inherent in visual representation: "If representational visibility equals power, then almost-naked young white women should be running Western culture" (ibid., 10).

Other areas of representation, subordinate to the main question of national ethnic depiction, must also be addressed. Issues and strategies of the representation or masking of gender and sexuality immediately arise in the embodied manifestation of dance, an art form exuding sensuality and appealing to the senses. Thus, dance is more often banned than any other form of aesthetic and cultural expression. For example, after 1979 the governments in Afghanistan and Iran banned the performance of dance. The government of Saudi Arabia does not permit women to dance in public; the Saudi national dance company is all male. For the careful observer of the Moiseyev Dance Company, the most striking aspect of the dancers, once their extraordinary technical and athletic skills are absorbed, is the utter lack of sensuality or sexuality they display. The interaction between the sexes resembles a schoolyard in the characterizations of boys and girls bashful in each other's company. In the written description of one of his choreographies, Moiseyev states: "The whole number is composed of such choreographic dialogues of joyful 'quarrels'" (Cheremetievskaya n.d., 7). The dancers all portray one-dimensional and interchangeable individuals, forever smiling and happy, who seem to be so doll-like as to have no bodily functions.

The contrast with Ballet Folklorico de Mexico in this respect is striking. In the dances found in the choreographies *Veracruz*, *Boda en la Huasteca* (Wedding in Huasteca), and *Boda en el Istmo de Tehuantepec* (Wedding in Isthmus of Tehuantepec), among others, a subtle but powerful sensuality pervades via the movements and attitudes of the performers, heightened by effective lighting. In the latter suite the dancers mimic the mating of turtles (and elsewhere iguanas or charging bulls) with unmistakable sexual references, and such reference is also evident as the groom carries the bride off stage at the end of the dance, prior to the wedding night. Similarly, a raw and powerful masculinity informs Amalia Hernandez's choreography (much copied by other groups) of the *Danza del Venado* (Yaqui Deer Dance). Such sensuality is totally absent from the productions of the Moiseyev Dance Company.

Of all the Soviet ensembles I have viewed, the only ones that display adult, powerful male sexuality in their performance are the Georgian, Armenian, and Azerbaijani dance groups. By contrast, female sexuality in these same ensembles is very muted, except for soloists in the Azerbaijani national ensemble. This muted female sexuality and the emphasized male role in the Caucasian companies accurately reflects the historical relationship between males and females in those societies. The dichotomy between male and female gender representation in the Georgian national company, which every audience member with whom I spoke emphatically noted, is further evident in the company's artistic personnel: fifty male dancers and only eighteen females. The spectacular and varied choreographic roles of the male dancers stand in stark contrast to the essentially monochromatic female choreographic duties.

Female sensuality, experienced in the Ballet Folklorico and some West African companies such as those of the Ivory Coast, Guinea, and Senegal, are absent from Moscow, reflecting the Communist state's prudish attitudes toward sex. Female sexuality exhibited in the Guinean national company, Ballet Africains, during a 1960s tour caused hypocritical puritanical reactions in the United States, where outraged middle-class sensibilities required the wearing of bras in some cities, but not in others. The incident was featured in numerous newspaper articles and became something of a cause célèbre. Bakhor, the Uzbek company, utilizes a highly understated sexuality that does not reflect the traditional Middle Eastern and Central Asian image of the dancer as a paid sex worker. The Reda Troupe of Egypt attempts to mask the very overt sensuality for which Egyptian dance is famous and substitutes sensuality with coy "fun in the village" high jinks.[10] While the peasant frolics of Bayanihan exhibit a Moiseyev-like lack of sensuality, the Muslim dances of the southern Philippines and some of the tribal dances of the northern Philippines display and celebrate female sensuality. But in the politics of representation, the Muslims of the Philippine southern islands constitute the cold, dangerous "Other," while the idyllic frolics of the Tagalog-speaking peasants, representing the "true" Philippine character, exhibit a display of adolescent coyness and innocence acceptable to middle-class values in both Manila and Kansas City.

Representation of class also forms an issue in several of the state-sponsored ensembles. As one might expect in the areas of Soviet influence, this became a state policy. "Certainly, folklore had to disdain the landowner, and the tsar as well. They mocked both the priest and mullah (not to mention the rabbi)" (Zemtsovsky and Kunanbaeva 1997, 5).

In the *Spanish Colonial Suite,* Bayanihan represents the former Spanish-speaking Manila urban elite in a positive light through sumptuous dance productions with the female corps all attired in black and white "Maria Clara" costumes creating a stunning and unforgettable experience. The elite display luxurious costumes, and their measured and elegant dance styles wistfully recall a more leisurely and golden time.

By contrast, the few depictions of the upper class in the Ballet Folklorico's Revolutionary suite *La Revolucion* or its *La Vida es Juego* (Life Is a Game) portrays them in a feckless, negative fashion as they disport themselves in a ballroom, ignoring life around them. The choreography focuses on and valorizes the heroic working peasant women who rudely burst in upon the ball and drive them away. Moiseyev pokes fun at the pre-Revolutionary petite bourgeoisie in his *Old City Quadrille,* while his stagings of an Argentine tango and *Back to the Apes, a Rock 'n' Roll Parody* form an outright satire of the "decadent" upper classes of the West, as viewed from the perspective of Moscow. During Professor Ljevakovic's era, which reflects the research interests of folklorists of the late nineteenth and early twentieth centuries, urban dances did not appear in the repertoire of LADO. Only the peasantry entered his representational field as embodying the "true soul" of Croatia.[11] This philosophical viewpoint was reflected in most of the Eastern European dance company repertoires as well as in the research concerns of dance ethnographers in the region (see Giurchescu 1999; Felfoldi 1999).

The Nation-State

First and foremost, a national dance company embodies a nation. This mission forms the basic reason for the formation of these companies, and each, in its own way, states this in its program notes and other publicity publications. The companies also attempt to find choreographic strategies to visually depict all of "The People" of the respective nation-state. The Ukrainian State Folk Ensemble, under the direction of Pavel Virsky, visually represented the entire Ukrainian nation through an opening choreographed spectacle in which all of the dancers appeared in the major Ukrainian costume types, representing villages and regions from all over the Ukraine. The dancers paraded impressively around the stage and, in a final gesture, symbolically presented bread and salt, the Slavic ritual of welcome and greeting, to the audience.

In the past few years many social scientists have begun theorizing the phenomenon of the nation-state on a number of levels, questioning its existence and the popular acceptance of the nation-state by the majority of the world's population as a given in their lives. Because the nation-state has formed the dominant political unit over the past century, scholars are beginning to question the "naturalness" of the nation-state as an entity. Sociologist Craig Calhoun remarks: "One of the ironies of modern social theory is that the 'natural' has come to seem the realm of the stable and immutable, that which humans must accept as given" (1995, 283). This reification of the nation-state and other such concepts has had serious implications for any study, such as the one that I propose here. Calhoun continues:

> This construction of "cultures," "societies," and "nations" as basic units of modern collective identity and of comparative social science research has significant implications. In the first place, it implies that each one is somehow discrete and subsists as an entity unto itself rather than only as a part of a world system or some other broader social organization or discourse that defines it as a constituent unit or part. This boundedness is suggested, in large part, by the sharp boundedness of modern states; the ideology of nationalism promotes the notion that each has its own singular culture (and vice versa). (1995, 53–54)

Ernest Gellner, the dean of nationalist studies, as well as many American politicians treat the nation-state and its centralized power as both natural and desirable. Give the minorities a folk dance company and keep them happy. "His hope that different cultures could be allowed to flourish did not diminish his insistence that power remain politically centralised. As the provision of opera houses rather than the acceptance of political autonomy, of folk-dancing rather than democracy, fail in both Austro-Hungary and the Soviet Union it is worth speculating as to why Gellner would not go any further" (Hall 1998, 15).[12]

One might add that such substitution of a folk dance company for political power sometimes result in World War II and ethnic cleansing in Kosovo. After all, KOLO, the Serbian state folk dance ensemble, offered two Albanian (Shiptar) folk dances in its repertoire, but the Albanians seemingly sought representation in other, more political playing fields as well.

Arjun Appadurai makes a distinction between a "nation" and a "state":

> The relationship between states and nations is everywhere an embattled one. It is possible to say that in many societies, the nation and the state have become one another's projects. That is, while nations (or more properly groups with ideas about nationhood) seek to capture or co-opt states and state power, states simultaneously seek to capture and monopolize ideas about nationhood. (1990, 13)

By "nation" Appadurai means ethnic groups such as the Kurds, Slovaks, or Basques seeking independent status or some kind of similar recognition, often by carving out an independent territory within a preexisting nation-state. I will not make the same distinction as Appadurai between the term "nation" and "state," but rather the two will be used interchangeably for a centralized government with some degree of legitimacy. For Appadurai's notion of "nation," I use the term "ethnic group" because in the former Yugoslavia, the former Soviet Union, and other areas such as Iran, which I will discuss in ethnic detail, there are so many "nations" according to Appadurai's definition that the term would engender enormous confusion. Additionally, among these various groups there are many degrees of aspiration and sophistication. There are some ethnic groups that do not seek independence or any specific political recognition and therefore would not fall under Appadurai's concept of a "nation," while others, such as the Kurds, willingly forfeit their lives over the concept of possessing a separate national homeland. The levels of ethnic consciousness among the various ethnic groups also vary widely, as Appadurai observes.

Appadurai makes a telling point, similar to that of Urban and Sherzer (1991), that is central to this discussion of dance as a tool of expressing ethnicity and the nation-state:

> States, on the other hand, are everywhere seeking to monopolize the moral resources of community, either by flatly claiming perfect coevality between nation and state, or by systematically museumizing and representing all the groups within them in a variety of heritage politics that seem remarkably uniform throughout the world. (Appadurai 1990, 13)

One of the major points that I make in this study is that national dance companies constitute an ideal vehicle for this type of demonstration of coevality. Appadurai adds: "Typically, contemporary nation-states do this by exercising taxonomic control over difference, by creating various kinds of international spectacle to domesticate difference, and by seducing small groups with the fantasy of self-display on some sort of global or cosmopolitan stage" (Appadurai 1990, 13).

I do not know if Appadurai had national dance ensembles in mind when he made this perceptive statement, but nothing could better illustrate his point than performances by such illustrious state dance companies as the Moiseyev Dance Company, Ballet Folklorico de Mexico, or the Bayanihan Philippine Dance Company. In regard to his point of uniformity, it is significant that the first tier of state ensembles that were formed were a command by the authorities in Moscow to their satellite states. Bulgarian dance scholar Anna Ilieva notes that "the first state ensemble [in Bulgaria] for folk songs and dance was set up in accordance with the Soviet model in 1952" (1992, 35). The next tier that formed (Mexico, Egypt, the Philippines, for example) sought the political capital that they observed with the success of performances by Moiseyev and other Soviet bloc companies. At first established by private individuals such as Amalia Hernandez or groups of students such as Bayanihan, their respective governments quickly realized the positive propaganda values that such visual spectacles provided.

In their representation of their respective nation-state, national dance companies visually epitomize and embody Benedict Anderson's famous study *Imagined Communities* (1991) in the essentialist manner of their choreographic portrayals, as the example of the Ukrainian State Folk Ensemble's standard opening choreography demonstrates. Anderson's potent image of individuals tied together through imagining themselves rising together and reading the newspaper over coffee replaces actual personal relationships, because in the nation-state one no longer has face-to-face contact with all, or even most of, one's countrymen. One must therefore imagine a similarity between oneself and one's largely personally unknown fellow citizens to establish a coherent society. The performances of state-sponsored dance ensembles putatively represent "all of the people" of the nation-state. However, such performances do not represent all of the people. Rather, choices are made, and in each of the following chapters in which I describe and analyze each ensemble, I detail and analyze those choices and their multiple meanings. Some of those choices stem from deeply held philosophical stances concerning which people represent the nation "properly." For example, a common choice for representing the "pure, noble" soul of the people through folk dances, music, and costumes is most often the peasant, a tribal group, or some other rural inhabitant.

As Herzfeld observes, "Nationalism is directly predicated on resemblance, whether biogenetic or cultural. The pivotal idea is that all citizens are, in some unarguable sense, all alike" (1997, 27). The dance companies representing multiethnic, multicultural entities such as Iran, Mexico, the Philippines, and the former USSR and Yugoslavia have been designed to demonstrate the essential equality of its entire rainbow of citizens. Dozens, even hundreds, of dancers, young, slender, energetic in traditional garb, represent millions of people. So powerful is the concept of the unity of the nation that it can sometimes be reduced and essentialized to a single individual as the embodiment and representation of the collective nation. The 1969–70 souvenir program for Ballet Folklorico de Mexico enthused: "And in her art, audiences around the world see the Mexico she [Amalia Hernandez, founder and artistic director] cherishes, the Mexico she celebrates in opulent theatrical terms, *the Mexico she is*" (Terry 1969, emphasis mine).

And most people accept such a fantasy masquerading as reality through claims of authentic representation of the national treasure of folklore in much the same way that two-hundred-pound women purchase dresses seen on anemic models in fashion shows: they imagine themselves as looking like and being those representational images. But as Strinati sagely observes, "Reality is always constructed, and made intelligible to human understanding by culturally specific systems of meaning. This meaning is never 'innocent,' but has some particular purpose or interest lying behind it, which semiology can uncover" (1995, 110).

Thus essentialism, epitomized by the presentations of these dance companies, becomes a strategy of representation of the State and The People. As anthropologist Michael Herzfeld observes, "Essentialism is always the one thing it claims not to be: it is a strategy, born ... of social and historical contingency. The agents of powerful state entities and the humblest of local social actors engage in the strategy of essentialism to an equal degree" (1997, 31). On the issue of representing the vast former USSR with its population of hundreds of millions, Igor Moiseyev claimed to build a "repertoire so broad that it would truly reveal the national character" (Libman 1986, 21). Thus, one hundred dancers may reveal "Soviet Man" through the colorful medium of "folk" dance. Igor Moiseyev holds the opinion that he can find the single essence of any specific group, such as the Tatars or Kalmuks, for use in portraying them in dance. "A people who are known for a fervent life of combat shows this fervor for fighting in their dances" (Cheremetievskaya n.d., 31). In this manner an entire group of people can be reduced to one character trait: combativeness. Thus, a choreographer can select from nationalist and ethnic stereotypes, either positive or negative, for their choreographic portrayals. A particular group such as Gypsies may be characterized as "fun-loving" or "lazy" while Estonians may be portrayed as "serious" or "industrious."

In contrast to these essentialist portrayals of the nation-state, dance companies also demonstrate the political and ethnic tensions inherent in the multicultural, multiethnic, multilingual states that characterized many of the contemporary nation-states such as the former Soviet Union and the former Yugoslavia. While the professional state ensemble embodies essentialism as it employs choreographic strategies to highlight that all Filipinos, Iranians, or Mexicans as the same, their programs must also show, and even celebrate, a rainbow ethnic diversity. This need to choreographically represent the diversity of the several ethnic groups in the respective nation-state creates an important source of tension that anthropologists Urban and Sherzer (1991) identified as the tension between "assimilation and differentiation." They point out contrasting methods that various nation-states in Latin America utilized for dealing with indigenous peoples: "assimilation" implies attempts at erasing local identity and culture, while "differentiation" suggests the highlighting of cultural differences. Such tensions, which the former Soviet Union and Yugoslavia attempted to balance by allowing dangerous feelings of nationalism to find outlets through seemingly innocent activities such as folk dancing and wearing national costumes, ultimately destroyed the state. In spite of inclusion and representation, at least the highly visible national dance companies and other folk-oriented performances, which displayed "the people" en masse, were heavily supported by the national governments of the former Soviet Union and Yugoslavia. Ultimately the choreographically represented individuals fell, often bloodily, into his or her respective ethnic enclaves.[13] The failure of these states is semiotically reflected in the various readings the public received from these dance companies. Their respective former governments "feared variant cultural readings—minority self-determination, youth nonconformism, cultural dissidence—that might undermine their universalist claims" (Herzfeld 1997, 27–28). Visual representation and inclusion in the official state folk dance ensembles, because politicians almost invariably undervalue and disparage and thereby underestimate the power of art (witness the radical Right's attempt in U.S. Congress to eliminate the National Endowment for the Arts because of the diversity, read un-American or non-American character, of its representation), seems an innocent and innocuous vehicle through which the politically powerless, especially ethnic and minority groups of various types, may be allowed some degree of representation. Politicians fostered the illusion that such representation could be equated with political and social participation in the nation-state. After 1948 when Russian political dominion had been reestablished in the Baltic states of the former USSR and in order to show a return to normalcy that included the domination of the Russians in the area, "Massive song and folk dance festivals began to be held, which included an increasing number of Russian songs and dances as well as those of other republics" (Misiunas and Taagepera 1993, 115).

Most politicians throughout the world view folk dance and music as an innocent form of nonpolitical expression but invariably attempt to harness its undeniable symbolic power for their own uses. The former Soviet government made the important and telling point that through these dance companies they respected and protected the primordial traditions of their many peoples—unlike the West, which the Soviets claimed has as an aim the eradication of the arts of the colonized peoples they politically dominated. This point of view resonated in countries such as Egypt, Mexico, and the Philippines. But in point of fact the Soviets had a "fear of the national uniqueness of other peoples, whose national folklore is quite different from the standard, sterilized, official folklore of their 'elder brother,' the Russian people" (Zemtsovsky and Kunanbaeva 1997, 8).

International world fairs and visits by heads of state are often accompanied by state dance companies with their heady mix of athletic and handsome youth, which sends the subliminal message that "we are a nice, innocent, welcoming people and our country is a nice place to visit." The visit of Anwar Sadat, former president of Egypt, to the United States was accompanied by the Reda company, one of the state dance companies of Egypt, which danced in the rotunda of the Los Angeles City Hall before the mayor and city officials. The slim, undeniably beautiful young Egyptian women, balancing candelabras on their heads, charmed their hosts, who watched the performance with rapt attention.

Thus, among the many questions that I will address in each chapter, one of the most important is who is represented in the repertoire of each of these dance companies? Once posed, this question begs, as Phelan suggested, two others: Who is not represented and why? And how are they represented?

Who Is Represented?

One of the first questions to be raised in the formation of a repertoire for a folk dance company is: Who are the folk? This is not an easy question, but one that requires choices to be made. The answer to this basic question differs from company to company and is frequently determined by a basic philosophical issue posed by the artistic directors. It is sometimes difficult for individuals who have never lived in nations with large peasant populations, or from which they have disappeared, to imagine the tensions between the urban elites and peasant majorities that obtained in most of the world, including Eastern Europe even after World War II. The founding artistic directors and choreographers of the state ensembles were reared in that atmosphere of urban dweller/peasant mistrust. Moiseyev, Hernandez, Reda, and others breathed the atmosphere in which urban dwellers regarded peasants as unwashed, impoverished, and unlettered.

The artistic output of such populations needed to be altered, cleansed, and "improved" for the eyes and sensibilities of modern middle-class audiences in the capital cities. For this they turned to the training in what was then (and is still) considered elite forms of art: ballet and modern dance in which they had received their formal dance training.

Thus, while the peasant is the focus of most folk ensembles, the philosophies of how these peasants are to be represented differs among these founding directors. For example, for Professor Zvonko Ljevakovic, former founding artistic director of LADO, the folk were clearly rural peasants. People from towns and cities were not, by his definition, "folk," and thus their choreographic expression did not merit inclusion in the repertoire showing the "pure" Croatian national spirit.[14] This position clearly reflected folklore scholarship and intellectual attitudes of Eastern European anthropologists and folklorists of the early part of the twentieth century, and consequently, as a member of that (exclusively urban) intellectual milieu, the repertoire he created for LADO reflected this attitude. "Ljevakovic belonged to a group of artists and intellectuals called *'zemlje'* (earth), which was active between the two world wars and which believed that the peasantry was the repository of the Croatian soul. Their art need no alteration" (Misa Sokcic, personal interview, October 17, 1999). The dance and song repertoire of the Croatian state ensemble almost exclusively represented regional rural expression. The repertoire of LADO has only recently added urban dances from Split, but to this day it still remains largely a repertoire representative of the peasantry.

The Moiseyev Dance Company also largely represents and celebrates peasant culture, valued for its work ethic and simple moral values, celebrated in dance by Igor Moiseyev. However, the contrast between LADO and Moiseyev forms a vast aesthetic and philosophical chasm. This gap is revealed in how their respective rural populations are represented and this, in turn, is reflected in the attitudes of the artistic directors toward issues of authenticity, a topic to which we will return often in the course of this study.

By contrast the repertoire of the Bakhor, the folk dance ensemble of Uzbekistan, primarily consists of dances created from the urban solo-improvised dance genre formerly performed by young male professional dancers as well as women in their own private quarters (Shay 1999a). Nothing approaching authentic rural regional dance appears in their repertoire and, significantly, the company is not called a "folk" ensemble. Between these two examples one finds Bayanihan of the Philippines and the former Mahalli dancers, both of which have a mixed repertoire of regional peasant, indigenous tribal, and urban dance genres represented in their repertoires.

Authenticity

The notion of authenticity touches the core of the topic under consideration, because many if not most audiences feel that the choreographic representations made by these companies are "authentic." There can be no issue taken with artists who utilize authentic sources as inspiration in order to produce art. Composers such as Copland, Liszt, Dvorak, and Bartok, among others, have appropriated, borrowed, and reshaped authentic melodies taken from various ethnic groups. Choreographers have also been inspired by native folk dances from the field. In the sixteenth century, Bahram Beiza'i points out, professional urban entertainers often included dances and movements from regional folk dances in their performances (1965, 169). Thus, this discussion should not be viewed as a criticism of the propriety of utilizing traditional music and dance as sources of inspiration. However, the efforts that I just described are more or less individual works of art that do not purport to represent "the *essentialized* people." In the case of choreographers and composers who work with state-sponsored national folk dance companies, there is an assumption that an entire nation is being represented. The fact that they are "official" representatives of their respective nation-states somehow endows these companies with an imprimatur of approval and authenticity in the eyes of many viewers. After all, the dancers are natives and representational of the country that is being displayed. As *Los Angeles Times* dance critic Lewis Segal observes:

> If something called the National Dance Company of China appears at the Los Angeles Music Center, we don't question its pedigree—until a so-called Mongolian Herdsman's Dance goes over the top, showing us nomads jete-ing out of their yurts with pointed feet, classical turnout, and Soviet-style placement. (1995, 41)

One can make the same observation of the Turkmen (*sans yurts*) who were displayed in a similar fashion by the now-defunct Iranian State Folk Dance Ensemble, the Mahalli Dancers, in Los Angeles in 1976. In this case the choreographer Robert De Warren made the strategic miscalculation of mixing authentic Turkmen with his ballet-trained dancers. In this way he created a startling visual mismatch of authentic native dancers with ballet-trained movers that clearly undermined the elements of authenticity he strived to obtain. The earthy dancing of the authentic Turkmen stood in stark contrast to the airy movements of the professionally trained company dancers, who were unable to accurately perform the earthbound movements of the native dancers. The difference between the two groups, mixed together on the same stage, was immediately obvious to the trained eye.

Once the issue of who is to be represented is decided, the next issue that arises is how they are to be represented. This question of authenticity goes to the heart of the notions of essentialization and particularization that I raised earlier in the chapter. As Andriy Nahachewsky observes, "One of the features that often validates national dance activity in the minds of the dance community is its 'authenticity'—its fidelity to the original forms" (1992, 73).

Igor Moiseyev, founder and artistic director of the Moiseyev Dance Company, had no interest in authenticity and declared this himself; he did not use authentic folk movements any more than nineteenth-century classical composers used authentic folk melodies. Rather, he utilized character dance, that form of classical ballet used to depict the so-called "national variations" in many nineteenth-century ballets in which a "Hungarian," "Polish," and/or "Spanish" dance variation appears. He greatly expanded and developed character dance to produce a folklorized dance style that became unique to the Moiseyev Dance Company, although many other companies both inside and outside of the former Soviet Union faithfully emulated it.

By contrast, Zvonko Ljevakovic, former artistic director of LADO, meticulously relied exclusively on authentic movements, costumes, and other elements to create his choreographies. He made the conscious choice to eschew the use of alien (i.e., classical ballet, modern dance, and other forms of Western theater dance), nonauthentic elements in his choreographies (personal interview, September 28, 1967). According to Nevenka Sokcic, one of the original dancers of LADO who frequently accompanied Ljevakovic on research projects, the director also considered steps and movements of neighboring regions as "alien" to a particular tradition. He conceived each district as distinctive. Even though shared elements such as the *drmes* (a shaking dance genre), for example, were common to most regions of Central Croatia, he attempted to teach his professional dancers how to distinguish minute differences in the execution of this widespread dance from district to district. He conducted original research and spent much time in the field learning the materials that he staged through witnessing and practicing the dances and music that were demonstrated for him by his many peasant informants (personal communication, May 21, 1968).

Amalia Hernandez, artistic director of Ballet Folklorico, stands somewhere between Moiseyev and Ljevakovic, but closer to the former. She has unabashedly stated that those who wish to view the truly authentic should go to the village in question and wait for several months until the dance in question is performed. "Authentic? You want authentic? For that you would have to go to the smallest village of my country at a certain hour on one certain day of the year. There, outdoors, in the shadow of the church, you would have a true folkloric experience. You might have to wait six months in that village before it happened, but it would be authentic." Clearly, regarding the degree of authentic elements she uses in her creative works, Hernandez makes choices: "There is no way to move village dancers directly onto a professional stage. Everything must be adapted for modern eyes—costumes, lighting, steps, *espectaculo*. Without stagecraft and adaptation for size and perspective, the originals look like nothing." Nevertheless, her program notes claim hours of research time expended in gathering dances in the field and studying historical sources for her pre-Columbian choreographic works, which, when viewed, arguably owe as much to Martha Graham techniques as they do to Aztec codices. As Hernandez added, "What we make are theater pieces based on folklore. We research carefully, and costumes are created in the particular style appropriate for the large stages where we perform" (Carriaga 1969, F1).

Underscoring the need to claim authenticity, Bayanihan spokespeople state: "'Take it from the people' became the PWU [Philippine Women's University, the home of Bayanihan] researchers' guiding philosophy, one which fired them through forbidding terrain, inhospitable weather and austere living conditions. The desire for authenticity in choreography, music and costumes for the dance repertoire that the PWU set out to develop saw a [research] team . . . touring the length and breadth of the country in succeeding years" (*Bayanihan* 1987, 83).

Issues of authenticity are raised in relation to all folk dance companies because of the idea that one is presenting an "authentic" representation of the nation by using its purest, most primordial materials: folk art. The artistic directors and choreographers of most dance companies that perform traditional dances expend a great deal of time conducting research or, conversely, at least attempting to justify and show their works to be "authentic." Often there is an inverse ratio between the amount of explanation and the actual amount of authentic elements the artistic director incorporates in her or his work. The degree of authenticity employed by each of these companies will be explored in detail in the relevant chapters.

At this point I will emphatically stress that Amalia Hernandez is correct in her statement that "Folklore exists only in its place of origin" (Flores 1993, 50). Every choreographer of a national state folk dance company or an amateur group from the village of origin makes crucial decisions about what to include and what to omit when dances are transferred to the stage. At the very least, the choreographer or artistic director will omit several "negative" elements that would prevent a professional theater creation. He or she might shorten a dance that could otherwise last for hours by omitting screaming babies and children; older people sitting on the sidelines (state folk dance companies are notoriously peopled by very young performers); poor dancers; the dirt and dust, if not mud, of the dancing space; and a host of other elements. The most important element that can rarely, if ever, be transferred to the stage is the total atmosphere within which the dance tradition developed. This is one reason why certain forms of dance such as flamenco, ethnic nightclub milieus such as Greek *tavernas,* and other similar heavily atmospheric locations are notoriously difficult to recapture on the stage.

Through these kinds of decisions a choreographic product is created. Sometimes, as in the case of Igor Moiseyev, little reference is made to the original dance tradition, if one existed; the Soviets did not hesitate to create dance traditions for its various nationality groups out of whole cloth. By contrast, Zvonko Ljevakovic and Dora Stratou attempted to include every authentic element possible that still permitted performances of highly professional technical presentation. Nevertheless, the result is never the village. At its very best, staged folklore can bring knowledgeable audience members the illusion that they are in the place of origin and provide an interpretation that evokes the excitement of the original.

In this chapter I have briefly touched on a few areas of representation found in the performances of state-sponsored folk dance companies, particularly the question of who is choreographically represented as a legitimate part of that nation-state. This is an issue that I will address in more detail in the specific studies of each of the six companies in the chapters that follow.

2

Anatomy of a Dance Company

For a fuller understanding of how folk dance companies, both state and private, consciously and unconsciously project the specific images that they convey to their viewers, one must take a look behind the stage curtains. Certainly some of the observations will be specific to some companies and not to others, but to mount productions of traditional dance, specific ingredients are required. These ingredients have a particular bearing on the final product and are crucial in creating artistic successes or failures. They include stereotypification; the selection and development of repertoire; methods of research to underpin the creation of dances; financing; the selection and training of artists; music; costume acquisition and production; creation and use of sets; behind-the-scenes support, both administrative and technical; and publicity.

The images created from these highly complex ingredients form a very different aesthetic project from classical ballet and modern dance companies that, for the most part, reflect and claim to project the personal images of specific individual choreographic artists such as Martha Graham, George Balanchine, or Mark Morris. In contrast to the "on-the-ground" aspect that folk dance claims to reflect, classical ballet and modern dance choreographies are created through a specific individual's aesthetic imagination, often representing that artist's emotional states, aesthetic interests, personal life experiences, and philosophical outlook, rather than any attempt at representing a particular group.

I certainly do not want to give the impression that these personal and highly individual elements are absent from the creators of traditional and folk choreographies. When one reads the highly dramatic and outspoken interviews of an artist such as Amalia Hernandez, her fierce individuality and creativity ring with the same aesthetic convictions as those of Martha Graham. Nevertheless, each of the state folk dance companies stresses and emphasizes the group: "the people's" art, the pure spirit of the aesthetic expression of a specific ethnic group of people. The artistic directors of the state-sponsored folk ensemble must, to some degree, efface their own contributions, thus creating a tension between the traditional elements and their own individual, highly personal choreographic and aesthetic vision. Like the creations of Martha Graham, Doris Humphrey, or Antony Tudor, the works of these artists are also highly unique. Make no mistake: had artists other than Igor Moiseyev, Robert De Warren, Mahmoud Reda, Mukarram Turganbaeva, Zvonko Ljevakovic, or Amalia Hernandez created works to represent the former Soviet Union, Iran, Egypt, Uzbekistan, Croatia, or Mexico, the results would have been dramatically different. Even in the most socialistic societies, the representation of the nation through the medium of a state-sponsored folk ensemble is produced through a single, unique artistic vision, but because the dances purportedly originate with "the people," the characters of the founder-artistic directors and choreographers are often more muted. Many individuals among the public largely believe the fiction that the choreographies they view on stage reflect actual dances as they would be experienced in a traditional field setting.

State folk dance ensembles often have one individual who is responsible for the entire choreographic creation of the company. Ballet Folklorico de Mexico, the now-defunct Iranian State Folk Dance Ensemble (the Mahalli Dancers), and the Moiseyev Dance Company are the creations of single individuals, in these cases, respectively, Amalia Hernandez, Robert De Warren, and Igor Moiseyev. Other companies such as LADO, the Croatian State Folk Ensemble, and KOLO, the Serbian state folk ensemble, had multiple choreographers. Zvonko Ljevakovic of LADO and Olga Skovran of KOLO certainly formed the artistic identities of these companies and created the overwhelming number of choreographic productions, but they nevertheless utilized other choreographers who were particularly knowledgeable in certain regional styles to enrich their company repertoires. The Dora Stratou Greek Dances Theatre constitutes an anomaly in that the ensemble has neither a choreographer nor an artistic director, but rather dance leaders who set the manner in which the dances of particular regions will be staged.

In Chapters 3–8, I will describe the following ingredients as they relate to the specific ensemble, its performances, and the images projected.

Stereotypification

I use the term "stereotypification" to refer to a phenomenon that has an enormous impact on the choreographic choices and strategies of creating repertoires that are designed for specific visions of national representation. Stereotypification here refers to the tensions and pressures placed upon the creators of the repertoire to represent the nation in a particular fashion. Each of the companies that I analyze in this study features works that fit into stereotypes that resonate both internally and externally. Every nation seems to have a geographic area, with the accompanying dances, music, and/or clothing, that are emblematic of the entire nation-state. Generally, there is also a secondary geographic area or dance style that forms a national icon.

Such symbolic representation occurs in almost every nation-state, no matter how modern and politically evolved. In the United States, many people—if not the majority of the population—think of square dance as the most representative dance and "the West" as the most stereotypically "American" area. Many attempts have been made to introduce legislation in the U.S. Congress to declare square dance as the official American folk dance, in spite of vigorous opposition by Native Americans, scholars, and other groups (Quigley 1992). Naima Prevots details some of the earlier efforts by the dance panel that advised the U.S. State Department to construct a professional folk dance company to send "abroad some representation of American folk or square dance, or a combination of the two," to represent the United States in answer to the formidable challenge of the Moiseyev Dance Company (1998, 116). This effort ended in frustration and failure. Since the panel consisted of dance artists, most of whom were incapable of seeing beyond classical ballet and modern dance as the only true choreographic art forms, the State Department opted to send mostly ballet and modern dance as the representatives of American culture.[1]

In the United States, Appalachia, with its running sets—a genre of country dances with many figures similar to those found in square dancing—and fiddling, is a secondary area, although the distinction between the music and dances of Appalachia and the western states seems blurred in the popular mind. This myopic and narrow but common view of dance in America excludes Native American, Puerto Rican, Tex-Mex, Hawaiian, Early Californian, Cajun, Georgia Sea Island, New England, and myriad other forms of dance that would have, in fact, created a rich repertoire of choreographic Americana in its widest sense.

In the repertoire of the Ballet Folklorico de Mexico, one finds the suite of the dances and music of the state of Jalisco, Amalia Hernandez's choreographic finale *Jalisco*, functioning as the most stereotypical suite of dances and music. In this region one finds the mariachi band, the china poblana female and charro male costume, and the hat dance and other jarabe dances.[2] These popular icons of Mexico form a de rigueur ensemble of symbols representative of the Mexican people and state. In fact, this suite of dances has been the finale of each and every concert of Ballet Folklorico that I have ever seen. After all, who would believe that they had seen a representative performance of Mexican folklore that did not feature these elements? Mexican products feature, perhaps more than any other figures, the china poblana and the charro as pictorial representations of their "Mexicanness." The state of Veracruz provides the secondary example with the internationally popular dance-song *"la bamba,"* virtuoso footwork and harp playing, and dazzlingly white costumes forming the ending number of the first half of virtually all Ballet Folklorico performances. Would the vast majority of viewers, Mexican or non-Mexican, believe that they were seeing a Mexican dance company and seeing a representative sampling of Mexican dance if they did not hear the strains of the *"jarabe tapatio"* or *"la bamba"*?

Many other nation-states have areas that have become emblematic of the entire nation. In Croatia (formerly a part of Yugoslavia) the main geographical focal point of national representation is the villages that lie in the hills above the capital city of Zagreb, known collectively as the Prigorje. The tourist shops of the capital and other tourist centers feature a variety of dolls, pins, and other objects depicting the costume of that region. Predictably, LADO's finale suite is the dances of Prigorje, *Prigorski Plesovi*. What I term the stereotypical secondary region of Croatia is Posavina, whose costumes also grace the tourist shops of Zagreb and are the most popular style of clothing among Croatian-Americans. *Posavski Plesovi*, the suite of dances of Posavina, often opens a LADO performance and was one of the ensemble's three original choreographies.

The dances of the villages of the Tagalog-speaking areas surrounding Manila and the *tinikling* (dance with poles) create through the lively finale of the concert the last impression for viewers of Bayanihan. This is the *Rural Suite*, which the program characterizes as "a panoramic view of the Philippine countryside, celebrating the *bayanihan*, communal spirit," from which the company takes its name (Bayanihan 1987, 124).

Diaspora groups often follow the cues from these national companies. Andriy Nahachewsky observes that among the Ukrainians of Canada the "basic national costume represented the dress of the Poltava region," while "a second costume common in the national tradition represented the Hutzul region of the Carpathian Mountains"

(1992, 77–78). In this practice of wearing the costumes of Poltava the dancers in the Ukrainian diaspora follow the examples set by the Ukrainian State Folk Ensemble, as well as that of Moiseyev who uses stylized Poltava costumes for his dazzling finale, *Gopak*.

While many state-sponsored companies follow this pattern, one striking exception is Egypt. As I noted above, the Egyptian authorities, and indeed many individuals throughout the Arab world, are uncomfortable with *danse orientale* (belly dance), the dance that often represents Egypt in the popular mind.[3] From the Victorian-era morality of colonial representatives' disgust with the open sexuality of dance and other arts and entertainments in the areas they ruled and administered, a pattern of subaltern reactions evolved among the elite urban middle classes that eventually succeeded them. This new class of administrators carried out the colonialist attitudes of suppressing or "cleaning up" the dance and clothing traditions that were considered sexual, crude, or representative of backwardness and created theatrical versions to make them acceptable to the newly Westernized middle classes of the capital city.[4]

Research Strategies and Methods

Because the directors and choreographers of these companies make claims of authenticity, research allows them to determine the most characteristic movements, steps, and poses found in a specific geographic area or among a particular ethnic group. Through research, however conducted, they can utilize the most "typical," "well-known," or "popular" dances in a specific area.

It is impossible to determine the actual amount of time and effort a single individual artistic director expends in research or which methodologies they pursue. The claims of many of them, at least insofar as the results of their efforts are demonstrated in the final product of choreography and staging of their companies, are certainly open to interpretation. Such claims are made to bolster claims of authenticity. All of the state dance companies, including the Moiseyev Dance Company, stress the amount of fieldwork the artistic director has undertaken. Referring to Mahmoud Reda, founding artistic director and choreographer of the Reda Troupe, Egyptian dance historian and scholar Magda Saleh states, "Reda undertook extensive field surveys and pioneered the use of traditional Egyptian folk forms to create theatrical dance spectacle" (1998, 496). Establishing the truth of artistic directors' claims does not form part of this study, because aside from being generally unverifiable, the claims that are made are of interest only insofar as they pertain to issues of representation.

The claims for research of these artistic directors are also not verifiable, because the directors have rarely published the results of their fieldwork. For example, Dr. Ivan Ivancan, who served as artistic director of LADO for some years and created a number of choreographies for that ensemble, as well as for his own company, Jozo Vlahovic, is the author of an impressive series of meticulously documented field studies. In these studies, Ivancan describes dances from several regions, both textually and using labanotation, and provides musical notation and in-depth descriptions of how, when, where, and by whom each dance is performed as well as descriptions of his informants. To conduct these studies, Ivancan posed a series of questions that he explored in the course of his research.

An artistic director or choreographer can learn dances by using a number of methods. By far the most satisfying is fieldwork, in which the individual goes to the place where the dance is natively performed. This method is the most satisfying because by seeing the dance in situ, one can obtain other important information. This might consist of, among other data, the relationship of the dancers to other dancers of the same and opposite genders, styles of movement when not dancing, and how clothing such as skirts, hats, kerchiefs, and shawls are manipulated during the dance. It is possible to learn in the comfort of one's studio by inviting an informant to demonstrate the steps and movements, and by interview the informant. However, the all-important subsidiary information is generally lacking or secondhand, and this information—details and aspects of which can be incorporated in a staging—in turn can bring a sense of verisimilitude to a work that has been removed from the field and brought to a concert stage. This latter problem—how to translate the field to the stage and at the same time retain the most unique and authentic elements—forms the greatest challenge to artistic directors of these groups, and all of them have stated this in interviews, or in program descriptions (Shay 1986). Additional methods such as books also exist for research, for there are many "how to" books and manuals that provide, with varying success, movements, steps, music, and other aspects of folk dances. Such books exist in all of the areas except Iran, although many of them appeared after the founding of these companies. Films taken in the field provide an alternative method to journeying to the field, and many governments maintain ongoing projects in many nations of the world to record the entire traditional music and dance corpus of all of the regions of their respective nation-states. Projects such as that begun by

Bela Bartok and Zoltan Kodaly for the Hungarian state, Dr. Vinko Zganec and Dr. Ivan Ivancan of Croatia, Ljubica and Danica Jankovic for Serbia, or Frances Aquino for the Philippines are impressive in their rigor, scope, and detail and cover many volumes.

While it is relatively easy to believe that individual artistic directors have spent at least some time in the field, the claims for research for choreographies purporting to be from ancient times form a particularly interesting body of questionable claims. Not all of the companies attempt recreating "ancient" dances, which often reflects the political attitudes of the respective nation-state. For example, neither the Greek nor the Turkish state folk ensembles, reflecting their nation-state's political priorities, represent the long Ottoman period in their respective repertoires.

On the other hand, among those ensembles that choose to choreographically represent historical periods, the choreographers obtain mixed results. Both the Mahalli Dancers of Iran and Ballet Folklorico de Mexico have attempted to culturally represent symbolic icons that resonate with their populations. Robert De Warren, former artistic director of the Mahalli Dancers, claimed to have laid a series of Persian miniatures side by side to obtain a clear picture of actual movement practices of four hundred years ago.[5] Other groups have variously claimed to study and utilize the results found in friezes from churches (Branko Krsmanovic, a semiprofessional ensemble from Serbia) and temple paintings and Aztec codices (Ballet Folklorico de Mexico). While not to my knowledge attempting to recreate ancient dances, the late Dora Stratou, founder and artistic director of the Greek National Dance Company, has made detailed claims for the ancient origins of contemporary folk dances (Stratou 1966).

Choreographic Strategies and Methods

Probably the most characteristic choreographic structure utilized by the dance majority of the companies under analysis in this study is the suite. Beginning with the Moiseyev Dance Company, all of the companies—with the exception of Bakhor, the Uzbek state company, which generally uses single dance works although suites are not absent from its programs—utilize the concept of the suite as a primary choreographic strategy for representation. These suites tend to represent a specific geographical region: a village, a district, a province, or even the entire nation-state. The Turkish State Folk Dance Ensemble has a wedding suite that encompasses customs and dances from areas across Turkey as well as suites of regional folk dances. In this manner, a choreographer can accomplish a number of goals. First, it enables the choreographer to utilize the widest range of movements and steps possible from the given area. This can be crucial if the steps tend to be simple. In LADO's suite from Posavina, *Posavski Plesovi*, there exist only four basic steps, including walking. The talent and creativity of Zvonko Ljevakovic turned these simple movements into an artistic masterpiece.

A second popular and effective format for the presentation of traditional dance is to use the context of a popular event such as a wedding or a national festival. In this way the choreographer can weave into his or her work customs, special songs, and a wider variety of festive clothing. All the world loves a wedding! The use of context tends to give the work greater verisimilitude. Other effective devices center around contexts such as work scenes, harvest festivals, rituals, holidays, and other daily activities.

Repertoire

Foremost in the thoughts of those who serve as artistic directors of dance companies, such as Igor Moiseyev or Amalia Hernandez, is the repertoire. Based on the decisions made as to which types of dances and the groups that they represent, choreographies, costumes, and sometimes sets are created to fulfill the mission of the company. Each folk dance company has a mission to represent certain "on-the-ground" realities, however fanciful the choreographic results may turn out to be. The mission statement in the Bayanihan company's thirtieth anniversary souvenir book encapsulates typical statements made by almost all folk dance companies, state and private: "Bayanihan . . . proved two things: [one,] that dance could be an effective medium for preserving—and showing off—the nation's rich cultural heritage; two, that a folk dance company could be a persuasive force in promoting the Philippines abroad. . . . Bayanihan has been cited for many things: awakening a new pride among Filipinos in their cultural heritage; preserving and adding a new dimension to the country's dance tradition; building for the country a rich reserve of international good will" (*Bayanihan* 1987, 6–7).

In the former Soviet bloc, the respective governments rigidly regulated the repertoires of both state and amateur ensembles. "For folklore this meant, for instance, an eventual codification of the repertoire of folk ensembles; changes had to be cleared with special Party/State committees that oversaw the work of such State-subsidized folk performing groups" (Gutkin 1997, 35).

It should be noted that as each company builds a repertoire, it becomes increasingly difficult to add new choreographies. This occurs for several reasons: (1) It is difficult to find the time to rehearse a new work and keep the performance repertoire in rehearsal at the same time; (2) When the repertoire is full, the choreographer/artistic director must subtract older, possibly very successful pieces from the repertoire; and (3) Finances may be difficult to obtain. The Dora Stratou Greek Dances Theatre, for example, is financially unable to add new works. One must convince investors, whether the state or other sources, of the need for yet another new work. In many of the socialist states, finances were extremely meager at different periods of a company's existence.

Dancers and Dance Training

In order for each of these companies to operate and perform, the most basic ingredient, after the construction of unique and successful choreographies, is the group of artists—dancers, musicians, and, in some cases, singers who can professionally fulfill the choreographer's images. In each respective section we will look at the sources of training, rehearsal schedules and practices, and the way in which each company searches for its artists. In addition, because it is pertinent to the discussion of representation, we will analyze when or if certain physical types of bodies, faces, heights, weights, coloring, etc., are required of dancers. Patrick Alcedo, Philippine dance scholar, described how many members of the Philippine public were upset that in the early days of the establishment of the Bayanihan company, many of the dancers had the appearance of the Spanish-looking elite of Manila rather than the more Asian aspect of the majority of the Philippine population (personal interview, June 5, 1997).

The technical skill of the artistic personnel can sometimes determine representation. A particular dance or piece of music may be so demanding as to be impossible for a group of dancers to perform it as it is performed in the field. For example, the LADO Ensemble attempted, unsuccessfully, to recreate the *moreska* from the island and town of Korcula on the Dalmatian coast. The native performers of this dance in the small city of Korcula spend hours of time on the performance of this one sword-dance ritual, which requires an evening for a full performance. A large military band that plays music from

Anatomy of a Dance Company 47

Verdi's operas is required to accompany the event. The cast of dancers is very large, as is the band. The ritual also features a lengthy dialogue between the opposing groups of dancers in Croatian that is unsuitable for touring abroad. The size of the cast, the skill needed for handling the swords, the hours needed for a successful performance, and the numbers of musicians needed to achieve the sound all lay outside of the technical capacity of most of the dancers of LADO (or almost any other company). Their attempt to recreate this work was not successful, and the choreography did not remain long in the repertoire.

I suspect that for much the same reason, Ballet Folklorico does not attempt to include the performance of the *voladores*, the famous "flyers" who suspend themselves by the feet from a high pole and spin through the air. No normal theater could accommodate the equipment required for such a performance. Professional dancers, who must master a large repertoire of dances from a wide geographical spectrum, simply do not have the hours and training facilities available to also master dances with such demanding special technical prowess. The native performers of these dances are often avid devotees, or religiously or spiritually inspired, and they spend a great deal of their free time practicing for this one ritualistic event. The possibility of accidents is enormous. Other examples of special skills are dancers who must walk through fire, such as the Anestenaria or Nestenarki event found in Greek and Bulgarian Thrace. In order to achieve this feat the performers must enter a trancelike state, and thus this type of ritual presents insurmountable technical problems. The Sufis of the Mevlevi order of Konya, Turkey, whose capacity to spin for long periods of time has attracted worldwide attention, spend years acquiring this skill as well as the control required to enter altered states of consciousness. The Mahalli dancers of Iran were unable to summon either the spiritual or technical skills to perform a convincing recreation of this ritual that was choreographed by Robert De Warren. Thus, representation or lack thereof sometimes takes on a technical or spiritual aspect that prevents the inclusion of dances of stigmatized minorities or socioeconomic classes; exclusion is not always a matter of political or cultural bias.

A critical factor in attracting the best dancers is the benefits, including prestige, of international travel and financial awards. For example, in the earliest days of LADO, attracting highly talented male dancers was relatively easy, because under socialism a dancer could earn the same, if not better, pay than an engineer. In addition, the company traveled widely, adding to the prestige and attractiveness of the position of dancer in the national company. In the 1960s as the

Yugoslav state turned increasingly to capitalistic incentives to reward highly skilled workers such as doctors, engineers, chemists, and others, the male talent pool upon which LADO relied dried up considerably. Men found it more advantageous to work in other professions, while women continued to find such employment superior to other alternatives.

Gema Sandoval, a choreographer involved for years in the folklorico movement, noted that in Ballet Folklorico, for many of the same reasons, the male dancers tended to come from the provinces where salaries were lower. The female corps were primarily made up of upper-middle-class individuals waiting for favorable marriage opportunities (private communication, 1998).

Music

The difficult and arduous training and preparation involved in multiple styles of movement and intricate choreographies almost pales when compared to the complex technical problems of providing musical accompaniment. This is particularly exacerbated in cases in which the artistic director insists on authentic, live music. Virtually all of the state ensembles utilize live music in their performances, although there are rare exceptions.[6] A prominent problem in these ensembles concerns decisions regarding music. Obtaining the most accurate music from the enormous diversity of musical instruments, vocal styles, and other ethnomusicological elements involves complex details, as we will see in all of the nation-states represented in this study. Sometimes wrenching decisions must be made in deciding which music to include, and which to exclude, in the repertoire. Not even the most highly financially backed dance company can afford all of the musical instruments needed to provide accurate music—there are simply too many instruments found in the countryside to be mastered by the number of musicians that one can afford to employ.

The various companies that we will investigate have made a variety of decisions. For example, the Moiseyev Dance Company employs a Western symphony orchestra with a few folk instruments, such as balalaikas and various types of accordions, to provide a bit of ethnic flavoring. When these are used, these instruments are often featured on the stage among the dancers, whereas the large concert orchestra of Western instruments that accompanies a Moiseyev concert are seated in a pit.

The Bulgarian Ensemble of Folk Songs and Dances, known as the

Philip Koutev Ensemble in the West, made a specific decision to create an orchestra of instruments based on the four most prominent Bulgarian native instruments: the bagpipe (*gajda*), the end-blown flute (*kaval*), the bowed instrument (*gadulka*), and a plucked instrument (*tambura*). In addition, the large drum (*tapan*) provided the percussion. This decision truly contains implications for issues of representation and essentialism. The pantheon of actual musical instruments utilized in the field by the rural population was extremely varied, but the instruments selected by the artistic staff of the Koutev ensemble were essentially perceived of as "Bulgarian," in contrast to instruments of Western origin such as the widely popular accordion and violin. Brass bands, *zurla* (double-reed instruments), and clarinets were often (and still are) played by Gypsies or had associations with only one region such as Pirin (as the Bulgarian government designated the Macedonian ethnic enclave of the southwest). In addition, these instruments—as well as the *oud* (a Middle Eastern lute), the *kanun* (a zitherlike instrument), and the *darabuka* (goblet drum) and *daf* (frame drum)—had Turkish and thus negative associations. They were not permitted in the golden circle of qualified instruments even though they had been popular in urban orchestras with Christians, Muslims, and Jews alike throughout the Ottoman Balkans.[7]

The Bulgarian state ensemble, and the numerous amateur groups following their lead, did not simply use the four instruments in the form in which they were found in villages, and traditionally played as solo instruments; they were altered in two ways. In their native state these are nontempered instruments, that is to say that they do not have the standard tunings found in a piano-based scale, with evenly spaced whole and half tones. Thus, in order for these instruments, which had generally not been played together before and certainly not in large orchestras, to play in tune with one another, they had to be specifically constructed to have the same pitch. Another alteration—or perhaps a better term is creation—was to take the *gadulka*, a bowed instrument held by the neck and played like a cello, but much smaller, and create instruments the size of cellos and basses in order to provide a bass and tenor sound to fill out the treble timbres of the original four instruments. The result is a massive sound that had previously never been heard in a Bulgarian village. Thus, the artistic staff of the Bulgarian state ensemble created an entirely new musical entity: a folk orchestra that represented all of Bulgaria—a truly invented tradition.

Vocal music is not utilized in all of the ensembles in this study. For example, the Moiseyev Dance Company does not use vocalists. But, in the Koutev ensemble the all-female choir had pride of place because Philip Koutev was the founder and overall artistic director of the Bulgarian state folk ensemble, in addition to which he served as vocal director, composer, and arranger for the choir. Here, too, while developing an essential "folk voice," Koutev provided three highly creative moving vocal parts not found in the overwhelming production of Bulgarian folk music as heard among the rural population. The chorus of forty-four voices sings with a professional unity that is truly unique and truly Bulgarian, but not traditional; nor, on closer inspection, does it resemble the singing found in the field, although vocal duets containing the traditional dissonances are featured like a heady spice in the performances. The musical style created by Philip Koutev remains popular with concertgoers and devotees of "world music" today. There is little attempt to produce the many regional styles that exist in Bulgaria; rather, the chorus produces a "Pan-Bulgarian" sound, where previously only regional styles existed. CDs of the choral music arrangements begun by Philip Koutev have large sales, and live concerts by vocal ensembles utilizing the style he originated are preeminent in world music performances.

By contrast, LADO, the company that by far attempts the most detailed regional musical styles through its own regular orchestra members, and very occasionally for very special events with guest musicians, utilizes a wide range of instruments. Croatia is by far the smallest of the nation-states represented in this study. Nevertheless, the complexity of musical types and instruments representing its various regions is staggering. Ljevakovic decided that he would stretch his regular musicians as far as he could to have the most authentic sounds possible. He occasionally chose to use recorded music for areas that his musicians could not master. For example, two double-reed instruments, *sopila* (plural *sopile*), traditionally accompany the dances from the regions of the Quarnero (*Kvarner*) Bay in the north Adriatic Sea (the regions and islands of Istria, Krk, Susak, etc.), which are constructed in minor sixths by master instrument makers of the region. The playing of these instruments, particularly because the two parts are equally difficult, requires hours of practice. For much of its career, LADO used recordings for these unique sounds because Zvonko Ljevakovic's exacting standards did not permit him to substitute other instruments. I also witnessed that two players from the island of Krk were employed for exceptional instances when LADO wished to make a particularly important impression, but they were never a part of the ensemble. By the time of LADO's 1992 tour of the United States, two of its regular musicians had mastered the instruments.

Costumes

In the performance of all folk dance ensembles, costuming is, after choreography, the single most important visual aspect of the performance. The costumes worn by the dancers signal, at least to the knowledgeable, the artistic director's attitude and philosophy regarding authenticity. Zvonko Ljevakovic declared himself dedicated to finding the most varied, valuable, and authentic costumes, and his knowledge of them was extensive (personal interview, September 23, 1967). Ljevakovic considered the costumes to be social documents and assiduously sought the widest variety of clothing suitable for representing a specific region. For those who study costume, this constitutes an understandable stance for an individual interested in showing the nuances of folk life. Clothing, and particularly folk clothing, constitutes an entire semiotic system. In rural life, during the period when traditional clothing is worn on an everyday basis, clothing, jewelry, and hairstyles reveal to the knowledgeable the exact social status of an individual: age, marital status, religion, and condition of emotion.[8]

This insistence on authenticity in the clothing or costumes worn by dancers in LADO contrasts with costuming practices in most other state-sponsored companies. As Amalia Hernandez stated, "In their original form, folk costumes, exquisite in their handiwork, often do not translate exactly to the stage. Our costumes are handcrafted, too, but for large spaces" (Carriaga 1969). As with the dances, Amalia Hernandez mistrusts the actual peasant taste and production and feels the need to "improve" upon them.

The former Mahalli Dancers of Iran wore costumes designed by a fashionable upper-class woman whose creations were loose translations of the original garments designed to make the dancers look attractive in twentieth-century terms. These creations were produced in modern fabrics in colors that harmonize to satisfy modern urban eyes. In this way, the Mahalli dancers, like Ballet Folklorico, mistrusted the aesthetics of the peasants and tribal people they claimed to represent. The costuming of the Mahalli Dancers often followed the practice found in the Moiseyev and other professional dance companies, where one finds three dancers in red, three in blue, three in green, and three in yellow (an actual practice with Moiseyev costuming).

The costumes of the Moiseyev ensemble make no attempt to project more than the sketchiest nod to the original clothes upon which they are based. This attitude serves as an excuse for the artistic directors to project more contemporary images to their audiences. Many of them dislike the "un-chic" aspect of actual traditional clothing because it impedes the modern aspects of their choreographies. Certain clothing does not lend itself to rapid turns, for example, a common feature of current folk choreography. Others, such as Mustafa Turan of the Turkish State Folk Dance Ensemble, find them inconvenient for fast changes and make alterations, such as sewing two or three garments together and using zippers that are not a feature of traditional clothing so that the dancers can change costumes rapidly. Costuming, too, does not escape the eye of officialdom. Horror stories abound regarding political decisions:

> Dr. Kunanbaeva has stories to tell from the Brezhnev years (otherwise known as the "stagnation period"), of how the wardrobes of a large folk ensemble had to be remade because of the color-code system imposed from above for national ensembles: the Kazakh performers had to be dressed in yellow and not green since the latter color was assigned to Kirghizia. (Gutkin 1997, 35)

Nicolae Ceausescu, the former Rumanian dictator, was rumored to have forbidden folk dance companies to wear peasant shoes because they made the country look backward, so the women wore red high-heel dance shoes with the heavily altered and glamorized "traditional" costumes. They certainly wore the cherry-red shoes in three U.S. performances that I saw in the 1970s and 1980s.

In the following chapters, I will discuss for each dance company the details of several costumes and how they are at variance with the original clothes that the dancers purportedly represent. As an overall observation, hemlines, silhouettes, waistlines, and skirt lengths are designed to please modern (mid-twentieth-century) tastes. The ubiquitous practice of using three yellow, three green, three red, and three blue costumes (or perhaps other colors) and the use of light, inauthentic fabrics pervades the costuming throughout the Moiseyev repertoire as well as those of other Soviet companies.[9] This latter practice was also utilized by the Mahalli dancers of Iran, who, like Amalia Hernandez and Igor Moiseyev, had fashionable dress designers redesign the costumes to look larger than life on the stage, eliminate inconvenient aspects of the original clothing that did not enhance the dance movements of a particular choreography, and, in general, appeal to twentieth-century audiences. Because the costumes convey the most important visual images alongside the choreographic elements, an analysis of the degree to which costumes should be authentic lies within all of the other companies under discussion in this study and creates an important topic under the rubric of projected images.

Like the technical difficulties that often limit certain types of representation in the abilities of dancers to perform highly specialized dance traditions, the physical complexities as well as the cost of creating or purchasing costumes can also present difficulties, affecting a company's ability to create a wardrobe. The funding of the companies that we will look at more closely varies widely. For all companies, considerable financial investment is made in even the least expensive costumes. For those companies such as LADO or the Dora Stratou Greek Dances Theatre that insist on a high level of authenticity in their clothing, the cost of certain costumes—for example, costumes made with real gold bullion embroidery—can range from exorbitant to prohibitive, placing the representation of certain regions beyond financial possibility.[10]

Finances

Since all of these companies, to some degree, constitutes an official arm of their respective governments, clearly some, if not all, funding comes from that source. This of course varies widely and in many ways reflects the economic philosophies and realities of each nation-state, raising a crucial issue: Since the government is footing the bill, to what degree does the government expect to influence the content and other aspects of the national dance company? In the former Soviet Union and Eastern bloc nations such as Hungary and Bulgaria, virtually all of the funding came from the government. According to many sources,[11] the government, through the appropriate ministries, dictated to a high degree all aspects of folkloric production, including professional and amateur dance groups and festivals.

Some of the companies, such as Ballet Folklorico, Moiseyev, and Bayanihan, earn important sums of money from touring. In addition, other assets—a theater, offices, and other valuable space—is provided by the state or a municipality for rehearsals, administrative functions, and storage of costumes and props. These funding sources impose restrictions and limitations, such as how many performers one may hire or the opulence of sets and costumes that a single choreographer may command at his or her disposal. The funding also dictates the all-important factor of how much the company can pay the individual dancers. As economies undergo changes, how much one can pay in a competitive economy influences how attractive dancing as a profession is to individuals who might otherwise turn to other career choices.

Some of the ensembles receive an important portion of their financing from tourist dollars. Almost all visitors to Mexico City are taken to the wonderful Bellas Artes, the old Baroque theater in downtown Mexico City, to see Ballet Folklorico and the theater's world-famous Tiffany curtain. One sees tickets for Ballet Folklorico, one of Mexico City's major tourist attractions, for sale everywhere. This provides the company with a never-ending source of new viewers. For many viewers the romantic performances presented by Ballet Folklorico embody and encapsulate the essence of Mexico. Such "authentic" and unforgettable depictions of Mexico will not be sullied by news reports from CNN. So immediate are the images projected by the Ballet Folklorico de Mexico that they remain forever fixed in the mind of the viewer, who feels that he or she has shared an evening of the "true soul of Mexico," as one friend remarked when leaving that impressive theater in November 1974.

The Dora Stratou Company is also a popular tourist attraction for the myriad visitors to Greece. My evening in 1959 at the ancient amphitheater in Piraeus was an unforgettable experience. As in Mexico and Greece, the many visitors who travel to Moscow and Tashkent are often taken to see Moiseyev and Bakhor, respectively.

By contrast, other companies—such as LADO from Croatia and the Mahalli Dancers of Iran—were not on any regular tourist itinerary. Zagreb and Tehran are not major tourist cities. However, LADO received a major portion of its financing by touring and performing each summer in hotels and theaters along the length of the Dalmatian coast that teems with tourists in the summer months.

Foreign touring was also a major factor in financing these companies. While the issue of representation of the nation remained the most important factor, the hard currency earned by some of these companies was considerable. Moiseyev, Ballet Folklorico, and Bayanihan in particular had major annual tours that earned sizeable incomes. The touring schedules of LADO and the Mahalli dancers were far more modest but nevertheless brought needed financial backing. In addition, the lure of touring foreign countries attracted talented dancers to these companies.

Bakhor's foreign tours were almost totally, with one exception of which I am aware, confined to Third World countries, because until 1989 they had not attained the "Academic" rating required for touring in the West. Outside of the former Soviet Union it is a little known fact that the USSR had a system of ratings that defined the scope of foreign touring. The Moiseyev Dance Company's appellation of "Academic" ensemble (shared with the Kirov and Bolshoi Ballets, the Piyatnitsky Chorus, and the Georgian State Folk Company) permitted them to be engaged for foreign tours in the Western world, thus providing a valuable source of hard currency. Companies such as Bakhor and the Armenian State Dance Company occasionally traveled abroad in the West, but these forays were usually sponsored by special interest groups abroad such as the Armenian community or the American Society for Friendship with the Soviet Union, a group that was politically supportive of Soviet interests. The concerts these companies gave were open to the public, but unlike an appearance by the Moiseyev Dance Company or the Georgian State Folk Company, booked months in advance by American impresarios, they were not managed or advertised in a professional manner. Outside of the special interest group that sponsored them, their appearances were poorly attended. Mukarram Turganbaeva, the founding artistic director of the Bakhor company of Uzbekistan, explained this situation to me in 1976; unfortunately, she did not live to see her company awarded the "Academic" rating a decade later.

Great hoopla and an impressive public ceremony in which government representatives officially bestowed the coveted honor always accompanied the designation of the all-important "Academic" title. By contrast the former Mahalli Dancers of Iran received the bulk of their funding through the Ministry of Fine Arts and the private endowment of the former Empress Farah. In capitalist nations such as Turkey and Mexico, grants and financial aid from corporations and foundations are also available, and Ballet Folklorico has used this source of support extensively.

Thus we see a wide range of funding sources that formed the economic underpinnings of these ensembles. In each chapter that follows I will analyze how the funding permitted or limited such aspects of each company, such as how new works were produced and mounted, how many performers the dance companies could employ, and how they purchased costumes, sets, musical instruments, and other assets. We will also look at the physical spaces provided by the states and how those influenced the company's performances and rehearsal schedules and other related activities.

Artistic directors of state dance companies, no matter how well endowed or how free to make aesthetic decisions, work under a series of restrictions. These vary from company to company, but they represent elements—such as costumes, musical instruments, and the physical capacity and technical skills of the company artists—that many observers might not have considered as restrictions. In any analysis of these world-famous companies one must take these elements, as well as the political and social contexts in which the companies work, into consideration.

3

The Moiseyev Dance Company: Ancestor of the Genre

It would be almost impossible for anyone not present in the audiences of the first visit of the Moiseyev Dance Company to the United States in 1958 to understand the impact of those appearances.[1] The Ukrainian *Gopak* finale serves as a familiar example of a typical Moiseyev choreography. It opens as a bevy of young village "girls" (I use the word advisedly for they are dressed in the costumes of unmarried girls) runs onto the stage and forms a loose circle, excitedly whispering in one another's ears. This constitutes what I call "it's fun in the village" choreography. Garbed in approximate copies of the costumes—adjusted at the waist and shortened for mid-twentieth-century taste—of the Poltava region, the primary costume icon of the Ukraine, the circle splits apart revealing a pair of male dancers. The music slows to a purposeful rhythm, and as the two men perform virtuosic squats and leg extensions, the girls retreat to both sides of the stage, strategically grouped in threes by the colors of their sleeveless jackets—black, blue, green, and red. Throughout the choreography they form a decorative element as male soloists and duos appear, each with a highly athletic choreographic skill. As the "boys" (I also use this word advisedly, for they, too, are dressed in the costumes of the unmarried) finish a series of increasingly intricate and difficult feats familiar to those who have seen "Fiddler on the Roof"—rapid spins, "coffee grinders," "pryzadakas" (kicking the legs forward while in a squatting position), squats, and other movements associated in the popular mind with Russian dancing.

Among the dancers are two or three "character" dancers who sport moustaches and are depicted as fatter, shorter, taller, and/or older, thus dividing them from the "innocent boys." They do not, however, exhibit a threatening masculinity, for they play the role of the village buffoons. As each soloist or duo finishes, the dancers move to form a line behind the women. As the last male soloist finishes, the music crescendoes and the tempo quickens. The company suddenly erupts

Moiseyev Dance Company. *Gopak*. COURTESY ICM ARTISTS.

The Moiseyev Dance Company: Ancestor of the Genre

into a series of trios (one boy between two girls) and revolves in a counterclockwise circle around the stage. You can feel the level of excitement rising in the audience. By a choreographic sleight of hand, the dancers move into a formation of three spokes and, by more legerdemain, they dissolve into a presentational formation of eight rows of six dancers each. With a flourish, the front row of dancers, raising their hands and forming a bridge, move rapidly to the side and, using a high-lifting run, move swiftly backward, followed by each succeeding row. As they arrive at the back, each row runs forward under the upraised arms of their comrades to regain their original positions, ending the dance with hands raised in the air. This spectacle has been followed by an instant standing ovation from every audience I ever sat in.

All of the senses were overwhelmed by the perfectly precisioned, over-the-top acrobatic prowess of a hundred brilliantly costumed dancers accompanied by a specially designed symphony orchestra, which aurally heightened the effect of the visual spectacle. Such a spectacle had never been seen before in the United States, at least not in my lifetime. During the Los Angeles engagement—which repeated earlier successes in New York, Philadelphia, and other cities, night after night, week after week—seven thousand eager and excited viewers thronged the huge Shrine Auditorium. The unusually large crowds, which numbered in the hundreds of thousands for the U.S. tour, were attracted partly by a foretaste of the company on "The Ed Sullivan Show," viewed by millions of American households, and partly by the illicit thrill of seeing actual Russians for the first time. At the height of the Cold War, many Americans did not realize that all Russians were not Communists. They also thought that everyone in the USSR was a Russian. In the years before the Moiseyev Dance Company appeared, Communists had been depicted in lurid images in Hollywood films and in the televised trials of the McCarthy era. Many in the audience wanted to verify for themselves whether, in fact, Russians, by which one meant Communists, had horns and tails! Virtually no one in the United States had seen so many Russians in one place. Braving picket lines of protesting patriotic believers of McCarthyist anti-Communist politics, bomb threats, and miles of walking to the theater from distant parking locations, eager fans clutched tickets that were being scalped for ten times their value to see the mythical dancers from Russia. The *Los Angeles Times* breathlessly followed the dancers on their adventures as they visited Disneyland, Hollywood studios, and other local attractions.

The impact of this troupe of vibrant, handsome young dancers, smiling and enthusiastically waving in a friendly manner at adoring new audiences, must have been equally edifying to both Soviet authorities and the U.S. State Department. Banished from the minds of those in the audience were the cold, cruel embodiments of beady-eyed commissars so beloved in Hollywood filmdom and the House of Un-American Activities (HUAC). The Moiseyev performances created a choreographed finale to Joseph McCarthy's theater of sinister politics.

As a child and teenager, I lived in an environment defined and bounded by HUAC hearings, homemade bomb shelters in backyards and basements, atomic bomb drills, and doomsday science fiction novels graphically depicting the end of American freedom at the hands of the evil Russians.

As a member of an amateur folk dance group, I was familiar with the Moiseyev Dance Company, although I did not know it at the time because the company I saw in the film was identified by a translation of its Russian title, the State Academic Ensemble of Folk Dances of the Peoples of the USSR.[2] I had watched them several times in a grainy black and white film, shot in 1937, provided by the Soviet consulate in San Francisco. But nothing had prepared me for the sheer physical impact of their actual theatrical performances. I left the Shrine Auditorium a convert. I returned several more nights, as many as the income of a poor student, shelving books in the library and waiting tables, would allow. My life had changed forever. This is what I wanted to do with my life: create dances, spectacular choreographies, like Igor Moiseyev.

After that first performance, the folk dance group to which I belonged hosted the Moiseyev dancers for an party at which we happily went through the figures of the Virginia reel (which they used in subsequent tours as a popular encore-tribute to their American audiences) and other dances. Each of us danced with a Moiseyev dancer as a partner.[3] The thrill of dancing with those radiant performers and knowing them by name was infectious. Had the opportunity presented itself, I would have defected and done the 1950s version of running away and joining the circus.

Since those first appearances, Moiseyev's company has toured widely in the West with at least ten tours to the United States. I have seen all of those touring programs as well as performances in Brussels, Paris, and Moscow. The most recent tour of the United States was in early 1999 and Igor Moiseyev, age ninety-two at the time, accompanied the company.

Colonizing Dance

While this book is not intended to be a political primer or geographic study, it is perhaps profitable to establish a brief background sketch of the ethnic composition of the former Soviet Union and the role of dance in the political economy of that now-defunct state whose ghost still haunts its successor states. In the case of the former Soviet Union, and even in regard to the Russian Federation, its central successor state, many Americans are unfamiliar with even the basic ethnographic details of both states. It was not an infrequent event to hear the terms "Russian" and "Soviet" used as interchangeable ethnic labels, in spite of the fact that Russians made up only half of the population of the former Soviet Union. There were more than a hundred ethnic groups in the former USSR, many rather small. Of the population of approximately 300 million, the Russians made up about 150 million, the Ukrainians 50 million, and the Byelorussians 10 million. The largest non-Slavic group was the Uzbeks, who numbered about 15 million, while the rest of the numerous non-Slavic groups numbered between a few hundred to 10 million.

The relations between the Russian and non-Russian populations of the former Soviet Union, especially as those relations were articulated in the various domains of power and symbolic manifestations of that power, were not generally well understood in the United States. Those few experts who were aware of the issues of Russian domination in non-Russian areas and how Russian colonialism operated in the non-Russian areas almost invariably turned their attention to the more overt issues of political domination and colonialism, such as the linguistic hegemony of the Russian language. This colonialist project was inherited from the tsarist regimes that proceeded the Communist period. This political and cultural domination manifested itself in folk dance and its modes of presentation as well. Russian domination was manifest in the performing companies that toured in the West. They were overwhelmingly Russian: the Moiseyev Dance Company, the Red Army Chorus, the Piyatnitsky Chorus, the Don Cossacks, and the Siberian Omsk companies, all of which featured folk dancing, and the Kirov Ballet and Bolshoi Ballet companies. Of the non-Russian groups, only the trusted Georgian and Ukrainian state folk ensembles made appearances in the West on a regular basis.

Much attention had been focused on matters of censorship in the Russian (as opposed to the other non-Russian nationalities) cinema, visual arts, news media, and literature, but almost nowhere is the issue of Russian political, cultural, and ethnic domination discussed in relation to the non-Russian performing arts. In fact, many in the West have felt that the performing arts have had untrammeled freedom throughout the former Soviet Union, both in Russia and in the other republics, because of their high status and visibility both at home and abroad.

Perhaps no nation in the history of the world has supported dance to the extent that the former Soviet Union did, both financially and politically. For example, to show just how ready the Soviet Union was to finance dance, Intourist guides and spokespersons from the Artists' Union proudly pointed out to me that no expense was spared in the production of dance (field notes 1986, 1989). The Bolshoi Ballet, a company on the same level as the Moiseyev Dance Company, employed more than two thousand people as dancers, musicians, costumers, scenery builders, wig makers, shoe and boot makers, stage personnel, and administrators. Dancers, both those who performed folk dance and those in the classical ballet field, were well paid relative to other professions, and they were able to travel to the West, a rare opportunity for Soviet citizens.

Folk dance, with its accompanying music, singing, and wearing of colorful costumes, must have seemed like a relatively safe outlet for pent-up nationalistic feelings and pride; Soviet authorities felt impelled to provide some kind of expression to non-Russian groups. Most of the publicity issued by the former Soviet state featured photographs of happy folk dancers, always young, always smiling. Political, military, and economic power, however, remained safely in the hands of Russians, with a few other token Slavs, Armenians, and Georgians also included. Each of the republics had a native first secretary, but the second secretary was invariably a Russian who controlled the actual decisions made in each republic. Baltic historians Misiunas and Taagepera noted that "native First Secretaries were now assigned Russian Second Secretaries to act as Moscow's watchdogs" (1993, 77).

Russian political domination could be seen in the linguistic policies that promoted Russian at the expense of other "official" languages, to the point that many of the intelligentsia in republics such as Uzbekistan and Tajikistan even today function better in Russian than in their native languages. Domination and colonization could also be seen in the economic policies that, among other disastrous results, devastated much of the environment of Uzbekistan through decades of demanding that Uzbekistan and other Muslim republics provide cotton and other raw materials for developing industries in Russia and the Ukraine.[4]

Technically speaking, under the Soviet constitution the republics had the right of succession. But in point of fact, as the world saw when the Baltic republics attempted to succeed, every effort, including force, was used to restrain any attempts at independence. There are still those in Russia who wish to regain possession of their former colonized republics, and it is most telling that the Moiseyev repertoire still includes dances from the now independent republics of Moldavia, the Ukraine, Azerbaijan, and Uzbekistan.

Why was dance such a potent symbol to the Communist state of the Soviet Union? The symbol of dance was not only a useful political tool for the Russians, but one to which they were strongly attracted. Decades before the 1917 Russian Revolution, as well as after it, Russian classical ballet companies were world famous for their high level of technique and performing élan, if not their creativity. Before the Revolution, such companies as the Ballet Russe de Monte Carlo were well-known for their creative flair as well.

> Previous to the 1917 March Revolution which deprived the Romanov dynasty of its throne, the addiction to ballet among the ruling circles of Russia cast many of them into the exclusive class of balletomanes. . . . For an understanding of the paths of development of ballet under the soviet government, it is indispensable to probe the history of the art under the tsars. (Swift 1968, 3)

That changed after the Revolution when the whole question of creativity became a government issue. It was a source of pride for the Soviet authorities to out-perform the Western nations in the field of dance, in much the same way they invested considerable money and energy in the promotion of their sports programs and sport stars in the Olympics. This superiority in the performing arena symbolized the moral superiority of the socialist system over capitalism.

Nevertheless, the Communist world, particularly the Russians, has always had a love-hate relationship with classical ballet because of its aristocratic connections. While the Russian Soviet intelligentsia was as attracted to the ballet as their predecessors, the Russian nobility, the Communists felt it necessary to develop tortuous arguments in order to justify ballet's existence. Although *Swan Lake* and *Sleeping Beauty* hardly qualify as "tractor" ballets, the official Soviet line is that such ballets are acceptable and even "Soviet" because they have been infused with socialist realism.

Classical ballet is clearly the major source of much of the technique found in folk dance companies throughout the former Soviet

Union. In Russia, ballet is widely considered a uniquely Russian expression. Even before the founding of folk dance companies such as the Moiseyev Dance Company, the Russians established local ballet companies in most of the republics. In addition to "white" ballets such as *Giselle* and *Swan Lake,* a nod to local tradition was encouraged through the production of native-themed ballets. It is difficult to describe the visual impact of the spectacle of Mongol invaders performing pirouettes across the steppes, or the local Uzbek cotton-picking crowd *en pointe* while wearing worker's tutus.

After 1936, folk dance, with its connotations of ethnic identity and "the people's" art, became a focus of Soviet government interest. Folk dancing from that period became almost a cottage industry. Throughout the former USSR, considerable government backing and financial support were given to create vast folk dance festivals and to establish myriad professional and amateur folk dance companies. Swift states that "in 1936, three million people were reported to have taken part in the preliminary contests in the USSR Trade Union Festival of Amateur Art" (1968, 241). Folk dance companies were found on collective farms and factories, and even the NKVD, the secret service agency, had one.

Colorful and visually striking dance companies were formed to show the multicultural, multiethnic composition of the USSR. They showcased all of the Soviet people living in brotherly peace and friendly coexistence under the benign but careful eye of Mother Russia, whose dances would receive pride of place. This was an important message to send to governments and people in the undeveloped world whom the Soviet Union wished to influence. The State Academic Ensemble of Folk Dances of the Peoples of the USSR, known in the West as the Moiseyev Dance Company, rapidly became the most important and visible manifestation of the Soviet Union's interest in folk dance as a political tool.

By the 1950s, all of the republics formed companies in the Moiseyev image. It is important to note that while a few of the companies, such as the Georgian State Folk Company and the Bakhor Folk Dance Ensemble of Uzbekistan, were able to resist some of the choreographic Russification that authorities encouraged to develop a specific style and look of their own, most looked to the highly successful Moiseyev Dance Company as their model. More importantly, in many Muslim areas dance was not only *not* an important art form, it was one that had been associated with low-class behavior, performed publicly by societal outcasts. Traditionally, these were young boys who performed in articles of women's clothing in such areas as Uzbekistan and Tajikistan.[5] The Russians deemed such behavior as "unhealthy" and thus recruited young women to perform. There was initially enormous resistance in Muslim families to having their daughters dance in public in front of strange men, and, according to Soviet sources, several young women were murdered for dishonoring their families. Women dancing in front of men who are not within specific degrees of familial relationship with them was (and in many Muslim areas of the world still is) considered a disgrace (Shay 1999a). Thus, the use of dance as a symbol of ethnic representation in the Muslim areas may be considered as a colonial act imposed by the Russians over the groups they dominated.

In addition to the issue of the propriety of dance as an ethnic symbol, the manner of staging traditional dance as a group in a mass form is largely alien to these areas. Dancing in most of the rural areas of Eastern European was a group phenomenon and an important social and ritual event. In the Muslim areas, solo-improvised dancing was the principal form of choreographic expression and was seen as a form of entertainment. Soviet authorities were so insistent upon having dances for each republic that Russian "brothers" were sent to teach the natives in the republics how to create authentic folk dances, suitable to each republic. For example, in Kazakhstan and Turkmenia "dance was not so widespread and so their Russian brothers taught their 'friends' how to have proper dances for their nationality." After the October Revolution, "the Russian Theatre gave brotherly help to the Turkmen nation and provided them with folk dances" (Tkachenko 1954, 199 and 536–37).

The practice of choreographic pride of place for Russia was reproduced in other professional companies of the former Soviet Union. Supreme Court Justice William O. Douglas described a dance performance he saw while traveling in the Soviet Union.

> The Uzbek Ensemble had a finale in which the dancers were dressed in the various costumes of different Soviet Republics and each group performed a dance appropriate to the Republic it represented. Finally, four dancers dressed in red to represent the Russian Republic entered and executed the rapid twirling and stomping expected of them. In the end, the four Russians formed the hub of a huge wheel around which the other dancers formed spokes. While the giant wheel revolved, Miss Russia was hoisted high in the center, representing the role of Great Russia in uniting the various racial and religious groups in the nation and also pointing to the predominant role of the Great Russian in the U.S.S.R. (Swift 1968, 241–42)

Thus we see that the Russians imposed and projected their own cherished icon of dance upon other ethnic groups who might have responded more positively to other art forms such as poetry, which has pride of place as aesthetic expression in most Muslim areas.

Igor Aleksandrovich Moiseyev, Founding Artistic Director and Choreographer

Igor Moiseyev's name suggests that he is of Jewish origin, although this is not mentioned in any of the several brief available biographies. He was born in Kiev, the Ukraine, in 1906.[6] Moiseyev's Jewish identity becomes important in light of the virulent Soviet anti-Semitism during the Stalin era, another legacy of the tsarist past, when the Moiseyev Dance Company was one of the most prominent dance companies in the world. Russian folklorists Izaly Zemtsovsky and Alma Kunanbaeva recently observed that "Jewish music was regarded by the Soviet regime to be as dangerous as Hebraic letters, and was considered as revolting to Soviet officials as the smell of incense is to the devil" (1997, 15). They noted as well that "so-called cosmopolitans [i.e., Jews, according to Soviet terminology] were ruthlessly denounced and expelled from their universities, institutions, conservatories, or colleges" (ibid., 16–17). It is noteworthy that one of Moiseyev's most recent choreographies, *Jewish Suite,* is a Jewish wedding composed after the fall of the Soviet Union.

Margarita Isareva in the *International Encyclopedia of Dance* omits from the entry on Moiseyev that shortly after his birth, the Moiseyev family moved to Paris. One wonders if this move was a response to the deadly pogroms that periodically swept Kiev and other Ukrainian cities in the first decade of the twentieth century like those that occurred in the wake of the notorious Beylis trial so movingly documented in Meyer Levin's novel, *The Fixer.*[7] Isareva states that Moiseyev "spent his childhood and adolescence traveling around Russia with his father, who was a lawyer, and becoming acquainted with the cultures of various ethnic groups" (1998, 443), thus suggesting for Moiseyev an almost mythic interest in folklore and researching authentic sources. Such an interest must have lain dormant, for he was attending rigorous ballet classes at the age of twelve and was a member of the Bolshoi Ballet company from 1924 to 1939, where he was a soloist in several productions. He also produced several choreographies, including *Spartacus,* for the company.

In 1936 Igor Moiseyev was charged with the job of organizing an

Moiseyev Dance Company. *Jewish Suite.* COURTESY ICM ARTISTS.

all-USSR folk dance festival. This was clearly a major turning point in his professional life, for the following year, according to all of the sources, he formed the professional company that, in the Westernized version of the company name, came to bear his name with a combination of professional artists from the Bolshoi Ballet and dancers "from among participants in the festival" (Isareva 1998, 444). His first performance featured thirty dancers, but in the wake of its success in its Moscow debut performance, the company quickly grew to one hundred. The impact of this company was barely felt in the beginning years, most likely overshadowed by the outbreak of World War II. Following the war, however, the impact of the Moiseyev ensemble was immense for every republic of the USSR. After several successful tours throughout the entire Soviet Union and Eastern Europe, all of the satellite states formed companies that emulated the Moiseyev model. Moiseyev's company appeared widely throughout the Eastern bloc.[8] A spate of books appeared throughout the Soviet Union and several satellite states that showed how to perform Moiseyev style dances for stage and included movements, steps, formations, and, finally, sample choreographies appropriate to each ethnic group.[9]

In the West, in spite of the enormous impact of performances by the Moiseyev Dance Company, for a wide variety of reasons none of the nations of Western Europe created a national company in the Moiseyev image. According to dance scholar Naima Prevots, in the early 1950s in the United States there was a great deal of discussion concerning the formation of a national folk dance company by the Dance Panel of the American National Theatre and Academy. This panel was under contract with the State Department to select dance performances for export and to advise the government on how to showcase American dance. However, the dance panel "never resolved the issue of creating a professional folk dance group" (Prevots 1998, 118). The performances of the Moiseyev Dance Company did spawn a small number of amateur and semiprofessional groups in the United States that either used exact choreographies of Igor Moiseyev or Moiseyev–inspired pieces.[10] Russian government leaders claimed that unlike the colonialist West, they venerated the folk traditions of their non-Russian populations. For viewers in the developing world, this claim appeared to be embodied by Moiseyev's spectacular dance company, which included dances from Tajikistan, Azerbaijan, and Uzbekistan as well as those of the Muslim minorities, such as the Kalmuks and Tatars, in the Russian Federation. Performances by the Moiseyev Dance Company created a response that resulted in the establishment of dance companies across the political landscape from Mexico to Iran, Egypt to the Philippines, Turkey to Chile.

There were two reasons that the Moiseyev company frequently toured in the West. First, the diplomatic results in the wake of the highly successful Moiseyev Dance Company paid high political dividends to the former Soviet Union. Second, and less well-known, the Moiseyev Dance Company has been amazingly successful in earning badly needed hard currency for both the former Soviet Union and now for the successor Russian government.

Moiseyev Dance Style and Choreographic Strategies

A movement analysis of Moiseyev Dance Company performances reveals that Igor Moiseyev has taken character dance, which is a subgenre of classical ballet, and reshaped and expanded it to create a unique movement vocabulary. Lisa Arkin and Marian Smith, in describing the "national" dances found in nineteenth-century romantic ballet, state that

> it would be naïve to suggest that choreographers of the period made a regular practice of transferring the folk dances of the countryside to the

professional stage without modification. . . . It seems highly likely that original folk dances were distilled to a certain repertory of steps, poses, and gestures that were recognizably associated with a particular culture—with technical virtuosity and the choreographer's own artistry being added to the mix.

A certain repertory of markers, then, was sufficient to function emblematically, reinforcing the spectators' sense that they were somehow gaining access to the essence of a culture or nation. (Arkin and Smith 1997, 35–36)

While Arkin and Smith have pinpointed many of the salient features of Moiseyev's work, such as the use of virtuosity and the emblematic use of movement to signal a particular ethnic group, a close analysis of his work compared to the many available field recordings[11] indicates that Igor Moiseyev used far fewer authentic elements than these authors seem to suggest. He often created dances from whole cloth utilizing his own unique character dance vocabulary. Further, in his pan-ethnic repertoire, the same movements, figures, and athletic solos function in works from all over the former Soviet Union. His infrequent guest soloists, such as the Tajik soloist seen in the video *Moiseyev Dance Company: A Gala Evening*, highlight how distant his own works from Central Asia are from the original dance traditions.

In the case of the Moiseyev Dance Company, I use the meaning of "character" differently from that of Lisa Arkin and Marian Smith. They use the term "character" as a synonym for "national" dance, as in the Spanish or Polish variation found in the romantic ballets of the nineteenth century (1997, 13).

> Thus we restrict the use of the latter term to its narrowest sense, meaning "folk," "national," or "ethnic." The term "character dance" is more inclusive than "national" dance because it can also include rustic dance, dances by older characters, and dances that show a character's occupation (e.g., dances of shoemakers, bakers, sailors). Our use of the term "character dance" or "pas de caractere" in this article, however, is restricted to national dance unless otherwise indicated. (Arkin and Smith 1997, 57)

Unlike Arkin and Smith, however, I must use the term "character" in its widest meaning. A Moiseyev Dance Company performance abounds in characters: old men performing buffoonery, Chinese magicians, young villagers, football players, photographers, sailors, skaters, decadent Westerners (in his Argentine tango and American rock 'n' roll choreographies), foolish petite bourgeoisie, and brave partisans, to name but a few. These characters are generally one-dimensional—they are not individual people, but rather types of people. Another borrowing from the ballet vocabulary of the romantic period emphasizes the stylization of these stereotypical characters. As in nineteenth-century ballet, Moiseyev uses considerable miming elements, the extended use of which can be seen in the opening scenes of the *Jewish Suite*, in which the fathers of the bride and groom are bargaining over the dowry, and in the *Old City Quadrille*, in which couples exhibiting the behavior of petits bourgeois are strolling in the park, eating sunflower seeds, and flirting.

The movement vocabulary and stylistic characteristics of the Moiseyev Dance Company underscore the points that I made in the introductory chapter that Moiseyev, like many others, has in fact created a new, and parallel, dance tradition or genre. It stands apart from dance in the field, and connecting points between the dances in the field and those found in the Moiseyev repertoire are nearly nonexistent. Igor Moiseyev would be the first to admit this.

The reliance on ballet vocabulary is particularly revealed in a choreography entitled *Road to the Dance*, in which the dancers perform their warm-up and exercises in rehearsal clothes. They use basic ballet movements as they perform at the barre, and Moiseyev, through his movement vocabulary, conducts the viewer from the simplest steps to the most complex leaps and turns. The trained eye immediately recognizes that what the Moiseyev ensemble presents is not folk dance but ballet-based character dance in Moiseyev's unique stylization. *New York Times* dance critic Anna Kisselgoff observed "that the Moiseyev Dance Company is, of course, a ballet company in disguise; it is a troupe of professional, ballet-trained dancers" (Kisselgoff 1991).

Isareva claims that Moiseyev's "basic goal was to develop perfect traditional folk dances." These were to be an "improvement" on the dances that the peasants actually performed in the field. "Moiseyev reinterpreted folk dances, integrating them into a single choreographic scheme.... Moiseyev became a genuine composer of dances. In his works folk dances underwent complex formations, enriched by professional art and imbued with an expressive contemporary flavor. ... He created a new Byelorussian dance, *Bulba*" in 1937 (1998, 444). Moiseyev wrote in 1937 that his intent

> was not to reproduce exact examples from the body of more than 3000 existing national dances, but to raise the skill of performance to the highest artistic level in order to influence the creation of new national

Moiseyev Dance Company. *Old City Quadrille.* COURTESY ICM ARTISTS.

dances. He sought to establish a unique style for his company that would be at once dramatic, entertaining in a theatrical sense and larger-than-life. (ICM Artists, Ltd., 1997)

Neither Igor Moiseyev nor the government of the former Soviet Union was interested in verisimilitude. They wanted the spectacle of masses demonstrating support for an embodied representation of the Soviet system.

> Thus, in words and on paper, folklore was respected and supported; but in fact, the Soviet government actively supported its own version of folklore. However, this particular version had little to do with the people's free creativity and everything to do with regime's aim of total control of all cultural activities. . . . The strictest censorship was imposed on everything that was published and performed, including every sound that was played. (Zemtsovsky and Kunanbaeva 1997, 5)

This uniquely created movement vocabulary infuses virtually every dance work created by Moiseyev from the inception of the company in 1937 to the most recent works some sixty years later. "The singular qualifications he brought to the project were his strong background in classical ballet, which would provide the basic training for his company" (ICM Artists, Ltd., 1997, 1). Most importantly, Moiseyev developed a total and complete movement vocabulary that is extremely unique and is emulated by many companies throughout the Eastern bloc. This vocabulary stresses a highly energetic and athletic interpretation of character dances that distanced the Moiseyev Dance Company from the ethereal image of classical ballet. Moiseyev's choreographic creations are far more earth-bound than the character dances found in classical ballet. The athletic vigor that Moiseyev injects in his dances underscores why viewers find his work so compelling. It gives the dancing an "authentic" flavor, redolent of the earthy quality that is often attributed in the popular mind to folk dance. And yet in regard to authenticity, Moiseyev states:

> To present it [folk dance] in its primitive [i.e., authentic] form would be undramatic, dull, not suitable for stage. Our aim was not to act as literal copyist, nor to collect mechanically, but to enrich and develop the form while preserving the national character and original coloring. . . . We were compelled to discover our own ways and creative methods for the study and staging of a huge variety of national folk dances, so diversified in their character and style. (Moiseyev Dance Company 1986, 18)

The movement vocabulary features very simple footwork such as *pas de basque* steps and similar simple step patterns, spectacular and highly athletic virtuosic solo figures, rapid spinning, and extremely fast tempi. A Bulgarian piece in the repertoire was danced at such a high velocity that the original source—a dance from the Shop region around Sofia, the Bulgarian capital—was barely discernable, even to the trained eye. The movements rarely derive directly from dances performed in the field.

Moiseyev's choreographies most often feature masses of corps dancers in highly precisioned and disciplined formations. These formations utilize simple, basic geometric elements with many lines and circles common in folk dance. His genius lies in his adroit transitions and his signature precision timing, clearly appropriated from theatrical dance sources. Many classical ballet companies would be proud to boast a corps as disciplined as that of the Moiseyev Dance Company, arguably the most precisioned dance company in the world. Igor Moiseyev turns the ballet format upside down by featuring the corps and punctuating the choreographic maneuvers of the corps with brilliant, generally multiple, and very brief solo gambits within the context of the group. Unlike classical ballet, the soloists step out from the corps with whom they have been dancing to execute a bravura movement, and return immediately to the corps's anonymity. So prominent is the corps that although the soloists are listed, their names are not truly well-known as is the case with classical ballet.

Throughout the former Soviet Union, but especially in Russia, many professional and semiprofessional companies were formed or reformed to emulate the success of Moiseyev. Some of the better known of these companies—such as the Omsk State Dance Ensemble, the Piyatnitsky Chorus (with a dance ensemble), the Beryozka State Dance Ensemble, and the Don Cossacks Folk Song and Dance Ensemble—continue to tour throughout the Western world. A recent program of the Don Cossacks supports my argument that the USSR attempted to regularize the output of all of these ensembles to conform to the "new" folk dance created by Moiseyev. This ensemble began as an attempt to produce music and dance of the Rostov-on-Don region: "The Don Cossacks Song and Dance Ensemble, established in 1936, has more than fifty years of performing activity behind it. In 1970, by a decision of the Ministry of Culture of the Russian Federation the ensemble was reorganized and quite a number of young talent—graduates of Russia's secondary and higher musical and choreographic education institutions—joined it" (Don Cossacks Song and Dance Ensemble n.d., 3).

The meaning behind the wording found in the souvenir program's official prose is clear: the dancers of the Don Cossacks utilized the same standard character dance style made famous by the Moiseyev Dance Company and taught in the "educational institutions" referred to in the program (Don Cossacks Song and Dance Ensemble, n.d.). Interestingly, the members of the singing chorus occasionally performed the individual, unspectacular improvisational style found in the traditional dancing in the field, in contrast to the ensemble of dancers, which performed the standard spectacularized choreographic fare.

An important aspect of Moiseyev dance style is the "emotional" dimension that determines how the Soviet people are to be portrayed choreographically. This is a crucial political element of the choreography. For his abilities in the depiction of "Soviet Man," Igor Moiseyev received the Hero of Socialist Labor award, in addition to other awards.

Ethnomusicologist Thomas Turino uses the term folklorization to describe the process of "the relocation of native customs (typically music and dance, but other art forms as well) from their original contexts to new urban contexts, usually under the direct sponsorship of the state" (Urban and Schertzer 1991, 10). This term perfectly describes the staging of folk dance by urban-based, professional state folk dance companies in the former Soviet Union as well as ensembles from other parts of the world. The dances distinguish "a subgroup within a national context, [which] become ... markers of a folk tradition—one of a number of such traditions—making up the nation" (ibid.). Turino further observes that "folklorization shares some properties with invented traditions. . . . [I]n folklorization the tradition is regarded as part of a menagerie, one of several semi–independent traditions that taken together make up the whole" (ibid., 11).

The Soviet expression of the ideology of the people as expressed in folk dance, and congruent with the Soviet Union's official socialist political philosophy, demonstrates Turino's folklorization concept with an almost Rousseauian "noble savage" aspect, as expressed by Moiseyev:

> Folk art, whatever its form, is always on the side of good, always wholesome and optimistic. In folk-lore we find the vices denounced and held up to ridicule while praises are sung to man's better instincts. . . . Folk art, the art of the people, is a splendid means of educating the masses, for it can speak their own language, simple, colourful, and replete with wisdom. (Chudnovskii 1959, 23)

Moiseyev wanted "not only to bring out the national features but common human traits possessed by all people. These are a joy of living, industry, a love of gaiety and a sense of humour, and a wholesome morality" (Chudnovskii 1959, 23).

Thus, Igor Moiseyev was able to articulate this notion of creating "socially responsible" dances for a greater good, at the same time expressing the philosophy of the Soviet state that generously rewarded his efforts.

Repertoire

First and foremost, the position of the Moiseyev Dance Company as the State Academic Ensemble of Folk Dances of the Peoples of the USSR required that the bulk of the ensemble's repertoire "represent" the ethnic diversity of the more than a hundred official peoples that inhabited the former Soviet Union. Clearly a hierarchy exists in which peoples will be represented in a typical Moiseyev performance. Echoing the political reality of the former USSR, Russia occupied (and continues to occupy) pride of place. Although theoretically the Moiseyev Dance Company represents all ethnic groups equally, in fact the bottom line appears in the company's official history, produced by the state printing house: "Russian folk dances occupy a place of primary importance among the dances of the many nationalities inhabiting the USSR" (Chudnovskii 1959, 42). Another source states that "the *Russian Suite* should be mentioned first. It reflects all that is best in the Russian character—its fervour and reserve, modesty and recklessness, pride and a sense of humour. Take any part of the *Russian Suite* and in it you will see a new facet of the national character" (Ilupina and Lutskaya 1966, 11).

Thus, in a typical Moiseyev program the opening number is generally an elaborate choreography from Russia. There are almost always a second and third Russian number in the evening's program, as well as the inclusion of a short number with a few dancers from non-Russian peoples within the Russian Republic, such as the Tatars or Kalmuks. Indeed, the Soviet state felt that all aspects of the arts of non-Russian peoples needed improvement to bring them up to Russian standards. These were the standards to which all others must aspire—those of "Soviet Man." Where dances did not exist that were suitable for staging, they had to be altered to fit this image; new dances and new dance traditions were created in the Moiseyev image.

In addition to Russia, the second republic of the former Soviet Union, the Ukraine, was invariably represented by the Moiseyev signature work *Gopak* (to use its Russian spelling), which forms the spectacular finale of every Moiseyev performance I attended. The other European republics are more often included than those of the other parts of the former Soviet Union; the *Moldavian Suite* and a Byelorussian dance are common in most Moiseyev concerts. The Baltic republics of Estonia, Latvia, and Lithuania, perhaps due to their choreographic similarities, were never all represented in a concert. Sometimes there would be a Lithuanian or an Estonian dance—not a mass number, but a small character sketch with a few dancers, perhaps representing the diminutive size of these republics relative to Russia.

In a similar manner to the representation of the Baltic republics, the Central Asian and Caucasian republics were generally represented by a single dance with a few dancers. Since Uzbekistan was one of the most important and populous republics, the *Cotton Dance*, with a large female corps, or the *Platter Dance*, a virtuoso solo male dance, were common items in the repertoire. *Three Shepherds*, a dance representing Azerbaijan, or *Khorumi*, a spectacular, highly athletic male dance from Georgia, were standard representative dances in the Moiseyev Dance Company repertoire and continue to be so.

A second class of dance appearing in later Moiseyev concerts, and far less prominent, was that of peoples outside the Soviet Union, used to demonstrate solidarity and fraternity with the peoples of the world. I have seen dances from Argentina, Cuba, China, Bulgaria, Italy, Spain, the United States, and (in 1999) a dance from Egypt, a sanitized belly dance performed by seven women.

A third type of choreography might be labeled as character sketches. These pieces often show the "fun and gaiety" of living in the former Soviet Union: a football game (soccer), a skating party, or sailors working on board ship and then going off for a night on the town all form contexts for choreographic high jinks.

Perhaps one of his most successful and beloved works from Soviet life is the spectacular and brilliant choreography *The Partisans*, a contemporary choreography depicting the guerillas of World War II. This piece never fails to evoke wonder from the viewers because the dancers appear to be galloping on horseback across the steppes, their long, stiff cloaks concealing their footwork. This choreography avoids the banal characters of the "fun in daily life" and "joy in work" episodes, but the dancers still cannot resist coy touches of mugging at the audience.

Moiseyev also produced a few pieces from the classical music repertoire, such as Moussorgsky's opus *Night on Bald Mountain*, that have received mixed reviews from serious dance critics. If his wish was to create a classical or contemporary interpretation of this well-known

Moiseyev Dance Company. *The Partisans.* COURTESY ICM ARTISTS.

musical opus, the choreographic elements utilized in his folk dances for this work created a simplistic treatment of a musical work requiring greater choreographic sophistication.

A fascinating aspect of the Moiseyev repertoire is the adherence to the choreographies that were composed in its first years. After the collapse of the former Soviet Union, Moiseyev continues to program dances from Azerbaijan, Georgia, the Ukraine, Belarus, and Moldavia, long after their cession from the former union. It sometimes resembles an eerie glance into a museum of political history, or perhaps reflects current yearning on the part of a particular population to once again dominate the area. At least half of the choreographies, *The Seasons, Zhok* (Moldavia), *Khorumi* (Georgia), *Polyanka, Old City Quadrille, Three Shepherds,* and *Gopak* have been performed in almost every concert since the first one in 1937. The dramatic political changes of the late 1980s and early 1990s seem not to have entered the rehearsal halls of the Moiseyev ensemble, or perhaps they await a better day.

Dancers and Dance Training

Throughout the former Soviet Union, in the capital city of every republic and occasionally in other major urban areas such as St. Petersburg, special schools for dance, similar to the high schools for the performing arts now found in some U.S. cities, were established. They were called *koreografski instituti* (choreographic institutes). Although the Russian name suggests that choreography is taught and created in these institutions, in fact choreography is not taught at all; rather, these institutes are large dance conservatories that train their students for a professional life in dance. Carefully selected children begin at an early age to receive dance training. Interestingly, in the choreographic institutes in Uzbekistan and Azerbaijan, which I visited in 1976, 1986, and 1989, the Russian children were assigned to ballet classes only, while the native children were enrolled primarily in both ballet classes and folk dance classes. At the end of their twelve-year schooling, the native young men and women would be assigned (or consigned) to folk dance companies throughout the republic. Successful ethnic Russians were slotted for regional or national classical ballet companies. Only the most extraordinarily talented native dancers—such as Rudolf Nureyev, who was a Tatar—would be assigned to the top classical ballet companies (for example, the Bolshoi Ballet or the Kirov Ballet) in Moscow or St. Petersberg. The most talented native children would be sent to the national state ensemble of the respective republic. Thus, the major classical ballet companies received the cream of the crop.

Virtually all the Moiseyev dancers are Russian. "Most students—and therefore later members of the ensemble—come from the Moscow area. The company does not actively recruit from other regions. Moiseyev denies the suggestion that such a policy could lead to nationalist resentment in the provinces. 'It's a matter of quality,' he said. 'If you dance their folk dances better (than the local troupes), they applaud. Those who don't start in our schools have a lower professional level,' he stated unapologetically, 'so a Russian girl in our school dances Moldavian dance much better than a Moldavian girl'" (Laine 1986, 60).

A quick perusal of names in the Moiseyev Dance Company's programs indicates that the dancers are Russian. As with many companies in Eastern Europe, the Moiseyev company maintains a corps of short men and women and tall men and women. This is clearly evident in the choreography *Road to the Dance,* in which Moiseyev uses the varying heights of the two groups of men, the shorter men in white shirts, the taller in black, to make a humorous choreographic point. This practice provides a uniform look to the dance corps and serves the immanently practical purpose of allowing one group to perform while the other changes costumes. It is a well-known practice in the professional folk dance world.

In this way, Moiseyev selects from dancers who have received almost the exact same training that he largely pioneered. New dancers arrive at the company with all of the basic skills necessary for quick integration into the ensemble. This contrasts with American classical ballet and modern dance companies, which often have dancers with highly diverse training histories who must be integrated into the company style through years of training.

Music

Like all other elements of a Moiseyev performance, the music also has little to do with the musical practices found in the field. Much of the music is composed, often with no reference to actual melodic or harmonic structure played by peasants or urban groups being portrayed. One of the most common forms of dance found throughout Russia, and many other Eastern European areas as well, is the *horovod* or *khorovod* (called by specific names from region to region, country to country). These are mass dances, most often performed in circles in which the dancers, almost always women, sing in accompaniment to their movements. The singing is the more dominant of the two elements. The movements are typically quite simple, but the intricately designed dance labeled *"khorovod"* in the Moiseyev repertoire, like all of the other dances, was accompanied by the large orchestra and no singing.

The typical orchestra used by Moiseyev is a large symphony or theater orchestra that plays in the orchestra pit with an augmented brass section to add to the feeling of bold earthiness found in his choreographies. A folk feeling is given with an occasional small orchestra, using accordions, balalaikas, and a tambourine such as the one used on stage in the *Old City Quadrille*. The members of the orchestra in the latter work rise at the end of the piece and, to the audience's immense delight, dance briefly and spectacularly. I cannot remember the use of any nontempered musical instruments, found in great profusion throughout the Soviet Union, ever being used in a Moiseyev concert.

Costumes

The costuming of the Moiseyev Dance Company, like the choreographies, is "painted" in bright primary colors. A typical color scheme found in several of Moiseyev's choreographies features the female corps in red, blue, green, and yellow, as in the opening Russian number. The Ukrainian *Gopak* finds the women clad in red, blue, black, and green costumes, in groups of three, four, and six, as does the *Moldavian Suite*. The men in the *Moldavian Suite* are dressed alike in black and white, while in *Gopak* the men wear blue or red trousers with contrasting sashes. During the course of the choreography the women in red dance together, as do those in blue, black, and green. In this way the groupings of dancers become color-coded, heightening the precisioned effect that this company so effectively performs.

Two other frequent color combinations inform the costuming of a Moiseyev concert. In one scheme, all of the dancers wear a single color. In the Russian "Winter" sequence, the female corps is all in white, while in the Georgian *Khorumi* all of the dancers wear black. The second typical variant finds each of the dancers in a different color. This occurs especially when there are six or seven dancers, as in an Egyptian dance I recently saw in which each dancer wears a bright primary color.

The costuming utilized by the Moiseyev Dance Company also reveals other major alterations from the clothing found in the field. The altering of the silhouette is one important area of change. For example, in Russian traditional clothing, the main garment for women is the *sarafan*, a jumperlike dress with no sash or belt. In the hands of costumers for Moiseyev and other companies such as Beryozka and the Piyatnitsky Academic State Chorus, the main dress has become cinched tightly at the waist in a manner pleasing to twentieth-century aesthetics. Over the years skirts and dresses, in the hands of dance company costumers throughout the Soviet Union, have also become shorter and shorter, the lengths rising through the years from floor length to well above the knees.

While these color combinations are theatrically effective, they do not reflect real life in the field where the interest of traditional clothing lies in the subtle differences, which often carry semiotic messages regarding social class, marital status, ethnic identification, and religious status, among others. For example, in the field the way the hair is worn and the type of head covering used are important indicators of marital status. All of this is sacrificed to choreographic spectacle and theatrical effect.

Igor Moiseyev is one of the world's greatest and most prominent choreographers. Aside from issues of representation raised in this chapter, some of Moiseyev's works taken as artistic creations rather than theatrical treatments of traditional folk dances—such as *The Partisans* and

The Moiseyev Dance Company: Ancestor of the Genre 81

Night on Bald Mountain—can be considered works that are intended as serious art. It is well-known that in the former Soviet Union, artists in all fields worked under creative constraints. For more than forty years, Igor Moiseyev portrayed the nation-state of the USSR in just the way that the government strived to achieve. For this he was substantially rewarded with medals and honors, and he became one of the most visible artists of his nation. The precision and power of his choreographies reflected the morality and superiority of hard work that the former USSR attempted to portray to the world. He was the creator of the representational image that the Soviet government imposed throughout the country. The Moiseyev Dance Company choreographically reflected the typical publicity output of the former Soviet Union depicted in tourist brochures and the popular magazine *Soviet Life:* all-smiling, all-happy, all-working—all the time.

4

Ballet Folklorico: Viva Mexico!

A scant three to four years after the first appearance of the Moiseyev Dance Company in 1958, the Ballet Folklorico first began to appear on the concert stages of the United States and Europe, presenting dance audiences with another style of nation-state representation. I was enthralled by the first performances that I saw at the Hollywood Bowl in Los Angeles in 1962 and a year later in Mexico City at the Bellas Artes. It was the first time I realized that non-European dance forms could lend themselves to the same kind of spectacularization that the Moiseyev Dance Company applied to dances of the former Soviet Union.[1]

Jalisco provides a representative example of Amalia Hernandez's choreography. This choreography has always served as the company's finale in every concert that I have attended as well as in the company's two films. *Jalisco* has undergone a few minor changes, although the broad outline of the suite remains the same as I first saw it. The largest change came about when the chorus was no longer used. The suite opens with the large mariachi orchestra playing a selection. In the early years when the chorus appeared with the company, the singers entered carrying candles and singing Christmas carols. Later that section was omitted. The chorus members assembled in the back of the stage as the men, wearing striking black charro costumes trimmed with silver buttons on the trouser legs and the jacket and sporting red neckerchiefs and large sombreros, enter on a diagonal line performing the dance *"la culebra"* and using larger-than-life zapateado (virtuosic toe-and-heel footwork that produces strong rhythmic patterns and varies from area to area). This is followed by *"el tranchete"* in which the men move into simple geographic formations, continuing to perform the rhythmic zapateado footwork and creating vivid designs with their sombreros.

The women enter with the strains of *"jarabe la negra"* wearing stage versions of the china poblana costume, white chemises with daggeted edges and skirts with added fabric to manipulate them in the fashion of "skirt work" that Hernandez has made one of her trademarks. The female dancers are all dressed in red skirts with black decoration, while the women in the chorus wear corresponding green ones. The women perform the intricate zapateado footwork with the men in couples, evenly distributed around the performing space. The familiar melody of the *"jarabe tapatio"* (known as the Mexican Hat Dance in the United States) crescendoes and ushers in the finale with the dancers executing the rhythmic steps of the familiar dance while the chorus throws confetti and streamers on the stage and into the audience.

In this work we see many of the figures that Amalia Hernandez, and indeed many choreographers such as Moiseyev, utilize in their stage adaptations of folk dances: concentric circles, couples evenly spaced around the performing area, diagonal lines, rows of dancers either in couples or alternating men and women. These are all basic elements that the choreographer deftly manipulates so that one figure dissolves into the other.

Amalia Hernandez added contemporary elements in the introduction to her *Tlacotalpan's Festival from Veracruz* in which a large number of young women appear in one-piece body stockings carrying large sea-life figures on poles. They move with tiny running steps around the stage until a group of young men dressed in form-fitting knee-length shorts appear carrying nets and surround the sea life, in the form of the female dancers, that they harvest. Like the *Jalisco* suite, this suite of dances has undergone changes during the years. At one period the famous gauzy white dresses were replaced with hot pinks, oranges, and yellows and the suite was renamed *Mocambo*. The *conjunto veracruzano* (an orchestra consisting of Veracruz harp, requinto, and guitar—all plucked instruments) opens the series of dances that feature highly complex and intricate zapateado figures. The dances follow one another in a suite structure: *"la morena"* with two women dancing on the wooden boxes *(tarima)* in striking gauzy white dresses with yards of material and a train requiring expert skirt work. Six men, three to a box, follow them dancing *"el pajaro carpintero"* with driving zapateado rhythms. The full cast arrives, all in white, to dance *"los abanicos," "el coco,"* and the culminating dance, *"la bamba,"* well-known outside of Mexico, in which two dancers, to the accompaniment of the group's zapateado rhythms, tie a large red bow.

At the end of *"la bamba"* the stage is suddenly filled with figures with gigantic heads *(mojigangas)*. The figures they represent for the carnival in Veracruz are less than innocent. Among them are negative Others: huge African-Mexican heads, a Moor (for centuries the Catholic

Ballet Folklorico de Mexico. *Jalisco*. The Mexican state of Jalisco is the home of the songs and dances of Guadalajara, a city well-known for its beautiful women, dashing caballenos, mariachis, and elaborate fiestas. The climax of this dance is the "Jarabe Tapatio," the Mexican national dance better known in the United States as the "Mexican Hat Dance." COURTESY BALLET FOLKLORICO DE MEXICO.

bugaboo), as well as assorted comic devils, clowns, death as a folklorized Grim Reaper, and other carnival figures. These characters soon mingle in the audience, causing great amusement; this choreography closes the first half. In spite of a significant but little-known African presence in the coastal areas of Mexico, I have never seen an Afro-Mexican among the Ballet Folklorico cast.

The differences between the performing styles of the Moiseyev Dance Company and Ballet Folklorico de Mexico, arguably the two most famous and influential national state folk dance ensembles in the world, provide a study in contrasts. These contrasts appear on a number of levels and dimensions. As we saw in the previous chapter, the Moiseyev Dance Company features a one-dimensional choreographic style developed from ballet-based character dance; one sound, a theater symphony orchestra with no vocal music; one style of costuming; and chorus line procedures performed in a relentless presentational style, the dancers always smiling and frontally facing the audience. The suites and dances, with one or two notable exceptions such as the *Old City Quadrille,* are presented almost totally devoid of social or historical context. In essence, all Soviet nationalities are choreographically and visually interchangeable on the Moiseyev stage with costumes serving as the primary marker to distinguish ethnicity.

By contrast, Ballet Folklorico de Mexico features several dance styles (at least three), a variety of costume styles, and a wide range of regional instrumental and vocal musical styles as well as four-part classical choral arrangements of folk and popular salon music. The elaborate sets, for which the company is justly famous, help establish an evening full of context. The point of convergence that ties the two companies together is the relentless pursuit of spectacle through fast pacing, polished dance techniques, and dazzling primary colors. Whereas the impact of the Moiseyev Dance Company brought the allure of the exotic and the dangerously unknown oriental Russia to American and Western European stages, Ballet Folklorico in its first appearances, and still today, spectacularized the familiar.

Largely through performances of the Moiseyev Dance Company, which featured clean-cut, energetic young dancers with winsome smiles, audiences throughout Western Europe and North America, at least, were won over to the notion that Russians were human beings just like us (white) Americans. Audiences in the less developed areas of the world were impressed by the ethnic representation of minority groups, especially Muslims and other non-European populations, and the respect shown for their traditions that were perceived to exist in the repertoire of the Moiseyev Dance Company. Even if the dances from the Muslim areas such as Azerbaijan and Uzbekistan may not have been authentic, they were at least included. By contrast, until the appearance of Moiseyev on world stages in the 1950s and 1960s, Western companies of dance and music displayed only Western art or presented demeaning orientalist portrayals of the East (at least in the eyes of people from Asia, the Middle East, and Africa). Moiseyev at least represented the non-Western peoples within the Soviet borders, and represented them in a positive light. In the early 1950s those representational strategies resonated deeply with many political elites in underdeveloped countries smarting from the colonialist attitudes of the West, stimulating the foundation of similar companies in Egypt, the Philippines, Mexico, and states in West Africa.

Ballet Folklorico de Mexico produced other, more ambiguous and complex emotions and reactions. In the United States, Moiseyev played to one audience while Ballet Folklorico played to at least two—Mexicans or individuals of Mexican ancestry, and non-Mexicans—and their performances resonated in different ways with each of them. While the Russians represented the potentially dangerous exoticism of the Red Menace, the Ballet Folklorico de Mexico brought a warm and sunny familiarity. Moiseyev performances kept the dancers and their audiences firmly apart, like the Iron Curtain that represented their political separation. Moiseyev audiences cheered the sheer bravura technique of the performers and the utter precision of their choreographies.

Ballet Folklorico relentlessly courts and engages its audiences. Non-Mexican audience members are both startled and delighted at the reaction of audience members of Mexican origin, who enthusiastically clap, whistle, and shout in response to the continual display of patriotic icons, both aural and visual, that the artists of the Ballet Folklorico provide in their typical two-hour concert. Ballet Folklorico's Mexican and Mexican-American audiences alike cheer, because they are designed to be a part of the event, an element duly noted by astute dance critics. "The more formal protocols of staged performance haven't cut down on audience-performer communication" (Fisher 1995).

White America has generally regarded Mexico and Mexicans with a guarded ambiguity in which segregation and division derived through racism and linguistic distance has played a role. Images of street gangs, run-down East Los Angeles housing, and zoot-suiters jostle against those of docile, simple, polite domestics, oppressed farm workers, and dusty villages in Mexico. Hollywood films have dramatically portrayed mustachioed cruel and lethal Mexican revolutionary bandits, such as Pancho Villa, Emiliano Zapata, and Santa Ana, fighting and murdering the beleaguered good (American) guys in the Alamo. These melodramatic images vie with other Hollywood-created images of the Cisco Kid, Zorro, romantic Old California, festive holidays in the sun in Acapulco, and Betty Grable falling in love with a series of dashing (and rich) Latin lovers that dominated musical comedy films from the 1930s through the 1950s.

Amalia Hernandez, founding director and choreographer of Ballet Folklorico, shrewdly selected the latter popular and positive images to amplify her vision of how to represent Mexico. Her vision of Mexico was far from the environmental degradation and staggering overpopulation of the capital city, raw sewage pouring out of the slums that surround the popular sea resort of Acapulco into the ocean waters, and revolution in Chiapas. In her company's performances both at home and abroad, Hernandez chose to send a tourist's picture-postcard to her foreign audiences and warm familiar images that evoked home and belonging in her home audiences. The first and all subsequent appearances of the venerable company, now approaching its fiftieth anniversary, features the light festive touch of a Mexican restaurant with margaritas and mariachis.

This, however, is only a small part of the picture. The impression of a lighthearted tourist postcard, which most members of the non-Mexican audience experience, belies the actual and very deep impact the performances of Ballet Folklorico made on the Mexican-American audiences of the Southwest in the early 1960s. In fact, these performances created a sense of pride and ethnic awareness in the Mexican-American/Chicano community that resonates to this day and was ignited by the social revolution of the 1960s that swept the United States and Europe. This impact resulted in the vociferous demand for the creation of scores of Ballet Folklorico look-alike dance companies. Students of Mexican heritage at universities, colleges, and high schools throughout the Southwest held demonstrations demanding the funding, teachers, and classes to establish these organizations, many of which still exist. All of the southern campuses of the University of California, and most of those of California State University, boast a Ballet Folklorico-style dance ensemble, and they often gather on an annual basis to provide exhibitions of the dances that each performs. Dozens of these dance companies exist in the Los Angeles Unified School District (Gema Sandoval, personal interview, June 20, 2000). The performances of the Ballet Folklorico de Mexico and the many local copies illustrate the cyclical model of field-stage-field that I described in the Introduction. This enormous grass-roots response to the Ballet Folklorico in the Mexican-American community of the Southwest demonstrates the political impact these national companies are capable of creating. These young Mexican-Americans, reveling in the newly evolving Chicano identity, were not interested in recreating authentic dances from obscure villages. They wanted to recreate the authenticity, *espectaculo,* and pride in heritage and ethnicity created by Amalia Hernandez.

In Mexico many folk dance companies exist, many of which, such as the Ballet Folklorico Nacional de Mexico, utilize a slight twist in the name to suggest the Ballet Folklorico de Mexico. Former dancers of the Ballet Folklorico de Mexico have founded many of them.[2] Others, especially those at universities, such as the University of Guadalajara, seek choreographic solutions utilizing more authentic or contemporary elements.

Ballet Folklorico was not the first company in Mexico to theatricalize and prepare folk dances for public performance. There were earlier attempts at staging folk dance in a theatrical setting. Oscar Flores cites the performances of Gloria and Nellie Campobello in the 1930s (1993, 35). However, these earlier performances were rare and excited little interest. It was the successful model and phenomenal international attention provided by Amalia Hernandez for the Ballet Folklorico de Mexico that served as an impetus for the proliferation of a large number of folk dance companies throughout Mexico. "Without her creation, Mexican folk dance would not be pursued the way it is now in both Mexico and among those of Mexican origin in the United States. Folk dance was not something that people in Mexico paid much attention to until Amalia created the Ballet Folklorico. Her contribution to Mexican dance as an art form can not be underestimated" (Gema Sandoval, personal interview, October 25, 1999).

The Politics of Mestizaje

The performances and repertoire of the Ballet Folklorico have also set off heated discussions in the national discourse of Indianness versus Spanishness, which has dominated Mexican political and social life for the past four centuries. This discourse of *mestizaje* (racial mixing) intersects along lines of race, class, gender, and political and economic empowerment. According to Mexican historian Enrique Krauze, "This process of mestizaje is absolutely central to the history of Mexico. . . . It permeated every area of life and became the framework and substance of a society" (1997, xiv). This topic, which is sometimes referred to and encapsulated as "La Maldicion de Malinche" (the curse of Malinche), refers to the Indian princess from Tabasco who became the translator and aide of Hernan Cortez and eventually his mistress and mother of his child, Martin. Martin Cortes became, for Krauze, "the first Mexican" because he was the first Mestizo (ibid., 53).

For centuries Princess Malintzin (La Malinche) has represented the treason of an Indian, a woman, who symbolically surrendered on every level to the Spanish conquerors. The controversy created by the historical and ethnic representational strategies of Ballet Folklorico centers on how Amalia Hernandez represents the nation-state of

Mexico that is the company's raison d'être. Amalia Hernandez's detractors have argued that her untrue representations of Indian cultures follow in the trend of Malinche. Her supporters claim that her representations celebrate the diversity of Mexico with its Spanish, Indian, and Mestizo roots. They add that her choreographies representing Mexican Indian cultures have made these cultures known throughout the world and have garnered good press and attracted tourists to the country.[3]

In print, Amalia Hernandez claims to celebrate both her Spanish and Indian heritages in her choreography and identifies herself as a Mestiza. Walter Terry enthused, "She needed the indomitable spirit of her Indian ancestors and the fire (and some of the fury) of the Spaniard in order to have her way" (Terry 1969).

In fact, as I emphasized in the beginning of this study, Amalia Hernandez, like most of her colleagues who direct other national companies, has created a representation of Mexico that is acceptable and appealing to the upper-middle-class elite of Mexico City, of which she is a member. There is no interest or profit in appealing to populations outside of the capital since the political and economic benefits flow from the elite of the capital city.

Mexico is a nation of nearly 100 million people—60 percent Mestizo, 30 percent Amerindian, and 9 percent Caucasian according to the 1999 *World Almanac*. The population is overwhelmingly young, and the economic plight of the country has served as minor items in evening news broadcasts for many years. The political scene of the country is also in a state of change, as Mexican voters increasingly question the leadership of the PRI (Partido Revolucionario Institucional), the political machine that has ruled the country for decades.

One of the principal elements of the national discourse centers on racial issues of Spanish versus Indian identities. Throughout the centuries, since the Spanish conquest in 1519, the nuances of ethnic mixing have formed a major thread in the fabric of national life. "It is noticeable that in Peru and Bolivia, and most strikingly perhaps in Mexico, the issue of cultural hybridization and *mestizaje* figures much more prominently in the relevant debates. In societies suffused with the shades of multiple social and cultural forms, concepts of national, or religious identity cannot be realistically separated from a mosaic of meaning and practice" (Slater 1994, 110). This is due to the fact that those of European backgrounds form the elite, and an obvious Indian racial identity can prevent an individual from moving up in society and attaining a state of economic well-being. This economic and social disparity does not begin to address the treatment of Indian peoples, who in some portions of southern Mexico were required to ride in the back of the bus at least into the 1970s. The issues of race in Mexico were, and are, dynamic, not static. At the beginning of the twentieth century, with valorization of the Aztec culture under Porfirio Diaz, "the dead Indian was a fossil from the remote and symbolic past almost totally alien to their everyday experience . . . but the memory of the dead Indian served the political purpose of legitimizing the State, while the living Indian was a blemish on the landscape of modern, progressing Mexico" (Krauze 1997, 39). The "backward" Indian was so much a blemish that Diaz "even banned the wearing of traditional white cotton clothes for Indians within the boundaries of Mexico City" (ibid.).

The development of *mestizaje* proceeded relatively smoothly, according to Krauze, in some areas of Mexico, especially the central portion, but in the southern parts of Mexico racial hatred engendered violence. I found the lilting choreographic scene from the southern state of Chiapas that Hernandez projected so jarring because I knew that "in San Cristobal de las Casas in Chiapas, where a closed group of white creoles (the *coletos*), with the aid of some mestizos (the ladinos), despised and exploited the Indians, who were not even allowed to walk freely in the streets" (Krauze 1997, 56).

It is important to realize that to become a Mestizo, what many claim to be a true Mexican, is a crucial and deliberate step by an Indian to give up his or her cultural heritage—especially language, but also lifestyle, including a change to the clothing of the Mestizo. This process was "marked always by a gravitation of the Indian toward the Spaniard" (Krauze 1997, 55). As anthropologist Manning Nash notes,

> South of the Gijalva river in Mexico and throughout the whole of that part of Mesoamerica there are virtually only two kinds of peoples—Ladinos and Indians. Ladinos are the people of the national culture, those in the Spanish version of Euro-American culture; and Indians are those who are in the tradition of the Mayan Indians. Ladinos speak Spanish, wear European-style clothing, are Christians in a recognizable Catholic or Protestant idiom, have social classes, and are members of and participants in the modern world culture and society of the industrialized Western world. They are Guatemalans and Mexicans, not Indians residing in Guatemala or Mexico. . . . Ladinoization is a matter of detachment of individuals from Indian societies and their transformation (or their descendants' transformation) into Ladinos. Whole communities of Indians do not become Ladinos. . . . Ladinoization is a process of individual detachment from an Indian society. (1989, 95–97)

Thus, the discourse of mestizaje, the fusion of races, pervades national life and the manner in which the dances of Ballet Folklorico are created. Anthony D. Smith, a scholar of nationalism, observes:

> In Mexico from the 1920s, the post-revolutionary regimes of Obreron [Obregón] and Vasconcelos framed an all-embracing policy of cultural nationalism based on the idea of a "fusion of the races" and a union of their very different cultural heritages under the aegis of the Mexican state. Making use of the archeological discoveries of Teotihuacan, the researches of such anthropoligists as Manuel Gamio and the talents of such painters as David Alfaro Siqueiros, Jose Clemente Orozco and Diego Rivera, the state commissioned and presented to the people a panorama of successive cultures through which a modern myth of the fusion of races, mestizaje, could be traced back to the pre-Colombian past, and in this way the lineage of the modern national state could be firmly rooted in a millennial Mexican past. At the same time, the modern national state could be presented as the legitimate heir and synthesis of the different successive cultures—Indian and Hispanic—that composed the culture area and heritage of Mexico, at the expense, one should add, of the indigenous "Indian peoples." (1995, 93–94)

In addition to the visual artists, we may add the choreographic creations of Amalia Hernandez.

Amalia Hernandez, Founding Artistic Director and Choreographer

Amalia Hernandez Navarro was born in Mexico City on September 19, 1917. Her father, a wealthy and prominent military and political figure, brought the finest teachers to the private dance studio he had constructed in their home with the proviso that she was never to dance in public, as befitted young, properly behaved upper-class women. She studied classical ballet and modern dance with an array of teachers in her childhood and as a young adult. These teachers came from a variety of traditions, and different individuals are mentioned in different sources. Among those teachers were ballet and modern dancers Hypolite Sybine (Hipolito Zybine) and Anna Sokolow; La Argentina, a flamenco dancer; and Waldeen, a pioneer of modern dance in Mexico in the 1940s and 1950s. Several accounts note that Hernandez also worked with Luis Felipe Obregon, a noted pioneer in the field of Mexican folk dance research.

Amalia Hernandez could not resist the calling of her muse and was determined to seek her fortune in dance. There she began dancing and teaching in the spectacular baroque Palacio de Bellas Artes, theater where she served as a teacher of modern dance. In 1952, with encouragement from her husband Luis de Llano, a radio and television executive, she eventually formed a small group of eight women dancers that began a series of television performances in Mexico City known as "Gala Performances." One of her first choreographies for that series, the *Sones de Michoacan*, still forms a staple of the Ballet Folklorico's repertoire. It almost always follows the opening piece, and according to the company's impresario, Julio Solorzano-Foppa, "it will always be included in the company's program" (personal interview, September 17, 1999).

Amalia was a dancer in Palacio de Bellas Artes in its early years and was a featured soloist, her photograph appearing several times in one of the company's first luxurious souvenir programs. While her name appeared as a dancer in that program, which accompanied a phonograph record of the company's music produced in the early 1960s, by 1965 her name no longer appeared in the company roster of dancers. From that point Amalia Hernandez's history is inextricably linked with that of the Ballet Folklorico.

Regarding her choreography, Amalia Hernandez has expressed several times that despite claims of copious research, like Igor Moiseyev she does not attempt to place actual folklore on the stage. "She was inspired by scenes of Mexican folklore, and recreated them with diverse techniques of classical and modern dance" (Cristiani 1994, 8).

> In a now famous interview published in 1985 by Felipe Segura and Rosa Reyna, under a series entitled *Charlas de Danza* (Chats about Dance) Amalia Hernandez revealed some aspects of her work process: "With the dance," she said, "the intention is very clear: to create a highly professional spectacle that had the techniques, the choreography, the lights, the wardrobe ... because the theatre is an art. Spectacle is an art. Authentic folklore only exists in its place of origin on the days of fiestas; the theatre is a recreation, inspired by folklore, that must develop by fulfilling the laws of the theatre." (Flores 1993, 50)

Like Igor Moiseyev, but with perhaps more subtlety, Amalia Hernandez attempts to find a core characteristic of a particular region, thereby reducing some of her works to the simplistic evocations her critics disparage. Describing her working process to *Los Angeles Times* dance critic Lewis Segal, she said, "So, I started looking for movement to develop that mood, to put the personality of that happy people on the stage" (1997, 67). The implications in that statement—that "the people" are in fact uniformly happy, that one can identify a single mood, and that "the people" have a collective personality that can be distilled into a single choreography—are staggering in terms of representational strategies.

As Oscar Flores observes, "Surrounding Amalia Hernandez a legend has been woven. . . . One thing is certain, if Amalia Hernandez had decided never to abandon Mexican modern dance, this and folkloric dance would not be what they are today. Her defenders, such as Jose Antonio Alcaraz, point out that 'although everyone criticizes her, nevertheless, they imitate her as much as they can'" (1993, 50).

Aside from her obvious skills as a choreographic artist, Amalia Hernandez, according to Solorzano-Foppa, is a first-rate manager and organizer, both of the artistic flow of the programs and also in the management of a large thriving business and artistic enterprise. Clearly, for a woman in her time and place, in a pervasive machismo environment, to establish a world-famous organization is a major achievement. She is a woman of enormous energy, focus, and drive.[4] Aside from her considerable ability and talent, there are two reasons for her vast success: Dance, particularly folk dance, was a marginal activity. And she comes from the upper classes, where her sex would not impede her success in a field not dominated by competing males.

History of Ballet Folklorico

Current programs date the founding of Ballet Folklorico as 1952 when Amalia Hernandez formed a small group of eight dancers, including herself, and performed for a special television series that consisted of sixty-seven segments over a two-year period and included a variety of modern and classical dance forms.[5] By the time that period had elapsed, Ballet Folklorico had grown to twenty dancers. In 1959, the Ballet Folklorico had fifty dancers and traveled to Chicago to represent Mexico in the Pan-American Games. Their huge success inspired the Mexican president, Adolfo Lopez Mateos, to request that the director-general of the National Institute of Fine Arts organize the group into an official national company.

In 1961 Ballet Folklorico won the coveted first-place prize in the

Festival of Nations in Paris, and the company's highly successful international touring program began. Nearly fifty years later the company maintains a busy and profitable touring program.[6] Ballet Folklorico dances three times a week, fifty-two weeks a year, and maintains two companies. One company tours while the other is a resident company that performs in the Ballet Folklorico's home theater, the beautiful Bellas Artes in the heart of Mexico City. The company also maintains two orchestras. Thus, with performers, a large behind-the-scenes support staff, and the staff of the school, employees of Ballet Folklorico number into the hundreds.

In 1964, Amalia Hernandez took the very important step of creating an independent company by privatizing Ballet Folklorico. It still bears the official governmental imprimatur and Mexico City serves as one of the most important sponsors of the company, but Amalia Hernandez wished to keep the fortunes of the company securely in her own hands and those of her family.

The company is very much a family affair. One daughter, Norma Lopez Hernandez, serves as the artistic director of the resident company in the Bellas Artes, while a second daughter, Viviana Basanta, directs the company school. A grandson, Salvador Lopez Lopez, serves as administrative director. A sister, Delfina Vargas, has created costumes for the company, and a brother, Augustin Hernandez, designed the Ballet Folklorico school. Norma Lopez Hernandez, Viviana Basanta, and Salvador Lopez Lopez have all danced with the company as part of their training, and Salvador performed and continues to perform the lariat dance, a tour de force second only to *Danza del Venado* (Yaqui Deer Dance), in male dance assignments.

Stereotypification

Addressing the concept of stereotypification in relation to Ballet Folklorico, perhaps as much as any choreographer, Amalia Hernandez has been trapped by, or allowed herself to be trapped by, stereotypical images. The repertoire of the Ballet Folklorico abounds in such images. After all, who would believe they were in the presence of the Mexican national dance company if we did not witness the Mexican hat dance, kissing behind the sombrero, Aztec warriors marching up a pyramid, a rope dance, or the tying of the bow accompanied by *"la bamba"*? In addition, for the audience members of Mexican origin, iconic images represented in *La Revolucion*, a suite depicting the Mexican Revolution of 1910 and glorifying the role of

Ballet Folklorico de Mexico. *Revolution.* Modern Mexico began with the Revolution of 1910, where for the first time in the country's history, Mexican women joined men in the political struggle. This ballet is dedicated to the "Soldaderas," the women who participated in the Mexican revolutionary movement as soldiers and supporters in the fight for liberty. COURTESY BALLET FOLKLORICO DE MEXICO.

women revolutionaries, resonate deeply. "Adelita," "Jesusita en Chihuahua," and other popular melodies of the period with the visual icon of women revolutionaries or the falsetto sounds of Huastecan vocal music touch deeply felt emotions. Thus, it is difficult to avoid the inclusion of these familiar choreographies and meet the expectations of the huge audiences that year after year look forward to appearances of the company. The financial repercussions would be enormous.

According to Julio Solorzano-Foppa, "Amalia created a new work, *Tlaxcala's Carnival,* that featured rock music and tangos that have become authentic in the fairs held in Tlaxcala, a town outside Mexico City. It was a critical success, but the audiences hated it because it did not fit into their ideas of folklore" (personal interview, September 17, 1999). Clearly, many audiences crave the quaint, stereotypical representations of Mexican folklore for which the Ballet Folklorico has become famous.

Ballet Folklorico Dance Style and Choreographic Strategies

Unlike Igor Moiseyev who relies almost exclusively on the vocabulary of character dance, which he reworked and developed into a unique vocabulary of movements that uniquely marks his company, Amalia Hernandez freely borrows from a wide variety of sources. She openly admits utilizing elements of classical ballet and modern dance, as well as regional folk dance movements and vernacular dance from the nineteenth and twentieth centuries. "She was inspired by scenes of Mexican folklore, and recreated them with diverse techniques of classical and modern dance" (Cristiani 1994, 8). Like Igor Moiseyev, she has, from the eclectic vocabularies of modern dance, ballet, and folklore elements, shaped a movement vocabulary that uniquely marks her company, as well as those many choreographers who imitate her.

An analysis of Amalia Hernandez's choreographic output reveals that she has created at least three broad vocabularies, with certain specific variations within each. The several dance styles and movement vocabularies that mark her works closely follow the classification of her choreographic output that I outlined above.

The viewer is first introduced to the style and vocabulary that marks her pre-Columbian dances. This dance style is clearly heavily informed by modern dance of several styles (since Hernandez studied with several teachers and developed a modern dance style of her own) and classical ballet movements and steps—pointed toes, turnout and balletic positions and attitudes—in which her dancers are intensively trained. Dance scholar and critic Jennifer Fisher noted that Hernandez's pre-Cortesian dances "strongly remind me of Martha Graham in her Greek period" (personal communication, September 22, 2000). These movements and steps, with perhaps the addition of contemporary regional dances that some claim to have descended directly from Aztec times, such as the *Quetazles of Puebla* or dances of *Los Concheros*, are designed, like revival Greek dancing or Hollywood depictions of biblical movies, to convey to modern eyes that the viewer is in the presence of ancient rituals and celebrations. In addition, stiff poses and attitudes are abstracted from the pictorial evidence provided by codices, paintings and decorations on ceremonial structures, and clay figurines of pre-Columbian dancers. All is ponderous, serious, and fraught with mystery. This movement vocabulary—the pointed-toe ballet walk, the bent-knee turn in place, the processional formations—

is very similar in all of these pre-Cortesian choreographies. And, in my opinion, that is why the two dance critics present at the performance of the *Great Tenochtitlan* sought reassurance that it was a new work. It appeared so much like the other works of that type, particularly *The Aztecs*, in its movement, music, and costume characteristics that the critics believed it was an old piece.

Mexican dance researcher Cesar Delgado comments that

> if we want to analyze why these reconstructions have been made, we must see the final product that has been brought forth. There are practical reasons, such as mounting a spectacle. One can cite the case of the Ballet Folklorico of Amalia Hernandez.... However, what are these reconstructions showing us? Simply, they are stereotypes of pre-Hispanic dances, closer to contemporary modern dance than the actual pre-Hispanic dances they attempt to reconstruct. (Flores 1993, 49)

The second type of movement vocabulary to represent the regional areas of Mexico—both Indian, such as *Los Tarascos* (The Tarascans) and *Danza del Venado* (Yaqui Deer Dance), and Mestizo, such as *Veracruz* and *Jalisco*—utilizes steps and figures from the specific region. Amalia Hernandez conducts copious research, which even her most determined critics admit (Flores 1993). In a typical Ballet Folklorico performance, a wide variety of traditional elements such as the intricate and technically complex zapateado (footwork with rhythmic patterns of heel and toe movements) and the equally complex use of skirts, a Ballet Folklorico specialty, are incorporated into the choreographies. All of these elements are danced in a style unique to Ballet Folklorico; one would not confuse the precise footwork patterns, showing hours of rehearsal time, found in Ballet Folklorico performances with the dances found in the field. As Gema Sandoval, an expert in Mexican traditional dance, states, "One can see that the attack, the positions and postures of the body and how the weight is carried, and other similar details are different from those of the dancers in the field because of the intensive ballet training the dancers receive which significantly alters the original movements" (personal interview, October 22, 1998).

This does not indicate that the use of ballet and modern dance are absent from these works. These Western elements clearly inform many of the movements found in *Sones de Michoacan, Boda en el istmo de Tehuantepec,* and the opening of *Tlacotalpan's Festival.*

In her more recent historical reconstructions such as the suite *La Revolucion,* in addition to the modern and ballet elements Hernandez

Ballet Folklorico de Mexico. *Sones de Michoacan*. The people of Michoacan express their happiness through dance and song. The rhythms that frame this colorful scenario make us want to stand up and follow as if the world were one large and glorious fiesta. The songs and jarabes of Apatzingan, classic in their movements and style, are evocative of this sun-drenched land. COURTESY BALLET FOLKLORICO DE MEXICO.

utilizes appropriate steps and figures from vernacular dances such as the polka from the nineteenth century.

Her third dance style, openly drawn from modern dance and classical ballet with a few vernacular and regional elements, is utilized for her contemporary/modern pieces such as *Tlaxcala's Carnival* and *Life Is a Game*. Amalia Hernandez fashions these works almost totally from modern dance and ballet sources, shaping them into a unique choreography. These choreographic creations are not based in any specific folkloric or regional traditions but rather, as with any creative artist, her own conceptual ideas of how to represent Mexican culture in a contemporary fashion. In the final analysis, there is no doubt that all of her works bear her own creative stamp.

Like Moiseyev, Amalia Hernandez comes from a time and place in which the very word "peasant" is derogatory. Regardless of claims of authenticity and copious research, Amalia Hernandez in fact does not trust the peasant sources. They must be cleaned up, dressed up, and "improved" for the middle-class eye of the beholder of her works seen in elite cultural palaces around the world.

Repertoire

Amalia Hernandez conceptually identifies two styles of choreographies that she has created for Ballet Folklorico. This is not a category based on movement: (1) "Choreography with an argument," by which she means suites that have story lines. Using as the starting point a series of dances and songs a story is developed that reflects the traditions and nature of a region. One could say that in these ballets the dances follow the story. *The Tarascans, The Revolution, Wedding in Tehuantepec* can be taken as examples of this type of choreography. (2) Selective choreography. This method of working projects the image of a region basically by means of a succession of fragments of folkloric dance adapted to the needs of the stage and in some cases very considerable adaptation is necessary choreographically to combat excessive simplicity. In these cases there is no continuous story. Typical of these ballets are *Sones de Michoacan* and *Guelaguetza* (Ballet Folklorico de Mexico 1967, 13).

The company repertoire, all of whose choreographic works have been created by Amalia Hernandez, has remained essentially the same from at least 1965, by which time three-quarters of the company repertoire had been created and developed. The Ballet Folklorico repertoire is one of the smallest and most stable among all of the companies surveyed in this study. A souvenir program accompanying the Ballet Folklorico record listed fourteen separate suites and single pieces found in the repertoire and on the recording. Of these, nine, or more than half, were staple items in the program and were still in the active repertoire of 1999, which lists seventeen pieces. A typical Ballet Folklorico program consists of between eight and eleven works.

Among these repertory pieces one can find several types of choreographies, which I would classify differently than Amalia Hernandez. The types of choreographies found in a Ballet Folklorico program consist of: (1) Historical reconstructions of pre-Cortesian dances and ceremonies. (2) Regional folk dances both from Indian communities—such as the *Guelaguetza* of Oaxaca, the *Yaqui Deer Dance* from Sinaoloa, and the *Quetzales* of Puebla—and the Mestizo areas of Veracruz, Zacatecas, Jalisco, and others. The dances from Indian communities are generally of a ritual nature, while those of the Mesitzos are social and recreational. These dances constitute nearly three-quarters of every program. (3) Historical reconstructions such as *The Revolution* from the more recent period. (4) Modern and contemporary choreographies such as *Life Is a Game* (sometimes called Toys) and *Tontinzintla*, which utilize a wide range of eclectic sources but are not actually based in any specific folkloric tradition, although for Amalia Hernandez they generically represent the (essentialized) Mexican character.

With one exception that I could discover through attending many performances and studying the printed programs, all Ballet Folklorico performances begin with a representation of pre-Cortesian Mexico. There is generally only one pre-Cortesian culture represented, and it features attempted historical reconstructions of the dances and ceremonials of the Olmecs, the Mayas, or the Aztecs. Four of these possibilities from the pre-Cortesian choreographies are listed in the 1999 program as part of the seventeen choreographic works in the active repertoire: *The Gods (Los Dioses)*, *The Mayas (Los Mayas)*, *The Olmecs (Los Olmecas)*, and the *Great Tenochtitlan*. Thus, subtracting the pre-Cortesian dances, this brings the total of the remaining active repertoire to fourteen choreographies, nine of which have been in common use since the early 1960s.

Amalia Hernandez stands in stark contrast to Igor Moiseyev and most other choreographers of national dance ensembles in her pursuit of historical reconstructions. This reflects the national mood of Mexico, with its fascination of and preoccupation with the pre-Columbian cultures upon which the very capital city is built. Every month, during excavations of building sites and public projects such as the subway, important archeological finds are made. These pre-Columbian cultures, and their tragic endings at the hands of the Spanish conquistadores, evoke powerful emotions with the Mexican public. As Krauze observes, "Ideological manipulation of the ancient past was an old Mexican custom.... The regime of Porfirio Diaz not only seized on the historical parallel between the Aztecs and the republicans; it converted indigenism, and particularly the mystique of the Aztecs, into an effective state ideology" (1997, 27, 30). It is no small wonder that Amalia Hernandez attempts to choreographically recall that past, because she is an inheritor of the generation that venerated an idealized Aztec empire.

This idealized pursuit of the past in national state dance ensembles is pursued in other nations such as Iran. By contrast, in Turkey and the former Soviet Union the newly constituted republics made clean breaks with their respective Ottoman and Romanov imperial pasts in an effort to consign them to historical oblivion. Every attempt was made to erase all cultural traces of them. Turkish and Russian companies show only stylized representations of the dances of the rural populations.

The second piece of a typical Ballet Folklorico program is the *Sones de Michoacan*, one of Amalia Hernandez's first choreographies. Seven women and two men, reflecting the early days of a smaller ensemble, and an accompanying regional orchestra of violins and guitars perform this work. The first two selections are often followed by *The Revolution*, which has been featured in every Ballet Folklorico performance that I have seen over the past forty-five years. The finale of the first half is invariably a suite of dances from the Veracruz region, which I described earlier in this chapter. This suite has undergone several renamings to match the changing of the introductory scenes. It has variously been called *Veracruz* and *Fiesta en Veracruz*, introduced by an instrumental ensemble featuring a harp and requintos (guitarlike instruments). A later incarnation of the Veracruz dances was entitled *Mocambo*, which was introduced by a Caribbean flavored jazzy blues opening featuring a torch singer. The normally white lace dresses of the women were dyed to hot pinks, reds, yellows, and oranges. *Tlacotalpan's Festival*, which is introduced with a purely contemporary modern dance in which the women, clad in one-piece bathing suits, carry a series of cartoonlike sea creatures on poles, while the men in knee-length white pants and carrying a large net gather them up, is the most recent entry. The basic core dances of *Veracruz* in these various reincarnations remain nearly the same with old favorite local tunes such as "Coco" and "La Bamba," with its famous knot-tying sequence, never failing to bring the audience to a high pitch of excitement. *Tlacotalpan's Festival* finishes with a carnival scene featuring the *mojigangas*, huge carnival figures that leave the stage and move into the audience, further accentuating the audience-performer connection.

102 CHOREOGRAPHIC POLITICS

The second half of the program always ends with the dances of Jalisco, called variously *Guadalajara, Christmas in Jalisco,* or *Fiesta in Jalisco,* which I described in some detail at the beginning of the chapter. The penultimate selection is the famous *Danza del Venado* (Yaqui Deer Dance). This means that there is only room in a typical concert for two to four other works. These dance numbers usually feature regional folk dances, with perhaps a contemporary choreography such as *Life Is a Game* included. These other pieces, in three-quarters of the numerous concert programs that I studied, are the *Wedding in Huasteca; Wedding in Tehuantepec; Zacatecas; Zafra en Tamaulipas* (*Sugar Harvest in Tamaulipas*); *Chiapas; Guerrero Guerrero; The Tarascans;*

Ballet Folklorico de Mexico. *Yaqui Deer Dance.* The dramatic and beautiful Yaqui Deer Dance is a myth that explains the transmutation of the personality of the hunter into the experience of the hunted. The dance explores the fear, survival instincts, and eternal struggle between life and death that link the warrior with the deer. The dance resembles a prayer honoring the spirit of the deer by the hunter prior to the hunt.
COURTESY BALLET FOLKLORICO DE MEXICO.

Yucatan: Danzon and Jarana; and *Tarima de Tixtla.* Two or three of the choreographies listed above have been circulated and fill the empty slots of the programs that I have witnessed throughout the nearly fifty years of the company's history.

Aside from the financing of a new production, the staples of the Ballet Folklorico repertoire—*The Revolution, Sones de Michoacan,* the dances of *Veracruz* (under different titles), the *Danza del Venado,* and *Jalisco*—are such icons that, according to company impressario Julio Solorzano-Foppa, they are extremely popular. "When there has been an attempt to replace them or retire them for a while the public outcry is enormous" (personal interview, September 17, 1999).

Nevertheless, the fact remains that aside from the *Tlaxcala's Carnival,* which appears to be a truly new work, it has been a consistent practice in the past few years for Ballet Folklorico to announce other works as premieres that are in fact revivals of earlier works. Over the past few years *Guelaguetza, Chiapas, The Tarascans,* and *Yucatan: Danzon and Jarana* have been revivals rather than new pieces even though some of them, such as the dances of Yucatan, had not been seen in the United States for years.[7]

Dancers and Dance Training

The dancers are uniformly young. A comparison of the cast lists of the programs over the years reveals a very high turnover. The vast majority of them do not stay with the company for long periods like the dancers of the state ensembles of the former Socialist bloc. In those countries, dancers made a career of dancing with the national company because they received many perquisites, such as traveling to the West, relatively high salaries (at least in their first decades), and the attraction of the artistic product. Several of the LADO dancers mentioned their love of Croatian folklore, as performed by LADO, as an important reason in their choice of dance as a lifelong career. Ballet Folklorico attracts cancers because of its high production values as well as its portrayal of Mexican culture.

Regarding salaries, the company spokesperson said that dancers earn approximately the same pay as a "skilled worker." This is a low salary. "However, there are many benefits. Traveling with a highly esteemed national dance company, staying in good hotels with good food, and the training they receive that provides the basic skills they need for those interested in pursuing dance as a career. The training in the Ballet Folklorico school is the finest in all of Latin America, and performing in the highly disciplined company makes the former company members welcome in dance companies throughout Mexico and Latin America" (Solorzano, personal interview, September 17, 1999).

Gema Sandoval, who is familiar with the internal operations of the company, stated:

> There are several reasons for the rapid turnover in the company. The company is largely populated by young men who come in from the provinces looking for a better life. Folk dancing, as opposed to other forms of dance, is the only acceptable vehicle for men to follow in dance. Later, they are sometimes attracted to other genres of dance. More often they leave after a few years due to the low pay. The women, often from the upper middle class, enter to pass the time in an artistic career while they wait for a suitable husband. They worry if they have not married by twenty-three. After marriage, the husbands do not want their wives dancing on public stages. Also, in Mexican society in general there is a deep-seated mistrust of large organizations. Loyalty goes to the family, not to organizations. Therefore, there is no true loyalty to the company, which is such an important element in the construction of *esprit de corps* within a dance company. (Personal interview, October, 26, 1999)

The company is highly disciplined, and Amalia Hernandez commands this ordered environment through a series of stringent rules. Those who are late, make mistakes, or commit other infractions of the company's rules can be fined or dismissed. Solorzano added, "If someone is ill or breaks the rules, he or she is sent home and a replacement who can take all of that individual's roles is flown back on the return flight" (ibid.). This ability to replace any individual maintains a businesslike atmosphere of professional discipline in the company.

I inquired of the company spokesperson if there were any physical or other requirements of the dancers. Aside from professional competence, he informed me that "Amalia demands no special physical appearance aside from preferring taller dancers for the touring company because they look 'better' there are none. The touring [company] is generally about two inches taller than the home company on average" (Solorzano, personal interview, September 17, 1999).

Music

It is in the music, especially the instrumental music that accompanies Ballet Folklorico, that Amalia Hernandez has remained most faithful to the original sources. For the most part very authentic, highly proficient musicians who are clearly steeped in the styles they portray accompany the regional folk dances. Occasionally, recorded music is utilized, as with the *Yaqui Deer Dance,* when original music is difficult to procure. The pre-Columbian pieces often combine recorded and live music. The use of this music heightens the effect of authenticity, and mariachi music certainly constitutes one of the most popular forms of world music; even non-Mexican audiences are clearly familiar with its unique sound.

In the beginning decades of the ensemble, a large chorus, classically trained and singing in nontraditional four-part harmonies, was a prominent part of the company. Amalia Hernandez used them in an interesting choreographic fashion, enabling her to people some of her productions with huge casts. This vocal music was sometimes effective, as in such works as *Wedding in Tehuantepec, Jalisco,* and *The Revolution* in which the European-style choral music was not obtrusive. However, the modern harmonies sung by the chorus add to the anachronistic quality of pre-Cortesian works. Attrition to the opera chorus of the Bellas Artes, to which many of Ballet Folklorico's choral members belonged, as well as the cost of maintaining the large chorus during the period when Mexico's economy declined forced the Ballet Folklorico to dispense with its services. The decades during the absence of the chorus allowed the more authentic musical ensembles to take center stage, and the outstanding performances highlighted this authentic element of the company.

In 1999 the chorus was reintroduced, performing in the *Great Tenochtitlan, The Revolution,* and *The Tarascans.* The chorus also joined the dancers in the *Jalisco* finale, not singing but peopling the stage.

Costumes

Like many of the choreographers and artistic directors this study seeks to analyze, Amalia Hernandez mistrusts her original sources perhaps even more than the mistrust that she exhibits in her use of choreographic elements. She has clearly expressed this viewpoint in a number of interviews.

> Back in Mexico City, she made a selection from the original steps and arranged for the costumes to be adapted from those she'd bought at the market in Oaxaca as well as from films and photographs.

Because she believed that the authentic decorations on folk costumes can either look too small to make any effect or seem impossibly fussy when presented on a large stage, Hernandez often enlarges the patterns for greater acceptability and theatrical splash. (Segal 1997, 67)

On the point of "greater acceptability," I return to the core audience that must accept her work: the upper middle classes of Mexico City and her international following. In order to achieve this theatricalization of the costumes to be worn in her choreographic works, she engages the services of high-fashion designers such as Dasha and Delfina Vargas. These designers, familiar with the lines and cuts of clothing that are appealing and acceptable to the modern eye, begin their alterations and redesigning. First, they harmonize the colors. In *Guerrero Guerrero* soft pastels in harmonizing tones of pale greens, blues, yellows, and oranges provide a soft, dreamy look. The pre-Columbian clothing appears in intense colors and hues and in synthetic fabrics that only aniline dyes and modern chemical techniques can make available. The men's spandex body stockings in flesh tones, visible from the back of the large auditorium in the recent *Great Tenochtitlan*, created a jarringly anachronistic element in the visual appearance of the company, as do the green ones in *The Olmecs*.

One of the most frequent alterations that designers create for Amalia Hernandez is skirts, dresses, and *huipil* (native tunics found throughout Mexico) with much fuller fabrics than the originals. This gives the choreographer and the dancers much more freedom of movement. The amount of bare leg that can be seen often startles audience members who are familiar with the original clothing and with the fact that women in those traditional societies would never show bare flesh in that fashion. The women's costumes from *Veracruz* typify the field-stage-field model that I have proposed in this study. Julio Solorzano-Foppa shared with me that the people in Veracruz who wear those costumes for dancing have abandoned the original clothing in favor of the more glamorous versions worn by Ballet Folklorico, which further illustrates the way in which elements of the field circulate back from the national company (personal interview, September 17, 1999).

Those familiar with the china poblana, the emblematic icon of Mexican costume that was historically worn throughout Mexico and Early California in the nineteenth century and associated, in its many forms, with urban centers such as Guadalajara will search in vain for this clothing in a Ballet Folklorico performance (Shay and Machette 1987). It has been replaced with a full red skirt with black trim for the dancers, and a matching green one for the chorus members.

Finances

Although the company was nationalized in 1961, in 1964 Amalia Hernandez took the bold step of privatizing the company as a nonprofit corporation. Revenues are received through several sources. The company's three-times-a-week performances in the Bellas Artes, touring receipts, and especially the grants and touring support of large corporations such as Honda, Telmex, and Black and Decker, as well as the Tourist Organization of Mexico City (all prominently featured in program advertisements as sponsors) provide the Ballet Folklorico with a handsome income. This enables Amalia Hernandez to maintain an independent status for her company.

Ballet Folklorico is one of the two most visible and venerable state folk dance companies in the world. Although controversy swirls around Amalia Hernandez regarding the manner in which she treats her sources, clearly she has created an impressive company against which all other folk dance companies in Mexico, and even the world, are compared. She will surely be considered one of the most important and influential dance makers of the twentieth century, when her company commanded most of the major stages throughout the world.

Amalia Hernandez passed away on November 4, 2000, at the age of eighty-three. Her lively and controversial choreographies of Mexican folk traditions and the Ballet Folklorico de Mexico de Amalia Hernandez will remain as her legacy.

5

LADO, Ensemble of Folk Dances and Songs of Croatia: Proper Peasants

Mi nosimo zelen vencec
Daj nam, Lado, lepi Lado
We bring green wreathes
Give to us, Lado, beautiful Lado
Opening verse of *Ladarke*, LADO
choreography of the Central Croatian ritual

As the curtain opens, the full cast of LADO, the Ensemble for Folk Dances and Songs of Croatia (to use its official name), stands revealed in the richly embroidered costumes of the Central Croatian district of Pokuplje. With full-throated Slavic voices, the company sings the opening vocal strains of *Ladarke*, a work that has become something of a company signature piece; performing the Midsummer's ritual, a group of maidens bearing green branches move with simple, ritualistic walking steps, placing the branches in the center of the stage. Through each of the three parts of the choreography the tempo increases, and one by one the cast members begin joining the slow circling in concentric circles. At the end of the second piece the dancer/singers all stop and a woman steps forth and asks, singing in a powerful voice, "*je'l vam se hoce, Lado, kaj nas bude vise?*" (Do you wish us to increase, Lado?) The chorus responds and the tempo moves even faster. A couple begins to whirl in the center, and the cast joins in concentric circles, moving faster and faster, ending in a vocal crescendo. In this choreography, except for the central whirling couple, the movement never moves beyond a mellow circling suitable to a ritual event; the vocal element has a pride of place over the dance.[1]

I first experienced a LADO performance on a crisp September evening in 1968 at the Greek Theatre in Los Angeles. Fresh from the Montreal World's Fair, LADO was scheduled for a full week of performances.[2] From the opening ritual, *Ladarke,* in which a cast of dancers opened their program with full-throated Slavic singing, I was riveted to my seat. Throughout its evening performance the company resolutely eschewed the use of spectacle, which, strangely enough, created a unique niche for this company in the minds of many viewers. Having experienced the spectacle of the Moiseyev Dance Company, Ballet Folklorico de Mexico, the Bayanihan Philippine Dance Company, the Ukrainian State Folk Ensemble, and the Georgian State Folk Company, among others, I was unprepared for the simple elegance and majesty of LADO. Others were impressed by the performance in the same way I was. Martin Bernheimer, *Los Angeles Times* Pulitzer prize-winning music and dance critic, advised those looking for the choreographic thrills provided by Moiseyev and other "Slavic troupes that have visited us in the recent past" to "gasp elsewhere." He characterized LADO's performance as "small-scale, low-key, non-bravura, non-spectacular, unslick and anti-commercial" (Bernheimer 1967).

Night after night for a full week of LADO's performances, I returned to this captivating company for the thrill of those voices, the majesty of attention to minute detail. For years thereafter I made annual pilgrimages to Croatia to experience, what was for me, LADO's magic. In contrast to the programs of Ballet Folklorico and Moiseyev, LADO continuously produced new works. Surprisingly, given the much more limited budget and financial resources of the Croatian Republic and Zagreb city government, LADO's primary funding sources, the LADO repertoire is significantly larger than those of Ballet Folklorico and Moiseyev.

The opening work marked a departure from all of the companies I had ever seen. Dancing and simple movement, rather than a stress on a "grab the audience" spectacular dance piece common to the vast majority of other companies, accompanied the singing. I have never seen any other state folk dance ensemble give equal importance to the singing and dancing and use the dancers as singers. The Bulgarian State Ensemble of Folk Songs and Dances (known as the Philip Koutev Ensemble in the West), the Pirin Ensemble of Bulgarian Macedonia (Pirin), and the Hungarian State Folk Ensemble all maintain separate choruses, and in KOLO of Serbia and Bayanihan of the Philippines the dancers sing. In the case of the first three companies, the singers support the dancers by singing with the orchestra, while in the case of KOLO and Bayanihan, singing is intermittent and incidental. After having experienced the spectacularized folk songs and dances of Mexico or Russia, I found that the highly nuanced and subtle performances of LADO reward the viewer with a full palate of folklore.

LADO, however, like all of the other professional and semiprofessional ensembles under consideration in this study, for all of its use of authentic elements is not "the village" any more than the performances of other professional dance ensembles. But LADO gives the impression of village dance events because of the passion and commitment of the company artists and choreographers to preserving the myriad, highly detailed, authentic elements that they have lovingly absorbed. LADO's performances are highly professional and precisioned choreographies. Numerous viewings of the company enable the observer to readily see that the creator of the staged pieces carefully crafts the apparent spontaneity of a village celebration. The professional artistry of the company performers creates the illusion of being in the midst of a village gathering.

The difference in the approach that LADO, under the artistic direction of its founder, Professor Zvonko Ljevakovic, has adopted and those of the companies that I have analyzed so far can be summed up by the reaction of the people themselves. Many years ago, in the early 1960s, I met a young Lebanese man who was an expert at performing the dances of his village, which he kindly shared with me. He was from "the field" and danced with spontaneity and improvisation, one of the main elements that identifies "in the field" performances. He characterized the dances performed by the *Firqat al-anwar*, a professional Lebanese national dance company of that time, as "new folk dances." In other words, he both foreshadowed and underscored the conception that I have formulated for this study, that of parallel traditions, although he did not articulate his thoughts in those terms. The Lebanese village dancer readily discerned that the professional company, which performed a highly spectacularized and contrived version of the *dabka*, was performing a form of dance related, if very distantly, to what he performed in his village. He readily understood that the state ensemble's choreographies of the *dabka* were conceptually different from his in-the-field experiences and style.

The reaction of the peasants in Croatia to performances of LADO is strikingly different from that of the Lebanese dancer. "LADO dances our dances better than we do," said a peasant woman in the video *Potret Zvonka Ljevakovica*. For the Croatian peasants, LADO performs "their" dances, which they immediately recognize. They understand that LADO gives a highly polished and precisioned version of their dances, creating a contact between the parallel traditions that becomes very blurred for the Croatian peasants and many audience members. In addition, they see that LADO performs their familiar dances in a style that was popular with older generations, thereby

LADO, Ensemble of Folk Dances and Songs of Croatia   111

LADO. *Dances of Prigorje.* Courtesy of LADO, FOLK DANCE ENSEMBLE OF CROATIA.

creating the further impression that the artists of LADO are keepers of the flame of old Croatia. In their eyes, LADO performs an older and therefore "purer" version of dances that had often become outmoded and had fallen into oblivion in many villages. Unlike the experience of the Lebanese dancer, the Croatian peasants conceive of LADO as a highly precisioned version of what they themselves perform.

The Rocky Road from Socialism to Independence

Croatia has emerged as an independent republic in the aftermath of the breakup of the former Yugoslavia. The Croatians, a Slavic-speaking people, arrived in the Balkans, the present-day Croatian homeland, during the Slavic migrations of the sixth and seventh centuries. By A.D. 900, the Croatians had established a kingdom taken over approximately a hundred years later by the Hapsburgs. Croatia remained a part of the Austro-Hungarian Empire under the Hapsburgs until 1918, when it became one of the constituent parts of the kingdom of the

Serbs, Croats, and Slovenes, later Yugoslavia. During World War II, the Germans established a Nazi puppet state that committed atrocious crimes against humanity, victimizing the Serbs, Jews, and Gypsies.

From the end of World War II until the breakup of the former Yugoslavia in the early 1990s, Serbs made up 12 percent of the population; following recent hostilities, however, few remain. Throughout most of its history Croatia has been annexed to stronger and larger neighbors. The Croatians in the last decade achieved their independence at great cost and engendered more mutual hatred with their greatest historical enemy, the Serbs. It is within the context of the ethnic tensions of the former Yugoslavia and the repression of ethnic expression that the performances and repertoire of LADO must be viewed and analyzed.[3]

Zvonimir Ljevakovic, Founding Artistic Director and Choreographer

Zvonimir Ljevakovic was born in Pipak, a small Slavonian village, in 1908. Little is known of his early education, but he was universally referred to as "Professor," a term that he encouraged people to use. He was esteemed as a colleague by Milovan Gavazzi, the renowned Croatian folklorist, whose theoretical works, based on the geographic distribution of cultural elements, is still largely followed by the generations of folklorists whom he trained.

Ljevakovic was a member of a group of interwar intellectuals and artists who were known under the rubric *"zemlje"* (earth) and profoundly believed in the lore and artistry of the Croatian peasantry, whom they believed were the repository of the Croatian national spirit. This belief clearly marked his choreographic output. Unlike the other choreographers analyzed in this study, Ljevakovic believed in and practiced the inclusion of all of the possible authentic elements in dance, music, and costume while maintaining and directing a company that performs with the highest level of professionalism and precision.[4]

Ljevakovic also differed from all of the choreographers and artistic directors of state folk ensembles in that he was also a highly proficient musician. (Philip Koutev was also a musician, but not a choreographer.) He is credited with both the instrumental and vocal arrangements of many of LADO's works. Later he employed the considerable talents of Bozidar Potocnik, who also contributed many vocal and instrumental arrangements and became the musical director of the ensemble.

LADO, Ensemble of Folk Dances and Songs of Croatia 113

Professor Ljevakovic was never a member of the Communist Party and he was a passionate Croatian patriot. For both of these reasons they [government officials] never trusted him. But they also recognized his talents and wanted to use them. Because he refused to join the party, he was denied the many honors and awards given to the artistic directors of the ensembles of Serbia and Macedonia, who were party members. But he never cared. His life was Croatian folk dance and music. I remember Professor Ljevakovic as an excellent folk dancer who understood every nuance of the traditional movements as well as had a thorough knowledge of the music. (Nevenka Sokcic, original dancer and vocalist with LADO, personal interview, October 14, 1999)

Another LADO performer observed that "Professor Ljevakovic was meticulous in every detail of a performance. He went to the field, not only to learn the songs and dances, but he would choose every single garment in the villages, and know which woman in LADO would wear which dress" (Andela Potocnik in videocassette *Portret Zvonka Ljevakovica*).

LADO. *Slavonian Kolo*. Courtesy of LADO, FOLK DANCE ENSEMBLE OF CROATIA.

Indeed, every individual performer in LADO, over the many years that I followed the progress of the company, held Zvonko Ljevakovic in awe and considered him a genius, the word that they frequently used in conversation describing him. His word was law, not because he was a tyrant—as some other directors in this study were and are—but because of a vast knowledge of Croatian folklore so profound that company members never questioned him or his decisions. The dancers also revered him, regarding him as a genius in theatricalizing Croatian folklore without compromising the authenticity of it. He was characterized as a "perfectionist" by almost every observer (videocassette *Portret Zvonka Ljevakovica*).

Although Professor Ljevakovic's name appeared on all of the numerous programs as artistic director, one can search in vain for a single word of his biographical background. This was a result of Ljevakovic not being a member of the Communist Party. In contrast to the programs of Ballet Folklorico and Moiseyev, in which highly polished biographies of the artistic directors are prominently featured, none of the LADO souvenir or regular programs contains any information about Zvonko Ljevakovic.

Professor Ljevakovic directed LADO until 1973, when he retired. He passed away in 1990, a scant few weeks after LADO's fortieth anniversary in November 1989, where I saw him in attendance at the gala performance. He was equally revered by many of his peasant informants who were also his friends. In the video documentary of his life, *Portret Zvonka Ljevakovica,* a group of Slavonian peasants sing a deeply moving, emotional dirge at his funeral.

History of LADO

LADO began its career in the wake of the devastation, ruins, and political and ethnic chaos that characterized much of Eastern Europe after World War II. In Yugoslavia this was a period in which the Communist Party was filled with idealism and hope but also pursued a policy of revenge that touched the innocent as well as the guilty.[5] In order to mobilize the youth of the nation whom the party hoped to shape and mold as workers and Yugoslav citizens (as opposed to Croatian or Serbian nationalists) in a new image of the party, the government founded many youth organizations and clubs that were devoted to athletic, social, political, and cultural activities. These organizations provided a place for young people living in the cramped, substandard housing that characterized war-torn Eastern Europe to pass their leisure time, play sports, and make contacts with the opposite sex.

LADO, Ensemble of Folk Dances and Songs of Croatia 115

The Young People's Society for Culture and Art (Jozo Vlahovic) became one of the most prominent youth organizations in Zagreb, the capital of the newly constituted Socialist Republic of Croatia, and formed an important link in this national chain of youth clubs. In 1946, the forty-year-old Zvonko Ljevakovic formed a cultural group of talented young people within Jozo Vlahovic whom he prepared for the presentation of traditional Croatian folk dances. This was a period of the frequent mass youth festivals throughout the Communist bloc, which were used to symbolize the political domination of the party and its support by the masses, all dressed in peasant costumes representing an ethnic rainbow of unity.

In its beginnings Jozo Vlahovic was enormous in size, because after World War II folk dance and music became highly valorized, heavily subsidized forms of "safe" Croatian nationalist and political expression. It had more than two hundred singers and dozens of dancers and instrumental musicians. Its first works, still in the active repertoire, were *Vrlicko Kolo*, the silent dance of Vrlika (an area in the mountains behind the Dalmatian coast); *Posavski Plesovi*, dances of Posavina (Central Croatia); and *Slavonsko Kolo*, the ring dance of Slavonija (Eastern Croatia), Ljevakovic's birthplace for which he always had a special fondness. In keeping with the political tenor of the time, Professor Ljevakovic created the choreography *Opsaj diri*, a suite of dances from the Pokuplje region (south and west of Zagreb), which, while retaining the original musical and choreographic elements of the region, featured newly fashioned panegyric lyrics extolling Communist Party leader and Yugoslav president Josip Broz Tito.

In the Jozo Vlahovic ensemble, Ljevakovic made musical arrangements and directed the dancers and orchestra. Emil Cossetto, a well-known arranger of Croatian folk music, usually directed the chorus. In 1947, Jozo Vlahovic, garnered the second prize at the huge World Youth Festival held in Prague.

> Of course, it was almost a law that the first prize would go to Moiseyev. First, they were a professional company, but more than that, the Russians had to win everything. Still, for us to take home that coveted second prize, over all of the other thirty-four professional ensembles from eighteen different nations participating in that massive festival was a great thing. (Misa Sokcic, personal interview, October 15, 1999)

In 1949, Jozo Vlahovic won the coveted first prize of the Yugoslav Government among all of the other professional and amateur dance companies from all over the country. At a time when socialist governments throughout the world marched in lock step with the Soviet

LADO. *Tanec from the Island of Krk.* Courtesy of LADO, FOLK DANCE ENSEMBLE OF CROATIA.

Union, the creation of a state dance company based on the Moiseyev model became de rigueur for every major political entity. In light of Ljevakovic's recent artistic successes, the Croatian government entered into negotiations with him and on November 11, 1949, Jozo Vlahovic was converted into a professional company. Shortly after, in 1950, the company was renamed LADO, an ancient word meaning "good" or "dear" and a frequent refrain in the folk songs of Northern and Central Croatia. The first program of the newly professionalized company dated February 4, 1950, does not carry the name LADO but announces only the State Ensemble of Folk Dances and Songs (*LADO 1949–1979*, III). "The choice of this name is an indication of how much attention LADO pays to its vocal expression" (*LADO U Svijetv/LADO and the World* n.d.).

The change to a professional company meant a reorganization of the formerly amateur Jozo Vlahovic. The chorus was financially impossible to maintain, and the corps of dancers was reduced to a group capable of the highest quality of performance. Nevenka Sokcic recalls that

> The first years were both wonderful and difficult. The wonderful part was that we were treated like movie stars. We had special rehearsal outfits and when we wore them, we had free access to public transportation and everyone admired us. The difficulties came from the [Communist]

Party. The party was everywhere. The party frequently dismissed good dancers. I remember one excellent dancer was thrown out because a relative had been a member of the Ustasha [Nazi Party in Croatia that ruled during 1941–1945] and another because he sang a patriotic song of that period when he was a little drunk.

Life was very difficult after the war. Food was scarce; the economy was in a shambles. We were to travel to London and Western Europe in 1950. The party ordered special fabrics from Switzerland to make us suitable clothes, and we were fed three square meals a day in the best hotel in Zagreb so that we would not appear emaciated and poor. In those early years when we traveled abroad the party sent agents to watch over us and report everything. In the beginning they were very diligent and reported everything. After that, those agents, who received far more money than we did, landed with us, went shopping, and never saw us again until we returned. In spite of those efforts, defections occurred on every tour. Usually one or two people defected from the company on each tour, but once, in Trieste, fifteen dancers deserted and we had to dress the musicians in dancers' costumes to fill out the stage because we had only three [of the usual seven] couples to perform Vrlika. (Personal interview, October 16, 1999)

Unlike the Moiseyev Dance Company and Ballet Folklorico, which are purely the artistic creations of single individuals, LADO, even in its beginning years, utilized the choreographic talents of other individuals. These works were not only the creations of individuals outside of Croatia but also of Croatian choreographers who produced such works as the dances of Baranja. After Ljevakovic retired, LADO continued to expand its choreographic repertoire with a number of works by different individuals. Particularly noteworthy in the repertoire are several outstanding works by the dean of Croatian folk dance research, Dr. Ivan Ivancan.

LADO, like the Moiseyev Dance Company and Ballet Folklorico, has toured extensively to every continent.[6] The world had a seemingly endless taste for the appearances of these national companies, one that continues unabated.

Dance Style and Choreographic Strategies

LADO can be said to use either one style or dozens. The company uses the multiple regional styles of Croatia, and, formerly, those of the regions of the former Yugoslavia. Ljevakovic placed much emphasis on utilizing only the steps and movements characteristic of a single district or region. Croatia has three broad regional styles. Briefly, the Pannonian area (Central Croatia) is characterized by turning, walking, and small *drmes* (shaking) steps utilized in endless permutations. The dances of the regions of the Dinaric Mountains (extending into Bosnia, Montenegro, and Albania) can be characterized by relatively large, heavy steps performed in circles, and more rarely in couples. The dances of the Adriatic coast can be characterized by both circle dances and dances in lines in which the dancers face one another, executing small steps, turning in place, and exchanging places, among other figures. For well over a hundred years the polka and waltz, among other Central European dance forms, modified by local dance styles, have been included in the dances of Croatia. In the nineteenth century, the elites of large urban areas such as Split hired dancing masters from Italy and France to teach their youth the latest fashionable dances. None of the choreographic traditions I described above lend themselves to spectacle of the sort that Moiseyev created. Neither Ljevakovic nor any of the other choreographers who created works for LADO attempted to use steps, figures, postures, or attitudes from outside of the regions or districts of the particular choreography that was being represented. Ljevakovic especially eschewed the use of Western theatrical dance forms such as classical ballet or modern dance.

In order to add to the picture of verisimilitude, Ljevakovic noted how individuals stood or walked in everyday life and incorporated this into his choreographies. He employed these everyday movements and postures when the dancers were standing still or strolling about the performance area as part of the choreography. Thus, when a woman stood on the stage not dancing, it was important that she walk in a particular manner and gait, place her hands either forward or backward on her waist, and hold her head properly. When she turned, it was important to turn at a particular speed in order to imitate how the peasants moved and achieve the aesthetic for which Ljevakovic strived—a peasant aesthetic. To attain this goal, every movement on the stage was a studied and cherished ingredient.

Repertoire

The repertoire of LADO is far more extensive than either the Moiseyev Dance Company or Ballet Folklorico. Because the company sings as well as dances, the possibility of aesthetic representation is greatly increased. In contrast to the Moiseyev company, the ensemble

LADO, Ensemble of Folk Dances and Songs of Croatia

includes a wide range of customs and rituals, as well as celebratory dances and songs, from throughout Croatia. Since the establishment of the Croatian Republic, LADO's creative output has included the singing of unusual regional folk masses and other religious music not encouraged during the Communist period.

The repertoire of LADO, twenty-five years after the retirement of Zvonko Ljevakovic, continues in the spirit of his quest for authenticity. A recent publicity brochure of the company articulates his philosophy (although it is not credited to him), which continues to inform the ensemble's repertoire:

LADO is a name of the clearly distinguishable quality, because
LADO fully respects the authentic folk art
LADO keeps behind the scenes all unsignificant elements, alien to the national tradition
LADO restrains itself from shallow formal aestheticism
LADO pays particular attention to the costume, and disposes of a considerable fund of authentic folk costumes
LADO breathes the life into all the components of the folk art, in their integrality and fullness
LADO gathers together the most prominent ethno-choreologists and choreographers, ethno-musicologists and score writers. (*LADO U Svijetv/LADO and the World* n.d.)

LADO's repertoire consists entirely of regional folk dances of Croatia, although formerly it included choreographies from the various regions and republics of the former Yugoslavia as well. Until the breakup of the former Yugoslavia, LADO maintained two separate repertoires, one for Croatia and one Pan-Yugoslav. There was no attempt to produce historical reconstructions. With the exception of the dances of Split, urban dances are not included because Ljevakovic and like-minded folklorists considered the Croatian peasant as the true spirit of Croatia (Dubinskas 1983). Thus, class is rarely displayed, either in a negative or positive fashion in LADO's repertoire in the manner of Ballet Folklorico, the Moiseyev Dance Company, Bayanihan, or the Mahalli Dancers of Iran.[7] The most reviled class under the Communist regime was the urban petite bourgeoisie, particularly of Zagreb, which has never been represented in the LADO repertoire. Every attempt is made to have representation from every part of Croatia. Unlike other companies, the ethnographic regions found in the LADO repertoire are often geographically very small, often representing the unique dances, customs, songs, and costumes of a small group of villages, or even a single village.

LADO. *Dances from Split.* Courtesy of LADO, FOLK DANCE ENSEMBLE OF CROATIA.

Dancers and Dance Training

Unlike the Ballet Folklorico and the Moiseyev Dance Company, LADO has never had a formal large-scale school that produces large numbers of well-trained dancers from which to draw talent. LADO had two sources for finding company artists. One source of new artists was from among individuals who were members of the many amateur ensembles in the Zagreb area. Another source for locating dancers was through training provided in classes, held in the afternoon after the regular company rehearsals. During these training classes, a few talented individuals who wished to enter the company were given special attention by senior company members.[8] Following the training period, an open audition would be held to fill the positions of the ensemble left vacant by an individual retiring or leaving for some other reason. Those wishing to enter the company had to sing as well as dance. The training consisted of the technical skill in steps and movements from the various choreographic traditions represented in the company repertoire rather than learning choreography.

Nevenka Sokcic recalls that

> I sat on a three-person selection committee, who along with Professor Ljevakovic selected new members from among the candidates. In the early days among the people whom we auditioned we were forced to accept some individuals who had party connections. That practice was dropped as life improved in the 1970s. On the other hand, being a member of the company had fewer compensations and the pay in other fields became more competitive. (Personal interview, October 16, 1999)

In the beginning when salaries were under the Communist system, the company artists earned a handsome wage and had many perquisites including the ability to travel to the West, a rare privilege in the 1940s, 1950s, and 1960s. However, as the party decreased its presence in the economic field, other professions became increasingly attractive financially, especially for men. The attractiveness of the artistic life and a passion for Croatian folk music and dance continues to draw individuals to LADO, but it is a difficult way of life. The company maintains a grueling schedule, especially in the summer, with days and weeks away from homes and families in Zagreb. This, and the relatively low pay, creates difficulties in finding artists.

Music

LADO is an ensemble in which music, particularly vocal music, is as important as dance.[9] LADO does not hesitate to tackle the intricacies of traditional harmony, using nontempered scales with microtones (intervals of less or more than the half and whole tones found on the piano).

> In the beginning of the ensemble we spent considerable time listening to field recordings or the peasants themselves in order to learn to sing in the authentic style that Professor Ljevakovic wanted. This style was alien to us because we were city dwellers and we had to work hard and spend hours perfecting the singing. It was much harder than learning dance, but over the years we developed the style for which LADO is famous. (Andela Potocnik, Nevenka Sokcic, and Mira Tunukovic, personal interview, November 5, 1989)

The instrumental ensembles vary from region to region. LADO musicians are expected to learn several instruments in order to maintain

LADO. *Dances from Baranja.* Courtesy of LADO, FOLK DANCE ENSEMBLE OF CROATIA.

the authenticity for which the company strives. In instrumental music, LADO is similar to Ballet Folklorico in employing different traditional ensembles to accompany the appropriate region. LADO differs from the many ensembles such as the Moiseyev Dance Company and the Philip Koutev Ensemble of Bulgaria, which use a single orchestra to cover all of the musical accompaniment.[10]

Costumes

LADO maintains an enormous wardrobe of authentic costumes from all over the former Yugoslavia. In the few instances where the costumes were prohibitively expensive or unavailable for other reasons, the company had the costumes copied in exact detail. The company is extremely proud of its costumes, many of which are of museum quality.

More than any other company except the Greek national company, the costumes are authentic in every detail. This includes the practice of using various modalities of clothing. For example, in traditional societies the married, the unmarried, and other social categories were marked by differences in clothing. Underscoring the importance of authenticity, great care and time are taken to teach the company artists in the correct wearing and tying of the garments and headpieces, some of which are difficult to learn. Women's headpieces in particular are often very intricate in the detail and wrapping.

Unlike Ballet Folklorico or the Moiseyev Dance Company, costumes are not altered to make them more appealing to modern eyes through shortening the skirts and dresses, harmonizing the colors, enlarging the designs, or adding extra fabric. Traditional garments are often constructed in such a way that the possibility of enlarging them is built into the original design. Shoulder straps are adjustable for length, and folding practices allow for greater or lesser girth (Gusic 1955).

Finances

LADO maintained an unusual financial arrangement for many years. The City of Zagreb advanced LADO's budget at the beginning of each fiscal year. As LADO was reimbursed through contracts and ticket sales by various sponsors and presenters, the company, in turn, reimbursed the City of Zagreb. Extra money made over and above the planned budget was then utilized to finance new productions. A committee from LADO created the budget and assessed the artistic value as well as the years of service of each performer in the ensemble to determine salaries.

A close reading of LADO's repertoire development provides support for one of the main theoretical viewpoints of this study: that the repertoires and performances of state folk dance ensembles reflect the political situation within which they develop. In its beginning years, following World War II, the ensemble's repertoire began as a purely Croatian one, emphasizing LADO's position as a cultural representative of the newly formed Socialist Republic of Croatia as well as the artistic priorities of its founding artistic director and choreographer. Some choreographies of this period are the *Silent Dance of Vrlika*, *Dances of Posavina*, and *Slavonian Reel*.

This was followed by a period in which dances and songs were reconstituted with new political meaning. They were choreographed and arranged to eulogize the Communist Party, Josip Broz Tito, and the partisans. Dance songs such as *Opsaj diri*, *Kozarsko Kolo*, and *Partizansko Kolo* as well as a large body of songs exemplify this period.[11] As the political domination of the party ebbed in national life, these latter works were quietly dropped or were brought out from mothballs for an occasional special event such as Tito's birthday.

Shortly thereafter, a period ensued when the national companies of Serbia, Macedonia, and Croatia began to tour widely. The government decided that each of these companies was to include dances from other Yugoslav republics in their repertoire. Sometimes the companies exchanged choreographies. For example, LADO performed dance from Serbia choreographed by Olga Skovran, the founding artistic director of the Serbian state company, KOLO. KOLO, in its turn, performed *Lindo*, a dance from the environs of Dubrovnik, and *Vrlicko KOLO*, a dance from the Dinaric Mountains, both choreographed by Ljevakovic. During this period Ljevakovic choreographed dances from Bosnia; the suite from Gorensko in Slovenia; the brides' dance from Macedonia, *Nevestinsko Oro*; the Vlah (a Rumanian-speaking minority) dances of Eastern Serbia; and the suite of dances from East Serbia ("*katanka*" and "*Trno Mome*"). Thus, LADO developed a Pan-Yugoslav repertoire, especially touring abroad, and an all-Croatian repertoire, which was more rarely performed. Usually, during their summer touring on the Dalmatian coast, two nights of performances in Dubrovnik were given over to the Croatian repertoire while two nights were devoted to the Pan-Yugoslav repertoire.

Finally, as the Yugoslav federation began to unravel, LADO began to perform only works from Croatia. In one particularly memorable work, which LADO premiered in its 1989 fortieth anniversary gala concert at the National Theatre in Zagreb, choreographer Dr. Ivan Ivancan showed the dances and songs of the Serbs and Croats in the Banija region of the Krajina in his dance suite *Na Baniji bubanj bije*. The symbolic union of the two peoples, shown in the finale of the dance when mixed couples danced together, if only briefly, before they again danced apart, served as a dramatic portent for the ensuing tragic conflict.

After the disappearance of the Communist Party and the former Yugoslavia, LADO began to expand its vocal repertoire to include several unique Croatian folk masses and religious works that would not have been encouraged under the Communist regime. Dances of Zagorje (northern Croatia) and the *Kalvarija* (Calvary), an oratorio from Hvar (one of the Dalmatian coastal islands), are examples of works created during this period. These political priorities were reflected in each of LADO's ten-year anniversary celebrations.

LADO, beyond its fiftieth anniversary, remains a major jewel of Croatia's artistic spectrum. In 1989, I witnessed a reception for the members of LADO on the occasion of the company's fortieth anniversary in which the mayor of Zagreb said that the City of Zagreb would ensure that LADO would always live.

6

Egypt: Bazaar of Dance

Fast by the opening of the labyrinthine alleyways of the Khan al-Khalili Bazaar in the heart of old Islamic Cairo stands the beautiful El-Ghuri Mausoleum, built in memory of an Ottoman official who died nearly five centuries ago. Its simple, elegant silhouette serves as a reminder of the flourishing economy of the early Ottoman period that lasted for four centuries in Egypt. Begrimed by centuries of wear from the ubiquitous dust storms brought from the nearby desert by the fury of the annual *khamsin* winds, modern construction, and the pollution of the more than 15 million (some knowledgeable insiders say 25 million) inhabitants of the contemporary city, the early-sixteenth-century structure, never used by its builder who died in a faraway battle, houses one of Cairo's several state-funded folk ensembles. Officially labeled "El-Tannoura, Egyptian Heritage Folklore Troupe" and known locally as *firqah ghureiyyah* (after the performance space), the all-male ensemble's performances eloquently display the ruling elite's attitude toward their own traditional performing arts. Western art forms—ballet, opera, symphony orchestra concerts—are given pride of place in the opulent new opera house built with funds from the Japanese government in the elegant district of Zamalek Island. Even though the traditional arts are relegated to substandard theaters, according to the *Egyptian Gazette*, the Minister of Culture is currently planning a second opera house in Central Cairo. The performances of the ballet and opera are listed on a regular basis in English-language newspapers for tourists and the large resident community of Europeans and Americans residing in Cairo. No mention of El-Tannoura is found in the quasi-governmental Egyptian publications such as the *Egyptian Gazette*.

Two hours before El-Tannoura's twice-a-week performances, which constitute the single free tourist attraction in all of Egypt, the small crowd begins to gather, for word is out among the knowledgeable that one must arrive early because of the limited seating (about two hundred spaces). The crowd overwhelmingly consists of young students and travelers from Western Europe, the United States, Japan, Australia, and New Zealand traveling on skimpy budgets with limited access to bathing facilities; New Age devotees; and the occasional older rugged individual for whom well-thumbed copies of *Lonely Planet* and *Open Road* guidebooks serve as travel gospels and promise their devoted readers an evening of spiritual experience with the Mowlawwiyah brotherhood dervishes. The two hundred or so young people remind me of the vitality that infused the 1960s, with its widespread soul-searching and seeking of spirituality.

Nowhere to be seen are the pampered travelers of the luxury hotels lining the Nile, their enormous buses disgorging them in the thousands at better-known sites. Nor do the Egyptian government or the thousands of private travel agencies promote these performances. The ubiquitous hordes of well-to-do and well-heeled middle-class tourists from the United States, Western Europe, Japan, Korea, and increasingly Eastern Europe, herded from monument to monument by impatient guides, are conspicuous by their absence. Also absent are Egyptians.

The large high-vaulted space inside the mausoleum darkens briefly and the lights of the performance area, which is thrust into the audience so that the audience surrounds it on three sides, focus on the twelve-man phalanx of musicians dressed in white turbans and galabiyas, the traditional robes worn by millions of men throughout Egypt, including Cairo. The audience holds its breath as a brilliant quivering sound from the orchestra of traditional instruments—bowed strings, winds, and a battery of percussion—unfamiliar to most of the audience members, rises and resonates throughout the vast chamber. The artistic director, Mahmoud Issa, playing the bowed instrument the *rababa*, fills the vaulted space with the plangent tones of an arrhythmic improvised piece (*taqsim*) followed by lengthy virtuoso musical demonstrations on the *ney*, an end-blown flute beloved by Sufi sects, and the stark tones of the double reed *mizmar*.[1]

Soon one of the percussion players steps out of the line into the performance area. With all of the flash and fury of a brilliant flamenco dancer, he brandishes his very large finger cymbals, the size of small saucers, in a display of virtuosic playing.[2] His solo-improvised dance consists of a dazzling display of rhythmic playing of the finger cymbals accompanied by a series of rapid turns and spins, followed by an abrupt series of dramatic poses. The entire dance, with its rich array of hand and arm movements, forcibly remind the viewer that the roots of much of the aesthetic and performative elements of flamenco are to be found in North Africa.[3]

This spectacular tour de force hardly prepares the viewer for the display on the *darabuka* (goblet drum), accompanied by a battery of percussion instruments and the two dances, associated with Sufi ceremonies, that follow in breathless succession, each choreographic display more spectacular than the last. The lights dim briefly and an improvised vocal selection in a classical Arabic modal scale *(mawwal)*, utilizing spiritual texts, ensues to set the stage for the coming dances.

Suddenly announced by a large fanfare of music, five men dressed in white turbans, robes, and trousers with red harnesses embroidered in yellow, white, and green appliqué embroidery leap out of the wings playing on large tambourines with rows of bangles. They dance for several minutes, forming simple figures and following the leader (the dance leader was the previous soloist with the cymbals), and they provide the only formally choreographed element in the program. These dancers continue to serve as a corps for the two soloists who follow. This choreographed aspect of the performance serves to remind the astute observer that this troupe is providing a spectacle, perhaps Sufi-inspired, but a spectacle nevertheless.

As the five men take up positions around the performing space, each of the two soloists, first one and then the other, wearing several skirtlike garments (known as *khamis*) over long full yellow shirts and trousers with a harness matching that of the five men, begins his spectacular series of movements that are more or less the same in each performance. Throughout nonstop spinning the two dancers, first one and then the other, manipulates their various skirts in a series of virtuosic movements that brings the enthralled audience to standing ovations. The skirts, known as *tannoura* (thus the name of the ensemble), are made of a heavy fabric in alternating panels of green, white, yellow, and red. The dancer, turning without interruption for twenty or more minutes, raises the skirt over his head, turns it horizontally, then vertically brings it down around his neck. After another series of figures in which he creates dizzying designs reminiscent of a top, still turning he folds the skirt, cradles it as if it was a precious child, and hands it into the waiting hands of the lead dancer.[4]

That this is a staged performance, a representation of elements from Sufi ceremonial practices, packaged as audience-oriented spectacle, in no way detracts from the vitality of this display of traditional Egyptian dance and music. The company does not rehearse in the same fashion as the Moiseyev Dance Company or Ballet Folklorico, in which every movement is choreographed and every musical note written. Performances of professional music and dance before audiences are ancient practices in Egypt. They are filled with improvisation and constitute a shared repertoire of tunes and movements by

Musicians of the Nile. *Tannoura* (skirt) *Dance*. COURTESY A. SHAFIE.

their practitioners, and as such the performances are highly fluid. No two performances are exactly alike, in contrast to the performances of the Moiseyev Dance Company, Ballet Folklorico, and LADO, as well as the nontraditional performances by Egyptian companies such as the Reda Troupe (*firqah Reda*) and the National Folk Troup (*firqa qawmiyya*).

Colonialism: The Gift That Keeps on Giving

Any study of the establishment of national state ensembles must take into account the political, historical, and social contexts in which they were established. To a great extent these elements determine the strategies of representation adopted by the various directors and choreographers in how they choose to represent their respective nation-states. In particular, the attitudes of the political and social elite become important since this sector of the population forms the primary source of support, both financial and political.

The central point that I wish to address in this chapter is the position that solo-improvised dance, belly dance in popular terms, occupies in the presentation of dance on the stage. It is the most widespread dance form in Egypt, indeed in the Middle East. In order to examine this topic and analyze the manner of its presentation, one must look at the phenomenon of colonialism. It is within the context of the continuing impact of colonialism, rather than Islamic law and attitudes—the reason that is often put forth by scholars as the overarching reason for negative attitudes toward dance—that one can discover the bases for the choreophobic attitudes that Egyptians (and other Middle Easterners) hold concerning dancing and its place in Egyptian life and on Egyptian stages.

Among the nation-states and their state-supported dance companies that this study analyzes, the imprint of Western colonialism has been most strongly felt in the performances—and attitudes toward them—found in Egypt. I wish to make clear that while the vast majority of Western and native scholars consider colonialism a British, French, and American enterprise, I strongly differ from this viewpoint. If colonialism is taken to mean the economic and social exploitation and domination of one group over another, then one must also examine, among others, the historic Aztec, Roman, Persian, Islamic, Spanish, Portuguese, Russian, and Ottoman imperial aims and practices. The difference between the earlier empires and those of Western Europe is the advanced technology and the degree and intensity of penetration with which the British and French have been able to dominate their colonized populations. Egypt almost more than any other area of the world has experienced centuries of colonialism. It successively fell under the colonialist rule of the Persian, Greek, Roman, Byzantine, and Ottoman empires prior to its experience of French and British imperialist rule. New studies (e.g., Brown 1996) are beginning to reassess the degree of penetration of Ottoman rule, now increasingly acknowledged by scholars as more intense than previously thought. Certainly many members of the elite classes of contemporary Egypt came into prominence during the Ottoman period, and they continue to constitute an important element, sometimes referred to as the "*efendi*" class, of the upper echelons of Egyptian society. Also, in contrast to British rulers, the Ottomans shared the Islamic faith and to some degree the same worldview as their subjects, in contrast to the utterly alien rule of the British. I will have occasion to address Ottoman colonialism in Chapter 7, on the Greek national dance company. In this chapter I focus on British rule, which I maintain left the most recent and penetrating effects on Egyptian society that continue to reverberate today.

As a starting point for the discussion of colonialism as it pertains to the representation of Egypt through staged folklore and folk-inspired performance, I turn to Timothy Mitchell's (1991) study, *Colonising Egypt*. Mitchell points out that in dealing with British colonialism, "the question of meaning or representation is an essential aspect of its structural effect" (ibid., xiii). Mitchell's admirable discussion of the process and penetration of Western colonial powers that created a "new binary order" (ibid., xii) within Egyptian society neatly summarizes the impact of colonialism. That order introduced many of the dialectical categories made famous by Edward Said's (1978) study of Orientalism: order-disorder, hygienic-dirty, Western-Oriental, industrious-indolent, material-spiritual that "spread over the entire surface of society" (Mitchell 1991, x). Mitchell, following Michel Foucault, argues that colonialism (and he writes only of English and French colonialism) "refers not simply to the establishment of a European presence, but also to the spread of a political order that inscribes in the social world a new conception of space, new forms of personhood, and new means of manufacturing the experience of the real" (ibid., ix). Thus, colonialism is not merely an economic, political, and military phenomenon, although one can argue that economic forces certainly created the impetus in its drive for new markets, cotton for England's burgeoning cloth manufacturing industry, and cheap labor. Mitchell's study makes clear that the British had convinced themselves that they were doing benighted natives around the world a service: they conceived of colonialism as a type of missionary effort to bring civilization to the natives. In passing, Mitchell notes that his study is "not intended as a history of this process, which remains even today something unaccomplished and incomplete" (1991, 14).

I wish to focus on three aspects of colonialism that play a role in the analysis of how Egyptian dance is represented. The first, well-documented by Mitchell, describes and analyzes how class cleavages were deepened by the colonial process. Members of the upper classes and elite (although other individuals were certainly coopted as well) adopted and were implicated in carrying out the colonial project, not only during the colonial period but afterward as well. Later, I will point out how individuals in the arts and entertainment utilized class and social status, both upper and lower, to position themselves in the nationalist discourse of Egypt.

Colonialism is often discussed and conceived of as a group phenomenon: that is, country A invades and colonizes country B, dominating the public spheres of life, exercising military control, and exploiting the economy of the oppressed population. Eventually country B succeeds in ridding itself of country A, the colonizers return home, and the colonial period is ended, leading to a new era of independence.

A little known and less discussed aspect of colonialism is the creation of colonized individuals, which Mitchell brilliantly analyzes through Michel Foucault's notion of the "disciplined body." The purpose of colonialism was "to create both a material order and a conceptual moral order" (Mitchell 1991, 15). Following Foucault, Mitchell describes this colonizing penetration of the individual by the colonizing power through the imposition of self-discipline. "Disciplinary power, by contrast, works not from the outside but from within, not at the level of an entire society but at the level of detail, and not by restricting individuals and their actions but by producing them. . . . [A] restrictive exterior power gives way to an internal, productive power" (ibid., xi).

This individual self-discipline was largely promoted through school systems established by the colonial power. "Upbringing and schooling were intended not only to discipline the body, but form the morals—the mind—of the child" (Mitchell 1991, 101). The British colonial powers firmly believed in the studies and books published by orientalist thinkers who, like mid-nineteenth-century observer Edward Lane, claimed that the immoral and libidinous nature of the Egyptians were out of control and must be brought in line with Victorian notions of propriety. As Lane commented, "In sensuality, as far as it relates to the indulgence of libidinous passions, the Egyptians, as well as other native of hot climates, certainly exceed the more northern nations" (ibid., 106).

The shaping of the colonized individual, a self-disciplined person who internalizes the colonizers' attitudes and moral system, is crucial for an understanding of the way in which Egyptian attitudes toward dance, particularly solo-improvised dance, are formed. These attitudes shaped by colonialism have a direct impact on the choreographic and staging strategies used by choreographers such as Mahmoud Reda, who spent his childhood and youth under British rule.

Under the joint influences of publications by orientalist scholars and politicians from England and France and the teachings in the newly installed school systems established in Egypt by the English during 1881–82, many Egyptians came to aid the colonialist project. This included the spread of ideas about the backwardness, indolence, and moral laxity of Egyptians and the need to adopt English morals.

The second aspect of colonialism that I believe adheres to the contemporary attitudes in Egypt, mentioned only in passing by Mitchell, is that the colonialist project "remains even today something unaccomplished and incomplete" (1991, 14). I want to expand on this concept of the continuing colonizing behavior because it has a major impact on the way in which Egyptians regard their own traditional forms of expression. Further, the colonialist attitudes toward Egyptian morality, which included shock and horror of the "naughty and scandalous" performances of belly dancing, stood in direct opposition to Victorian notions of sexual prudishness. Turkish dance historian Metin And wryly noted that the European observers could not "hide from their descriptions the breathless interest that they took in these performances" (1959, 24). These attitudes still operate in Egyptian society today, long after the English and other Western Europeans have abandoned them for freer expressions of sexuality. As Morroe Berger noted, "As the fame of belly dance spread to the Western world, it became something of an embarrassment to the cultural and political custodians of the East, who began to consider themselves above their own popular arts.... This is because the government encourages instead the performance of a sort of folkloric dance that only vaguely resembles the belly dance" (1966, 43). Thus, the imprint of colonialism lingers on, manifesting itself in choreographies reflecting colonialist attitudes, later embedded in nationalist rhetoric. Long after the actual colonizers have physically quit the country, the ruling elite continues to carry out their colonial project.

The city of Cairo is a physical reminder of this continuing colonial project. As in many colonized cities, the British tore up sections of the city to create "new cities" and enclaves to separate themselves, and those native individuals who became recreated in the British image, from the riffraff and natives of the *madina* (the old city). Revolutionary writer Frantz Fanon scathingly characterized the *madina* from the viewpoint of the colonizers as "a place of ill fame, peopled by men of ill repute" (qtd. in Mitchell 1991, 20–30).

> The native town is described in terms of the fears and prejudices of the colonizers, who represent those whom they exclude as the negatives of their own self-image: the natives crowded together like animals, they are crouching and kneeling like slaves, they are without sexual restraint. ... The identity of a modern city is created by what it keeps out.... In order to determine itself as the place of order, reason, propriety, cleanliness and power, it must represent outside itself what is irrational, disordered, dirty libidinous, barbarian and cowed. (Mitchell 1991, 165)

In other words, any site such as Cairo that is Oriental and in need of British order and authority. In addition, anyone who has not experienced colonialism must take into account "the penetration of these mechanisms of reality by recalling the extent of Orientalism to which the truths were reproduced under the British in political debate within Egypt" (ibid., 168). Thus the current president of Egypt, Hosni Mubarak, expressed the colonialist inspired choreophobic notion that the recent riots in the Imbaba (a district in Cairo) were instigated not by radical Islamists but by indecent and troublesome elements of the local district. "And who are they? Bellydancers [sic], drummers from the slums" (*Egyptian Gazette* 1995).

In theorizing aspects of colonialism that have an impact on the way in which the elite regard folk dancing and solo-improvised dancing specifically, Mitchell demonstrates that as individual Egyptians adopted and internalized colonialist attitudes, these attitudes also enabled individuals from the upper classes to distance themselves from their own urban underclasses and the rural peasantry. Like the English, they came to regard the lower classes as unruly and morally lax, as Hosni Mubarak stated above. Through the adoption of English attitudes and morals and a European-style education, the upper classes felt themselves to be freed from the lower classes, which they regarded as still mired in oriental backwardness. Within a decade of the British takeover, we find Egyptians writing against their own customs in such books as *Madar al-Zar* (The Harmfulness of the Zar), published in 1903, in which Muhammad Hilmi Zayn al-Din criticized the well-known and still popular exorcist ceremony.

A third element that must be considered alongside any discussion of colonialism is the countercurrent of nationalism. In many ways the nationalist discourse is embedded in the phenomenon of colonialism and always in tension with it. Mitchell makes clear that colonialism was never monolithic and that space for nationalist resistance existed within it. After Nasser's revolution in 1952, the nationalist and modernist discourse changed the way in which artists positioned themselves. As Walter Armbrust observes concerning popular movie and vocal idol Abd al-Wahhab, he "risked acquiring the reputation of being a pet of the aristocracy—truly the 'singer of kings and princes' rather than a symbol of burgeoning Egyptian nationalism. Association with the aristocracy was chic in the 1930s and 1940s, but acquired a very different significance after the 1952 revolution" (1996, 73). Aristocracy with its openly colonialist implications was out, Soviet-style socialism was in. And as was the case for their new patrons, the Soviets, in the new Egypt authentic folklore was of no interest—an embarrassment, an attitude that remains until this day. It is within the context of the colonialist discourse and the nationalist reaction to it that the meaning of what is authentically Egyptian is structured. Within the modernist context, folklore took on new meaning and newly created forms, such as the choreographies of Mahmoud Reda, based on Soviet models in keeping with the new middle-class outlook.

In this way the upper classes turned their backs on their own indigenous forms and created, with government support, especially after Nasser's revolution of 1952, modernist interpretations of what Egyptian culture should be. It is within this context that Mahmoud Reda and his many imitators created a "new" Egyptian folk-inspired dance genre—in Hobsbawm's terms an "invented tradition," acceptable to the colonized upper middle classes, now turned nationalist, that assumed control of the country (Hobsbawm and Ranger 1983). But this modernity was redolent of colonialist morality; all signs of lower-class vulgarity had to be banished. The issue of class forms an important element in how dance, the most vulgar and déclassé form of expression in Egypt (and many other Islamic countries as well), was to be portrayed on theater stages and by whom.

Under British colonial rule, the Egyptian elite began to believe that they were no longer a part of the rabble, whom they came to despise and depict as disorderly and uncontrollable crowds in novels and short stories (Mitchell 1991). Thus we find the imagined revolutionary vanguard made up of "bellydancers and drummers" that threatened the very existence of Mubarak's regime and merited front-page coverage in his tame press.

These attitudes of Victorian British morality continued under a new guise with the advent of nationalism. According to political scientist and long-time Cairo resident Nicola Pratt, these attitudes "are still strongly felt among the upper classes here in Cairo. The government fears the underclasses in districts like Imbaba [a poor district of Cairo] that they barely controlled during rioting there in 1994–95" (personal interview, January 24, 2000). Pratt confirms my observation that what I call the divorce between the upper and lower classes, rural and urban, is nearly complete. These classes were and are characterized as wild, libidinous, and immoral by the upper classes (and ironically the Islamists), striving to achieve an air of European bourgeois morality and respectability.[5]

Armbrust observed that in post-1952 Egypt, "Heritage is not simply there, but something to be properly organized. Vulgarity should be struck from the record and the folk be admitted to Egypt's heritage on condition of 'authenticity.' 'Scientific' methods sort the crass and regrettable from the sources of refinement and of inspiration, and modernist language defines the residue of this operation by equating the lowly and peripheral, wherever they are found, with the backward. This used also to mean the rural" (1996, 38). "Abdel Nasser's government," Armbrust adds, "from 1952 glorified 'the peasant,' though the peasant was of course to be drawn to modernity by revolution" (ibid., 39). Luis Awad, a prominent Egyptian literary critic, characterized as "the low regard intellectuals have for the culture of 'the folk'" (qtd. in ibid., 40) the way in which urban choreographers portray folk dance on urban stages in Cairo. Thus, as Armbrust shrewdly sums up, "Folklore is safest as a relic, never to be shown as important in its own right, but to be represented as a picture of where the viewers (modern folk) have come from" (ibid., 107), a dictum that Mahmoud Reda and his many imitators followed.

As has been the case in many nations with a large peasantry, while despising the peasant as unlettered, poor, and dirty, urban upper-class individuals also romanticize the peasants and their supposed bucolic lives. Awad writes that "a certain degree of romanticism has entered our outlook on the peasants and simple people since we have adopted the principle of glorifying the masses.... I am not innocent of this romanticized view of the people" (qtd. in Armbrust 1996, 39).

Both of these elements—the romantic and the avoidance of actual peasant movements, music, and costume—are woven into the choreographies of Mahmoud Reda. Like Igor Moiseyev and Amalia Hernandez, Reda clearly manifests a need to "improve" the original materials through the use of fantasy stories, urban-designed costumes, large theater orchestras, and sanitized movements. Typical Reda choreographies feature such hoary themes as flirtation between the peasant boys and girls (never men and women) in what I call "it's fun in the village" choreographies with work themes such as girls going to the well and dancing with the boys (which in fact would never occur in an actual village). Reda completes this romantic and rosy picture of the peasant by showing "the mannerisms and typical behavioral movements of the different (village) characters [who] are parodied and elaborated without being distorted by mockery.... The characters that Mahmoud Reda depicted in his work are, for example, the village yokel, the village policeman, and the mayor" (Fahmy 1987, 36).

The manifestation of class difference in the formation of how "folk" dance is portrayed on the stage is nowhere so strongly expressed as in the descriptions of the workings of the Reda Troupe. In comments echoed in the adulatory tones of American anthropologist Marjorie A. Franken (1994, 1996), Farida Fahmy (1987), a featured dancer and sister-in-law of Mahmoud Reda, states: "The social status of the founders of the troupe, and the recruitment of potential dancers from the educated class, as well as Mahmoud Reda's theatrical creations, brought forth a genre of dance that became accepted by Egyptians from all walks of life" (ibid., 20). Further, "his social and cultural background endowed him with an understanding of the movement preferences of the Egyptians" (ibid., 23). Fahmy never explains how or which qualities of being an upper-class individual bestows this understanding.

Franken, in an essay and later an article about the role of Farida Fahmy in the nationalist discourse of Egypt, compares Fahmy to the Egyptian icon Umm Kulthum, arguably the most famous singer in the history of Egypt and the Arab world. According to Franken, "Women performers of national stature had become possible with the introduction and spread of modern media—Umm Kulthum, the star radio performer of the entire Arab world, being an outstanding example. Farida Fahmy became her counterpart as a dancer, her image spread by cinema and television" (Franken 1996, 368). Franken states that Fahmy achieved her fame "for a brief period, but only because she was the 'right' woman—a member of the Westernized urban elite" (ibid., 274).

However, in making these comparisons, Franken undermines her own argument that the two are comparable artists. In the first place, anyone familiar with the arts of the Middle East is aware that "dance," in the words of Iranian choreographer Jamal, "is the least of the arts, if an art form at all" (personal interview, April 4, 1994). This statement echoes, a millennium later, the opinion of a famous medieval scholar. "In a brief passage of his major treatise, *The Grand Book on Music,* al-Farabi classifies dance with drumming, hand-clapping, and mime as inferior to the arts of singing and playing, which are higher in the hierarchy" (Shiloah 1995, 137). This attitude still resonates throughout the Middle East today. Whereas in the West one might compare the careers of a singer with a dancer, a Middle Easterner would find such a comparison highly problematic. In addition, as Franken's states, Fahmy's career was brief whereas Umm Kulthum's spanned three-quarters of a century. And more than twenty-five years after Kulthum's death in 1975, her work commands the airways and, as I found in Cairo, every taxi driver's cassette deck. When Umm Kulthum died, millions attended her funeral, rivaling that of her good friend Abdel Gamal Nasser, and the world press, including *Time* magazine, covered the event. Fahmy's funeral, I predict, will not occasion such a response.

Finally, Franken's comparison between Fahmy and Umm Kulthum founders on perhaps a more subtle issue: the way each self-identifies along class lines. As described above, Fahmy's brief career was built on her image as an upper-class individual who, in Franken's accurate depiction, challenged the old disreputable image of the belly dancer as prostitute, enshrined in the Egyptian film industry as a fallen woman, dishonored and doomed to a fate worse than death. According to Franken, it was because of her upper-class status that Fahmy could achieve this degree of fame. In other words, only a woman of the upper classes could achieve an honorable reputation as a dancer, the lowest possible social category in Egypt. It is to Fahmy's credit that she created a space for a degree of respectability in a milieu in which "music was considered the most respectable art form, followed by singing, acting, folk dancing, and finally, belly dancing" and in which "son of a dancer" (*yabn il-ra'asa* or *yabn il-ghaziya*) is a serious term of abuse (Van Nieuwkerk 1995, 129, 110). Such taunts caused one woman I met to quit the profession because her son was coming to blows with his schoolmates.

By contrast, Umm Kulthum, as portrayed in Virginia Danielson's masterful biography, no matter how fabulously wealthy and sophisticated she became always positioned herself as a country woman, *bint al-balad*.

> When Umm Kulthum talked about herself, she emphasized these aspects of her background, she linked herself in the *mashayikh* and to *fellahin* (peasants) and *abnaa' il-riif* (sons and daughters of the countryside). Her public image, built from song and speech, linked to these two concepts. . . . Both the religious *shaykh* and the *fellah* are important images in Egyptian society. The models are strong characters, men and women alike. In a simple, direct way, by describing herself in this language, Umm Kulthum correctly identified her cultural and social background as one shared with hundreds of thousand of Egyptians. In effect she produced herself, visually, aurally, and conceptually, from these ideas. (Danielson 1997, 187–88)

Thus, we can see that Umm Kulthum as a singer was able to position herself as other than elite, one of the people. However, Farida Fahmy, because dancing is a dishonorable profession, chose to portray herself as an upper-class elite individual in order to achieve her status, in effect canceling any comparison between the two figures.

Islam

Although a lengthy discussion is beyond the scope of this project, at this point a brief discussion of Islam, as it regards dance and its legitimacy, is in order. Many observers of dance and music in the Middle East, including not a few distinguished scholars, have cast Islam as the villain and the major reason for the negative attitudes of Middle Easterners toward their own indigenous dance form (Berger 1961; Shay 1995, 1999a, chap. 3). This is a simplistic analysis. Muslims, like other human beings, inherited pre-Islamic attitudes wherever they were. Attitudes toward dance in Indonesia, Afghanistan, Iran, Bosnia, Turkey, and Egypt vary widely. There is no specific proscription regarding dance or music in the Koran. There are ambiguous hints in the *hadith* (the reported speech and actions of the Prophet Muhammad by individuals who were present and reported them). Studies and interpretations of the *hadith* consume, to this day, much Islamic literature. Given that there is no supreme head of the Islamic faith, such as a pope, but rather many local influential leaders and scholars, the interpretations vary widely. In short, Islam is a highly contested field of learned and not-so-learned opinion. One cannot deny, however, that Muslim fundamentalists in Egypt have targeted belly dancers with physical threats, which has changed the professional dance scene in Cairo (Daniszewski 2000).

In Egypt, and perhaps the entire Sunni world, for more than a millennium Al-Azhar University in Cairo has been the seat of the most learned and respected scholars in Islam regarding issues of jurisprudence. Their pronouncements, therefore, carry a great deal of weight throughout the Arab world, in particular. The relationship between Al-Azhar and the government, well defined in a recent article by Tamir Moustafa (2000), has made clear that among both the scholars of Al-Azhar and the various Islamist groups the field of Islam is a highly contested one. "Moderates," "conservatives," and "radicals" exist in both camps alongside the government with its largely secular programs, all attempting to gain the high ground in piety and authority in decision-making matters pertaining to Islam. The Al-Azhar scholars have been maneuvered, through coercion and reorganizational strategies, into a cooperative arrangement with the government for more than a century, but especially after the Nasser revolution of 1952. According to Moustafa, the government is desirous of the pundits of Al-Azhar bestowing their approval on their socialist and secular programs. An important aspect of this relationship is the threat to its authority that Al-Azhar feels from the Islamist movement—a threat that comes from this perceived cooperative relationship with the government. All of these positions are highly fluid and dynamic.

In 1995, this threat led to what "exemplified Al-Azhar's highly virulent condemnation of militant Islamists and the recent violence in Egypt" (Moustafa 2000, 12). According to Jad al-Haqq:

> Those who [commit violence] are not Islamists and do not represent Islam. They are criminals who must be punished. Every individual who challenges public order and the state's authority and power must be punished. Such an individual is not an Islamist at all. Those who make mischief in the land are the enemies of God and his prophet. (Moustafa 2000, 12)

All of this dynamic tension plays a role in the way in which dance is perceived at different periods and the conditions under which both professional and nonprofessional performers negotiate a careful path in terms of performance. But dance continues, now stronger, now weaker, as the struggle continues. As the case in Iran shows, people will always find a way to dance, even if in secret (Shay 1999a). It also serves as a reminder that Islam can not serve as a monolithic, unproblematized reason for negative attitudes.

Egyptian Dance in the Field

As all students of Egyptian history know, the Nile defines almost every phase of Egyptian life. More than 98 percent of the population lives within a few miles of its banks, including the delta, and historically the two major regions were the South (known as *sa'idi* in Egypt) and the Delta (north). A few tribes and small sedentary populations live in oases or follow regular nomadic paths. Unlike many countries such as Iran, Croatia, Greece, or Turkey, Egypt does not boast a rich tradition of unique regional folk costumes and dances specific to small districts. Its geography, with the population along the Nile in constant communication with one another, mitigates against the kind of development of small ethnically and culturally distinct regions found in the aforementioned countries where significant geographic barriers separated relatively small populations into definable regions. Ergun Ozbudun describes Egypt as a country with a unique "socially homogeneous population produced by the ecological homogeneity of the Nile valley" (1996, 142–43).

For the classification of Egyptian dance in the field, I rely on Magda Saleh's (1979) extremely detailed study with its accompanying filmed field recording (available in the New York Public Library Dance Collection). In practice, solo-improvised dance for both men and women is the primary dance form, with much individual and some local variation, throughout Egypt. This dance form is perhaps the most misunderstood dance tradition in the world. In one of its myriad forms it is known as belly dance, or *danse orientale* or *raqs sharqi*, as its practitioners prefer. It has been widely described in romanticized and sometimes titillating and frankly orientalist terms from Flaubert's memoirs and Ingres's paintings to contemporary journals addressed to belly dance hobbyists (Said 1978, Shay 1998, Van Nieuwkerk 1995, Saleh 1979, Sellers-Young 1992).

This dance form is characterized by articulations of the torso, especially the shoulders and hips. It is a single form, performed by both men and women under a variety of names and musical genres, that ranges in its degree of elaboration depending on the skills of the dancer and the context, social and economic, in which it is performed. This dance genre is performed throughout the Middle East, North Africa, and parts of the Balkans, under names such as *ciftetelli*, *kuperlika*, and *cocek*. Many individuals in other Arab countries call it *raqs misri* (Egyptian dance) or *raqs sharqi* (Oriental or Eastern dance), and it is thought by many to have its origins in Egypt. What I call the domestic version of this dance, which is seen in almost every joyful occasion in Egypt, is called *baladi*, or dance of the countryside, by many individuals. In short, it is the quintessential Egyptian dance. As Morocco (Carolina Varga Dinicu) observed, "There is only one dance form that everyone, male and female, young and old performs and that is *raqs sharqi*, oriental dance which is the people's dance" (personal interview, January 19, 2000). This causes discomfort among many of the elite, Westernized classes, a point to which I will return shortly.

It is important to emphasize an often-misunderstood point about oriental or belly dance. The movements of the dance are not considered shameful (unless they are highly transgressive), but for a woman to perform this dance in front of males who are not in a proper kinship relationship with her, as set forth in Islamic law, is considered shameful and a dishonor. Dancing at weddings is common. "Girls and women who dance at weddings, however, should wear respectable clothes and move within proper limits. Professional dancers performing at weddings, although they interpret and bring out people's happiness, transgress these limits" because "women who work in the male public space are all suspect" (Van Nieuwkerk 1995, 131, 183).

Mahmoud Reda Troupe. *Stick Dance.* COURTESY MAHMOUD REDA.

The second most widespread choreographic form is the men's dancing with sticks *(tahtib)* and canes or short sticks *('asa)*. In January 2000, in a village wedding in Ghurna across the Nile from Luxor, I saw a large number of men and boys perform these two dances, and in Cairo I saw three parties in which men, and a few women, performed the domestic form of belly dancing.

In addition to these two ubiquitous dance forms, Saleh identifies several traditional dances that can be characterized as regional folk dances found in specific smaller towns in the extreme south in Nubia, north in Suez and Alexandra, and among the oases such as Siwa and Bahriyya in different parts of Egypt. Most of these dances are also characterized by improvisation.

Dance Bazaar: A Tale of Four Ensembles

When I first undertook this project my plan had been to profile and analyze the company known as the Reda Troupe *(firqa Reda)*, which is the first of the four companies that I discuss in this chapter.[6] After a short time in Cairo, I found that to discuss this one company, which

Musicians of the Nile. *Tannoura* (skirt) *Dance*. COURTESY A. SHAFIE.

has fallen on hard times, without at least briefly describing and analyzing the others would deprive the reader of examining an interesting situation. Four state-supported folk music and dance companies coexist in a nation of limited financial resources. The fragmented and ambiguous dance scene that presents itself to the observer contains, like the bazaar at Khan al-Khalili, twisted alleyways of social and political patronage, and complicated and tangled political and economic relationships that, to a large degree, exist outside of the framework of this study. Nevertheless, these murky relationships determine such issues as who directs the various companies, when and where they perform, and how much state support they receive.

The most interesting aspect of this situation is that two of these companies, El-Nil Folkloric Troup [sic] and El-Tannoura Egyptian Heritage Folkloric Troupe, can be placed at the extreme end of the scale that I created in Chapter 1, toward the performances of traditional music and dance in the field of which they are an extension. The performers are traditional musicians, vocalists, and dancers who are native to the traditions they perform. The other two, the Reda Troupe and the National Folk Troup *(firqa qawmiyya)*, exist at the polar end of the same scale in which character dance, as an invented tradition, rather than traditional elements is the primary movement vocabulary employed. Their performers are professionally trained urban dwellers who have learned specific choreographies and musical scores through formal training procedures. These companies also incorporate the use of designer costumes, composed music on largely Western instruments, and Western staging techniques. Thus the four companies stand in startling contrast to one another.

Mahmoud Reda, Founding Artistic Director and Choreographer of the Reda Troupe

Nearly everyone who is knowledgeable about the staging of Egyptian traditional dance and music acknowledges that it emanates from the same man: Mahmoud Reda, both in the two character dance troupes, as I call them in this chapter, and in the two traditionally oriented companies. Mahmoud Reda, a charming, gracious man who appears much younger than his age, was born in 1930. This date is significant because he was born during the British colonial period and was a young man when Abdel Gamal Nasser took power in 1952. Nasser's relationship with the Soviet Union is important in the establishment of folk dance companies, since the Soviet colonizing project gave folk dance priority as a means of propagandizing the Soviet system as representative of "the people."

To begin my discussion of Mahmoud Reda's specific choreographic strategies, I turn to Fahmy's study of the choreographic works of Mahmoud Reda in which she makes the astute observation that reflects the assimilation of colonialist attitudes I discussed above: "The elite

Mahmoud Reda Troupe. *Al Mowachahat.* COURTESY MAHMOUD REDA.

and upper classes of Egypt typically express embarrassment toward their native dances in general and towards belly dancing in particular. One of the causes of this embarrassment is the impact the West has had on Egyptian culture. Many of the educated Egyptians to this day aspire to, and imitate the Western way of life" (1987, 12).[7]

In order to attract audiences from the elite classes whose support and approval he sought for the success of the fledgling company that he had created in 1959, Reda felt compelled to create a new and hybrid genre of dance to fit in with the modernist version of folklore that was the fashion in Egypt in that period. In every sense of the word, this new dance genre constitutes an invented tradition. That this created genre fulfills the definition and concept of an invented tradition is underscored by its widespread emulation both within and outside of Egypt and Mahmoud Reda's own stated goals. As Reda himself said, "I had no example to follow. What I did was my own invention. Artists throughout Egypt follow me. They think it is authentic" (personal interview, January 10, 2000).

And yet, as Franken states, "A dance troupe performing Egyptian folk dance, modeled after Eastern European troupes so popular within the Soviet bloc, seemed appropriate as an expression of patriotism and nationalism of the times" (1996, 278). This coupled with Mahmoud Reda's frequent trips to the Soviet Union in the 1950s argue for the Moiseyev Dance Company serving at least as a conceptual model that

Reda followed, albeit using Egyptian motifs. However, in the Egypt of the 1950s, nationalist rhetoric precluded any claims for non-Egyptian inspiration. With all of his use of ballet, show dancing, and other Western choreographic strategies, it was important to appear Egyptian. "The hallmark of this newly defined identity was confident possession of such European customs as were deemed desirable, coupled with a fine discrimination of how far one could go in such behavior and remain truly Egyptian" (Armbrust 1996, 84).

Also in that period, authentic folklore would not have been acceptable. "Others consider 'folklore' an evil to be stamped out by a benevolently modern state, and encourage the substitution of almost any cultural model that is not the traditional 'backward' one. But both views of 'folklore' and the people who practice it leave ambiguous 'them' (the folk) and the mass culture fantasies that intellectuals themselves produce" (Armbrust 1996, 37–38).

Any discussion of the work of Mahmoud Reda and his role in the development of traditional dance for performance must begin, as it does with Igor Moiseyev and Amalia Hernandez, with his specific history and training in dance that have shaped his attitudes toward traditional dance. He expresses his attitudes both in his own words and his writings, as well as in his choreographies. In regard to authenticity, he stated: "We are not supposed to do folk dance that is anonymous—they [the folk] do not do it on stage. We don't do that. My work is inspired by folklore, but I did my best. I depended on my being Egyptian for the authenticity of spirit. But it is my own unique creation" (Reda, personal interview, January 10, 2000; see also Fahmy 1987, Reda 2000).

Fahmy sums up Reda's philosophy and the artistic goals that characterize his choreographies, including the most recent one, *Al-ginniyat al-bahr* (The mermaid), that Reda generously showed me a video recording of in Cairo.[8] "Mahmoud Reda's goal was creating a new theater dance form rather than transplanting dances from their local setting onto the stage. His works were never direct imitations or accurate reconstructions. They were his own vision of the movement qualities of the Egyptians" (Fahmy 1987, 24).

Reda echoes Amalia Hernandez' opinion regarding the performance of traditional dance on stage. "In his book, Mahmoud Reda points out that it is not possible to transport dances that are presented in their local setting onto the stage without having them lose many of their original characteristics. 'Once a dance is taken out of context and placed on the stage,' he explains, 'the change of environment and circumstances would naturally produce a dance very different from that which was performed in its original surroundings'" (Reda 1968, 45; Fahmy 1987, 24).

All of Mahmoud Reda's stated viewpoints of his relationship with dance in the field raise the question of what characterized the final choreographic product that Reda developed to represent Egypt and how far does it deviate from dance in the field. Part of the answer lies in Reda's socioeconomic background and his beginnings as a choreographic artist. Like Igor Moiseyev and Amalia Hernandez, Mahmoud Reda did not begin his career in folk dance. "In the beginning I never thought of Egyptian folklore," he said. Mahmoud Reda and his older brother, Ali, were consumed with a passion for dance as it was presented in musical films from the United States in the 1940s and 1950s. "We would dance in the streets on the way home from the cinema trying to remember the steps and movements we had seen in the film." During World War II, Ali became a very good ballroom dancer and won prizes in the military milieu of Cairo, where ballroom dancing was popular among the troops stationed there. Mahmoud Reda said of his own training, "Except for ballet classes for children, there were no dance classes in Egypt when I was young; I am self-taught. I was a gymnast and was a member of Egypt's Olympic team in 1952 in Helsinki. In that same year I auditioned for an Argentine company that was performing in Cairo, and for the next six months I toured Europe with them. One night in Paris I asked myself, 'Why am I doing Argentine dance? Why not Egyptian?' I returned to Egypt to form my own company, but that would take several years" (personal interview, January 10, 2000).

Reda's first opportunity to choreograph a work came when he was asked to choreograph some Egyptian dances for the operetta *Ya 'ain, ya leil*.[9] "They actually wanted my brother, Ali, but he was engrossed in directing films at this point, so I took the job. It was a great success and the Egyptian government selected the work to be performed at the World Youth Festival in Moscow in 1957" (ibid.).[10]

Even though this work was a success, the government gave him no help and showed no interest in his project of forming a dance company to perform Egyptian dances. "The most important reason was that the reputation of dance in Egypt was terrible and associated with prostitution" (ibid.).

Mahmoud Reda began his own company in 1959. "Even though I avoided the strong movements of the belly dance and covered the dancers, the government was uninterested in helping me at first" (ibid.). Morocco added that "the Egyptian government could not conceive of a private individual forming a dance company of any stature or artistic value. To have both, it had to be formed under the auspices and direction of the government or not at all" (personal interview, January 19, 2000).

Reda persevered and gave his first performances, with wide public acclaim, in 1959; in 1961, the company became a part of the Ministry of Culture and received financial support and subsidies. The Reda Troupe, under Reda's personal direction, maintained a cast of 150 dancers and musicians in the 1960s and 1970s, its peak years. Sadly, Reda felt forced to leave the company he founded because of disagreements with the current Minister of Culture. Although he still provides new works for them, he feels that they no longer have the technical skills that they possessed under his own direction, and certainly they are unable to attract audiences as they had in the past.

Among the many specific choreographic strategies that he utilized, in my opinion his most striking modifications, alterations, and inventions relate to his treatment of solo-improvised dance, the general term that I employ to cover the most widespread Egyptian dance genre, of which the best known example is belly dancing. First, Mahmoud Reda did not permit males on his stage to perform any of its movements, thus following the colonial gaze, now shared by the elite decision makers in the Egyptian government, of what constitutes proper and improper movements for the male (English, and now Egyptian) body. Mahmoud Reda's new theatrical genre thus attempts to erase the actual performance practices of the people, both urban and rural.[11]

Reda said, "The Fellahin men of the Delta did not have their own dance. They did *baladi* dancing and had no distinct male style. I did not want to leave the region without a dance, so I created a style from everyday work movements" (personal interview, January 10, 2000). Thus, he borrowed a leaf from Moiseyev and invented a new dance tradition when the existing one did not suit his purposes.

A second strategy that he adopted was to sanitize the movements of belly dancing. "We avoided the strong movements of the belly and hips" (Reda, personal interview, January 10, 2000). Fahmy observed that "Mahmoud Reda did not change the quality of the movement in this genre of dance, but was selective in his approach to it. He discarded elements which his artistic integrity deemed inappropriate to the context of the Reda Troupe. For example, he altered the movements he found sexually suggestive, by changing the way that they had been executed originally.... He refined and innovated new figures in the hip movements. He added and polished turning.... New pivots, swivels, and turns were devised. Mahmoud Reda also introduced various types of traveling turns" (Fahmy 1987, 68–69).

Mahmoud Reda Troupe. *Candelabra*. COURTESY MAHMOUD REDA.

A third modification that Reda employed was the use of groups to distract and subtract the "solo," as well as the "improvised," from solo-improvised dancing, since, according to Reda, belly dancing was always associated with soloists. He was able to utilize soloists, of which Farida Fahmy was the most prominent, by creating story line choreographies and having the soloist dance with a chorus. Every observer of popular culture in Egypt quickly becomes aware of the low position of dance. "Professional dancers in Egypt have traditionally been associated with prostitution, and though attempts have been made to adapt certain folk dances to the stage, the dances selected tend to be rural, communal (Reda 1968), and not at all sensual" (Armbrust 1996, 117). But as I pointed out, solo-improvised dance, especially the domestic form *baladi*, is the most widespread dance form in Egypt, both rural and urban. Reda chose to portray it as a communal dance through the use of a chorus line with a soloist.

In fact, Mahmoud Reda's alterations and modifications have produced a pale and anemic version of the vital dance form that the interested observer can see in the field at urban and rural wedding celebrations. As Morocco observed, "in groups like Mahmoud Reda's troupe, the work is created under a Victorian colonialism and

Mahmoud Reda Troupe. *Candelabra*. COURTESY MAHMOUD REDA.

features ironed-out torso and hip movements" (personal interview, January 19, 2000). However, he succeeded in his main goal of satisfying the needs of his elite Cairene audiences. "The manner in which steps and movements were interwoven, and the way Reda's dancers were able to use and shape their bodies, transformed the negative connotations that had stigmatized this dance genre for many years" (Fahmy 1987, 73).

A final element that removes Mahmoud Reda from traditional Egyptian practices is the choreographic concepts that he uses. Fahmy remarks that "Mahmoud Reda never restricted himself to a standard formula in his choreography, nor did he conform to a single identifiable style or form or representation" (1987, 25). She classifies his works under three broad categories:

1. Dramatization: sketches or tableaux, short stories that contain "elements of mime, gesture and narrative.... The story must be simple, and its meanings clear, so that it is possible to be depicted through movement.... Three youths flirt with a country girl" (35).
2. Imagery: "small dances with fewer dancers." Imagery and symbolism as a choreographic device. "By the late 1960s, its use had

been expanded into a number of elaborate dance productions using nationalistic and patriotic events, folk tales and myths" (57), and
3. Folklore: "includes the dances that were inspired by indigenous dance events and characteristic movements in the various provinces of Egypt" (45).[12]

I am at a loss to separate Fahmy's "Dramatization" category from "Imagery," since both characterize Mahmoud Reda's extensive use of narrative in his work. He showed me his most recent work (from 1999) on a video recording. It took him more than a year to create and rehearse it for performance "because the dance troupe was in terrible shape and required months of rehearsal and training before I could even show them the choreography" (personal interview, January 10, 2000).[13] It is called *Al-ginniyat al-bahr* (The mermaid), and he wrote the script, created the choreography, and designed the lighting for it. It is a three-hour choreography in four acts and has many dances and changes of costume (designed by Farida Fahmy). It requires a cast of ninety—twenty women, thirty men, soloists, and a large theater orchestra. The story line goes something like this: A young fisherman loves the village daughter of his boss. The young man goes to sea with the other village fishermen. A mermaid, a kind of *jenn* (from which English derives the term "genie") or malevolent spirit lures the young man into the sea and enchants him to fall in love with her. He forgets his boss's daughter. The father decides that she must marry her cousin (who is in love with another girl). The young village maiden, unhappy that her young fisherman no longer loves her, sells her heart to the *rubabkia*, a sort of itinerant peddler. Meanwhile, the young fisherman manages to escape from the lure of the mermaid, only to discover that the young maiden can no longer love him because she has sold her heart. He sets off with the peddler to retrieve the heart, traveling to all parts of Egypt where they see many dances. They cannot find the heart, and he returns to the village to see that the young maiden is about to marry the cousin. He throws himself into the sea, but he is saved by the wedding guests and the young maiden finds that she has a heart after all. She and her young fisherman, and the cousin with his beloved, prevail upon the father to let them marry the love of their choice. The work ends with a large celebration.

From this narration one can see that the choreography follows closely the types of story lines and fairy tales common to nineteenth-century European ballet. The use of European story lines is one of the elements that both Al-Faruqi and Morroe Berger used to criticize

Reda's troupe. Fahmy attempts to refute Al-Faruqi's assertion that Mahmoud Reda's work is, in fact, "European and alien to Egyptian dance practices" by both questioning Al-Faruqi's credentials and producing two or three isolated cases of mimetic practices in Egyptian dances. But, in fact, her arguments totally fail to convince since the story lines of Mahmoud Reda's choreographies follow the format of nineteenth-century fairy tale ballets such as *Sleeping Beauty* and *Giselle*, and has no precedent in traditional Egyptian storytelling and narration practices. Also, the mimetic movements he selects are not culturally specific to Egypt.

The Reda Troupe made two films in the 1960s that were directed by Ali Reda, choreographed by Mahmoud Reda, and starred Mahmoud Reda and Farida Fahmy. These films made the Reda Troupe famous throughout the Arab world as well as Egypt, and they are still shown on Egyptian television and beloved by all classes of people (see *Igazah nisf as-sinah* 1961, *Gharam fi al-karnak* 1963). These films follow Hollywood musical formulas popular during the heyday of Judy Garland and Mickey Rooney and can be summed up by the cliché "let's do a show."[14]

Fahmy summarizes her study of Mahmoud Reda:

> No other prominent theater dance company has appeared on the scene since 1959. Many choreographers have emerged from the Reda Troupe, and have worked in musical theater, cinema, and television. The new choreographers, however, have not introduced any remarkable innovations in the field of dance in Egypt. Their works continue to perpetuate Mahmoud Reda's style and choreographic techniques, and their efforts are but imitations or extensions of Mahmoud Reda's school of dance. This raises the pertinent question of why no innovative choreographer has appeared on the scene since the founding of the Reda Troupe. (1987, 77–78)

While Fahmy's ultimate question may never be answered, Reda remains the major figure in Egyptian theater dance. The National Folklore Troup, which travels widely, and which I briefly describe next, is very much a company in the Mahmoud Reda mold—so much so that when I inquired of a number of individuals what the differences between them might be, I was given several different answers. Morocco observed that "the dancers are trained in the same place." However, Abdul Rahman Al-Shafie, the director of the traditional ensemble, Festival on the Nile, declared flatly, "There is none" (personal interview, January 28, 2000).

Dancers and Dance Training

According to both Reda (personal interview, January 10, 2000) and Fahmy (1987), the most difficult task that faced Mahmoud Reda in the beginning was finding dancers of proper social background to join the company due to the association of dancing with prostitution that Fahmy described as obstacles to finding dancers because of public disdain of dance and dancers.[15] Farida Fahmy states that it was the high social status of both her family and the Redas that enabled the company to attract suitable dancers an in its ultimate popularity with the urban elite of Egypt.

In her study of Mahmoud Reda, Fahmy describes the training of the company dancers in some detail. Training consisted of equal parts ballet class and a special set of movements, developed by Reda, utilizing folk elements. "As a new genre of dance was evolving with different styles, and as a vocabulary of related movements was accumulating, Mahmoud Reda began his own method of teaching and training his dancers. . . . [B]allet was used for warm ups and exercises. The movements he introduced were segmented, codified and all variations were extracted, then developed into warm up exercises and various routines. Mahmoud Reda wrote that, 'all training must retain the traits of folk dance. That is, all folk movement that can be collected from all parts of Egypt must be studied, codified, and developed into exercises that are performed every day'" (Fahmy 1987, 25).

Attracting new dancers to both the Reda and National Folk troupes has become difficult for a number of reasons. The salary for a dancer is very low. Mahmoud Reda said it is ninety Egyptian pounds (less than thirty dollars in early 2000) a month. Others I interviewed concurred that the salaries were unusually low.[16]

The appearance of the Islamist movement in Egypt, with its harsh moral codes, has made it difficult to attract qualified female dancers to both the Reda Troupe and National Folk Troup. According to Morocco, "many families consider it too dangerous to permit their daughters to dance" (personal interview, January 21, 2000). Indeed, videocassette vendors in the bazaar have ceased selling dance films for the same reason (personal interview, January 24, 2000).[17]

In addition to the low pay for dancers, there is the question of esteem, especially in the case of men. "There are no [professional] male belly dancers anymore—only male folk dancers in theaters and in wedding processions exist. They are not highly esteemed, yet this is not on account of their immorality but because they do 'women's work'" (Van Nieuwkerk 1995, 132).

Music

Like the costumes, the music is composed and arranged for large theater orchestras by well-known composers. These orchestras, made famous in the accompaniment of Egyptian vocal stars such as Umm Kulthum and Abd Al-Wahhab and consist of mostly Western instruments with a large violin section, cellos, string basses, accordion, brass, oboes, flutes, and sometimes a native instrument such as the kanun. The orchestras read from musical scores and employ Western harmonies and scales, and sometimes Arabic scales and modes. "The music chosen was either new renditions of popular urban and folk melodies, or newly composed pieces appropriate to the setting of the dance" (Fahmy 1987, 8–29).[18] One need only view the videocassette *Egyptian, Nubian & Sudanese Folkloric Dance* (1984) produced and narrated by Morocco (Carolina Varga Dinicu) and featuring the Reda Troupe, accompanied by the relentless sounds of a Wurlitzer organ and native percussion, to realize that the music, while perhaps utilizing some folk melodies, is also an invented tradition.

Costumes

One can look in vain for a collection of traditional clothing in an Egyptian museum. That is not to say that some of the few tribes and oasis dwellers do not boast unique clothing traditions, but among the bulk of the population—rural, urban, and oasis—men wear galabiyas (robes) and women wear a type of loose dress, yoked at the bust. The men wear forms of caps and turbans, and the women—even the wealthy, except for those with an urban upper-class background—cover their hair with a snood or a scarf. Both the dresses of traditional cut and the snoods can be extremely elaborate and expensive, as I observed at a large wedding on the Nile. Thus, the wearing of these traditional garments does not mark economic class, but contains semiotic information about the degree of Westernization an individual expresses through his or her clothing. Some men also wear galabiyas on some occasions and Western clothing on others.

The costumes utilized by the Reda Troupe and the National Folk Troup follow the same style of modifications as the dance and form an invented tradition. Fahmy claims that they kept "the designs as close as possible to the original. . . . Traditional dress was never radically changed. . . . The alterations were made to enhance rather than distort the original cut and outline" (1987, 29). In fact, the careful observer discovers that it is difficult to find a semblance of the original clothing in a Reda production; even the galabiyas are amplified through the addition of extra fabric for greater mobility. Indeed, Fahmy contradicts herself. She states, "Costumes were designed to emphasize the shapeliness of the women's figures rather than [to] disguise them" (ibid.). Five minutes in any street in Cairo will enable even the casual observer to see that in fact Egyptian clothing for women is designed to do just the opposite: to cover and conceal all aspects of a woman's body, including her hair. While the Reda Troupe and the National Folklore Troupe do not use the floor length bikinis and bras that Western audiences have come to associate with belly dancers in nightclubs, nevertheless, bare legs, exposed arms, and other nontraditional practices mark the costumes of both companies. The costumes, like the dances, might be said to be "folk inspired," but more often they are figments of the costume designer's imagination. In regard to women's clothing, hip-hugging skin-tight pants with bell bottoms, featuring rows of ruffles from knee to ankle, do not qualify as peasant clothing in any Egyptian village.

National Folk Troup

I will discuss the National Folk Troup (as it is titled on its official souvenir program) but often called the National Folkloric Troupe (Al-firqat al-qawmiyat al-funun ash-sha'biyah) very briefly because it resembles the Reda Troupe in almost every element. The National Folk Troup was founded in 1961 under the direction of Boris Ramazin, a former Moiseyev company dancer provided by the Soviet Union to the Egyptian government in order to establish a company in the image of Moiseyev, with an Egyptian flavor (Saleh 1979, Fahmy 1987). According to Farida Fahmy,

> Soon after the Reda Troupe appeared in the theaters of Cairo, the Ministry of Culture imported Russian experts to teach and establish an Egyptian folk dance company. These experts were former members of the Moiseyev Ensemble. . . . This attempt ignored the physical aspects of the Egyptian people. Their movements, gestures, and their physical and emotional drives, were forced into the balletic form. What ensued was a quasi-ballet that remains, to this day, alien to the Egyptian public at large. (1987, 15–16)

Clearly elements of Moiseyev training still linger in their performances. For example, in a January 9, 2000, performance of the company the men entered the stage performing a *dabka,* a dance not indigenous to Egypt but to the Levant, and the dancers performed steps and figures more in keeping with Bulgarian and Macedonian folk dances in costumes that had a faintly Ottoman cast. A well-known choreography that was a direct copy from the Moiseyev repertory featured a dancer, dressed to represent two short boys, wrestling around the stage. Morocco characterized their choreographies as "Moscow on the Nile." She states:

> The last part of the Kaumiyya' [sic] fantasy version of the *Haggalah,* the "dance" the men are doing is pure Ukrainian Hopak and the "tableau dramatique" with the man wooing the woman and throwing down the dagger is a direct and total steal from Soviet Georgian Ensembles. In the "real" Haggalah, the men *only* clap and chant encouragement to the *one* young girl who dances. In this the Reda version is truer to the reality by using one female dancer. (Personal communication, May 20, 2000)

In a recent performance that I viewed, the movements certainly contained strong influences from the Soviet companies, but the costuming and music owed much more to Mahmoud Reda than to Moiseyev (see the videocassette *Funun Sh'Abiah, Misriyah*).

Following Fahmy's classification of Reda's choreographies, the National Folk Troup uses his third type—"Folklore"—in which folk-inspired renditions of traditional dances from the field had been spectacularized for the stage, utilizing all of the elements of invented tradition I described in the previous section.

The government constructed the Balloon Theatre (so called for the large dome-shaped roof) in the Agouza district, right on the border of Imbaba, to house its new companies. Tourists are not found in these audiences either. The performances were announced in Arabic signs so that only the occasional non-Arab who can read Arabic, or an oriental dance enthusiast, armed with information from the belly dance journals, would be aware of the performances.

From the numerous films of these two companies, as well as live performances, it is clear that Reda has developed a set of folk-inspired movements and choreographic works that are based more in European traditions, especially ballet, than Egyptian ones.[19] Like Moiseyev, he has utilized ballet movements and created a unique Egyptian vocabulary of character dance, or "theatre dance" as he and Fahmy refer to it. This new Reda genre has been widely emulated both in Egypt and abroad by his sizable foreign constituency, whom I will discuss later. In spite of Fahmy's disclaimers that "when Reda adopted movement to the stage, he paid particular attention to how Egyptians utilize their energy and shape their movement" (1987, 24), little of the movements seen in the field are found in his productions. In addition, she claims that "he selected and manipulated traditional elements to varying degrees in his choreographies. When he evolved new dance movements, he strove for what was culturally consistent and relevant to the premise he was working on." But, in fact, Fahmy herself refers to Reda's dance vocabulary as "a new genre of dance" and that "the basics of classical ballet and barre were still part of the training" (ibid., 25).

What Mahmoud Reda and those who emulate him have produced is an urban fantasy of village life, a form of self-exoticism designed largely for the urban elite as a charming form of village life that scrubs over its actual unpleasantness. Many Westerners are of the opinion that these dances were created for the tourist trade, the major economic force in Egypt today. Concerning a tourist show of Reda-inspired choreography that she saw in Aswan, Egypt, Deborah Root, a scholar of postcolonialism notes:

> The circle dances and songs flow together at this distance, but one scene has remained with me: the identically costumed dancers pretending to be drawing water from a village well. They teasingly splashed each other, intended (I suppose) to add charm to the scene as a way of lending veracity to the display of village life. It was all very irritating. Nobody in real life wears identical costumes, so why were they part of the dance? More important, however, the dancers were going beyond folk dance in order to construct a simulacrum of village life, complete with nonexistent water from a nonexistent well, a village life that was under pressure from both the tourist presence and foreign agricultural concerns. My mind kept drifting back to the other display that had been mounted for the tourists—the guard and his gun—and to the extent to which that exhibition was connected to the smiling dancers. . . .
>
> The Nubian dance evening not only entertained at least some tourists with its vision of happy villagers, but it also exemplified the displacement of these same villagers, a situation not entirely separate from the presence of the tourists at the dance event. (1998, 84)

But Root, while understanding the fantasy aspect of the dancing that glosses over the misery of village life, misses the point. These dances were not created for tourists. They were created for the Egyptian urban elite who run the tourist industry and feel that tourists ought to love these fantasies as much as Egyptians do. In fact, Westerners in general tend to prefer the more traditional companies that I describe below, regarding their performances as a more authentic Egyptian experience.

Traditional Music and Dance Ensembles

El-Nil (The Nile) Folkloric Troup

This company is perhaps better known in the West as the "Festival of the Nile," the title under which they travel in the West, where they have performed to critical and public acclaim. The company has had three directors and at least as many names (such as Musicians of the Nile). It was founded by Zakariah al-Heggawi in 1956 as the *firqat al-Fellahin* (Peasants' Troupe). He was succeeded by Suleiman Gamil in 1970, and the company became known as the *firqat al-ala'at ash-sha'biyah* (Troupe of Folk Instrumentalists). I found them housed in the Balloon Theatre in their present form, the El-Nil Folkloric Troup, supervised and directed by Abdel Rahman Al-Shafie. He was appointed to the position in 1975. Al-Shafie, a dapper, energetic gentleman in his early sixties, has skillfully shaped this group of professional-level traditional native performers, largely in response to the two companies in the Reda mode, into an exciting, world-famous music attraction. He fears that the colonial process, which I discussed above, was, and is, eroding Egyptian folklore. His is a rescue operation. In the year during which he took reins of the company, folklorists from the Smithsonian Institution were organizing performances of traditional artists from several parts of the world for the Bicentennial Celebration to be seen both on the mall in Washington, D.C., and in various venues throughout the United States. According to Al-Shafie, the Egyptian government, predictably, wanted to send the Reda Troupe, but the folklorists of the Smithsonian refused to countenance the appearances of companies that manifested a patently nontraditional representation of Egypt.

Al-Shafie painstakingly gathered groups of traditional artists from various parts of Egypt and welded them into a performing ensemble in which each group maintained its regional identity while playing a few well-known pieces—of both popular traditional folk melodies or composed songs sung by popular icons such as Umm Kulthum and Abd Al-Wahhab—for the opening and closing portions of the performance. Since then, he has managed to keep these programs fresh by utilizing a fluid collection of groups of traditional singers, musicians, and dancers, but with certain of the groups serving as a core, being employed year after year.

Of all of the groups, the El-Nil Folkloric Troup has been the most significant and well-received group outside of Egypt, but its existence in Cairo goes almost unnoticed. Egyptian dance scholar Magda Saleh notes: "Its success abroad is not reflected in Egypt, where native arts do not have any cultural cachet but are regarded as primitive and non-aesthetic. The theatricalized versions are, however, considered a substantial improvement in the drive toward refinement" (1998, 496).

They have toured the United States four times, the last time in 1995, and often tour in Europe. Obtaining exit visas from the Egyptian government and squeamish European and American embassy staffs for traditionally dressed individuals, particularly dancers, presents a major problem for the company. According to Morocco, "they wanted to bring the Banat Mazin, ghawazi dancers [professional performers of solo-improvised dance, but not in the urban cabaret style] from Esna-Luxor, but the government would not grant them exit visas because they are held in low esteem as traditional dancers. Since they are considered to be Gypsies, there is also a racist element in these decisions. They had to take a dancer from the National Folk Troup trained in the Reda Troupe style, who was not well received by the Western press" (personal interview, January 26, 2000).

Al-Shafie has worked hard to keep the idea of traditional performance alive. "There is a problem for us [Egyptians]. We want to imitate the West and we regard our own art as backward. We did not work hard to develop our own art. We went directly from Turkish colonialism and influences to British ones. Now the people see television and want to imitate what they see there. Globalization is a danger. We must protect our own arts and traditions or lose our identity. My goal with these artists is to present living traditional Egyptian music and dance" (personal interview, January 27, 2000).

Preparing for an upcoming tour, the company does not rehearse in the way that the nontraditional companies do because the performers have total control of their performance techniques. Rather, the rehearsals establish where the performers will stand, which pieces they will play as separate units, and what the program order is, then rehearse the few big ensemble pieces that open and close the program. The night that I attended, the full ensemble played a well-known Umm Kulthum song with an older woman singer in traditional everyday clothing. Songs that had been sung by Umm Kulthum have the important quality of *asil* (authenticity) from an Egyptian viewpoint and are well-known to everyone. They had one *mizmar* ensemble from the southern regions and another from the eastern region; a *rababa* ensemble from the Delta; players from the Suez area playing *simsimiyas*, strummed harplike instruments; a range of end-blown flutes; and a dozen men playing a variety of percussion instruments. The solo dancer performed a typical domestic version of solo-improvised dancing and served as a visual accompaniment to a vocal piece rather than as a featured performer. In this ensemble, the music is the thing.

El-Tannoura Egyptian Heritage Folklore Troupe

The latest addition to this array of state ensembles is the *ghuriya* troupe, which I described in the opening portions of this chapter; it was begun in 1988. That ensemble of twenty men fills the specific performance slot at the El-Ghuri Mausoleum, and in most respects it can be characterized as a chamber version of the Festival of the Nile. Some of the performers from that group—such as the tannoura (skirt) dancer who brought audiences through America to its feet—occasionally accompany the Festival of the Nile. Traditional performances are fluid—that is, aside from a few core individuals who serve as leaders and soloists, the performers are interchangeable.

The Raqs Sharqi Diaspora

In each of the chapters I have included how diaspora communities of immigrants—Russians, Mexican, Croatian—have been affected by performances of their respective nation-state's folk ensemble. As we saw with the first appearance of Amalia Hernandez's Ballet Folklorico, the Mexican-American community of the Southwest was galvanized by ethnic pride to reproduce its spectacle. Many Croatian immigrant community groups attempted to develop miniature versions of LADO, while the Russian émigré community has been less affected, probably for political reasons.

In the case of the Egyptian community, the vast majority of the immigrants are Coptic Christians who are leaving Egypt in increasing numbers because of perceived religious persecution. Violent confrontations between Muslims and Christians have been on the rise since the Islamist resurgence. There is no large Egyptian immigrant community in the West. Los Angeles is home to one of the largest; several Coptic Christian churches exist there, but the population has not yet reached a critical mass to create dance companies.

There is, however, a raqs sharqi community of more than a million women in the United States, and throughout Western Europe a similar population of hundreds of thousands.[20] With the allure of the romance of the East—sheiks, harems, caravans, and minarets—raqs sharqi has been taken in turn from the "hootchy kootchy" first seen at the World's Fairs at the end of the nineteenth century in major European and American cities, next Hollywood movies, and then was made popular by the women's liberation movement of the 1970s. However, "these 'modes of presentation' are [not] representative of the form as it is performed in its indigenous cultural environment" (Sellers-Young 1992, 141). In other words, as with the Mexican, Croatian, and Russian immigrant communities, these individuals have no wish to replicate actual folkloric practices from the field, but rather seek the spectacularized choreographic theater genres of Egyptian choreographers such as Mahmoud Reda.

This is the overseas community that I would define as patrons and devotees of the Reda Troupe and Mahmoud Reda's choreographies. This overwhelmingly female community stays in close contact through web sites, periodicals, conventions (which invariably include dance concerts by the students and their instructors), and dance workshops and classes. I would liken this to Anderson's (1991) "imagined community." During the 1970s and 1980s, several master teachers, including Morocco, conducted tours to Egypt, and concerts of the Reda Troupe and the National Folk Troup were staples of these journeys to the "home" country for these avid enthusiasts. Morocco adds, "These tours also included public and private performances of raks sharki, the Ghawazi, tahtib, and dance seminars taught by people such as Mahmoud Reda, Hassan Khalil, Nazial el Adel, Nadia Hamdi, and other working female performers" (personal communication, May 20, 2000). This tour activity has greatly subsided since the Islamist resurgence in Egypt, and dance activity is much less than it was.

Mahmoud Reda, according to many individuals from the raqs sharqi community and Reda himself (personal interview, January 10, 2000), is in high demand throughout Europe and North America. He has videos available using dancers from his ensemble to teach his technique (but not his choreographies). He has several women throughout the community who act as his agents in various geographic areas. Among this community his name is a household word.

In the beginning belly dance was largely taught as a solo form, but as time passed many teachers and other individuals began to form groups for performance purposes, as well as to teach theatricalized "folk dances," especially at belly dance conventions. In the beginning of the 1960s, choreographies were taught by these teachers. "The exceptions are dances choreographed for the theatre by dance ensembles in the country of origin and then retaught and reshaped in the United States, such as those of the Reda Company in Egypt" (Sellers-Young 1992, 147).

Thus, in a unique way, the enthusiasts for Mahmoud Reda's choreographic art are found perhaps in greater numbers outside of Egypt, and they are not Egyptian by origin.

Franken notes that performances of the Reda Troupe have also had an impact in other countries in the Arab world. She states, "Not only did the Reda Troupe symbolize the new Egypt at home and abroad; it inspired the formation of folkloric troupes in Lebanon, Jordan, Saudi Arabia, and other Arabic-speaking countries" (1996, 283).

Colonialism and its impact are still felt in Egypt long after the departure of the colonial establishment itself. It is a bitter double-edged sword, similar to the phenomenon recounted by long-held individual prisoners who both loathe, and then come to desire and love, their jailers. The colonialized populations both hated and wished to eject the colonial powers on the one hand, while simultaneously emulating aspects of their behavior in order to win their respect and approval. In the case of an embodied form such as dance, this attempt to elicit colonial approval by making it acceptable to middle-class eyes of the Edwardian period has had profound repercussions that have affected the manner in which Egyptian dance is portrayed before its own audiences.

Colonialism produced new class differences and moral standards, including altered concepts of gender and sexuality. For example, while there is one solo-improvised dance tradition in which all participate, its depiction on stage departs from traditional practices, sanitizing it for the moral standards of the postcolonial elite.

Will the future of traditional dance performances that receive government support be the traditional style followed by the El-Nil Folkloric Troup? This would require a movement toward the rediscovery of authentic traditional performance by the Egyptian elite that Al-Shafie is striving to promote, but it has yet to materialize. Or, will it be dance in the Reda mode? There is no way to predict.

7

Greece: Dora Stratou Greek Dances Theatre, A Living Museum

More than forty years ago, in 1958, under an appropriately romantic full moon, I sat in rapt attention on ancient stone bleachers in an amphitheater constructed two millennia ago in the port city of Piraeus waiting for a performance to begin. The evening breeze coming off the nearby sea felt cool on my face after the day's intense heat in which I wandered among the ruins of classical Greece on the Acropolis.[1]

Suddenly from behind the ancient pillars, a lone drummer appeared and set a dramatic and solemn rhythm. A pair of double-reed *zurna* players soon joined him, their penetrating sound echoing throughout the outdoor amphitheater. Stately processions of men and women wearing somber black and white costumes from the blood-drenched northern mountains of Macedonia evoked a history of enormous depth. The women, wearing helmet-shaped headpieces that recalled ancient Greek soldiers, entered first, performing three variations of the simple dance steps of the region. The men followed, performing a simple line dance in which the leader signaled the few changes in variations. As the dance picked up in tempo, the leader performed special steps as a solo. The men and women then performed a couple dance together.

Choreographically, the dancers never left the form of a semicircle. The men and women dancers simply circled around the performance space, joined in various handholds and performing dance figures that ranged from a walk or the basic dance figure found all over Europe and the Middle East (step right, step left, step right, simultaneously lifting the left leg, step left, simultaneously lifting the right leg), to somewhat more intricate steps. Many, if not the vast majority, of the group folk dances from the Balkans, Turkey, the Levant, and Iran are danced in lines, circles, and semicircles. The dancers utilize a variety of hand and shoulder holds and perform a basic, fairly simple step, such as I described above, and then continue the dance by performing ever more elaborate variations of the basic simple steps. From time to time

Dora Stratrou Greek Dances Theatre. *Tsamikos*. COURTESY GREEK DANCES THEATRE.

the lead dancer left the semicircle formation to perform highly athletic solo figures. Occasionally, the men would perform squats and turns together. The group dance was performed with the couples spaced evenly over the dance area. The dances generally began slowly, speeding up in tempo (Petrides and Petrides 1961, Raftis 1987).

As the first group exited, a line of women entered in a slow procession dressed in the colorful female costumes of the Corfu Island: velvet jackets elaborately worked in gold bullion embroidery, pleated skirts in primary colors, and hand-worked aprons, topped by a confection of a headpiece in flowers and ribbons. This dance, accompanied by sprightly melodies played by violins and the lutelike *lauto*, contrasted with the doleful sounds of the *zurnas*, giving the music an Italian quality, as did the male vocal quartet that preceded the dancing. Throughout the choreography, the women execute sedate dance steps—barely more than walking steps—while five men in baggy black trousers and matching vests, white shirts, and straw hats executed a variety of athletic squats and turns.

Throughout the evening, the dances were accompanied by a variety of instruments, such as the bowed *lyra* and Macedonian bagpipes, which I had never seen or heard before. The men in straw hats and baggy trousers and women with elaborate headpieces and Italianate costumes from the Corfu Island breathed life into the images of the sunny shores and blue seas for which Greece is famous. During the performance, the large company of more than fifty dancers and twenty musicians displayed a panorama of Greece, ending in a flurry of fustanellas and wailing clarinets as the entire cast executed the exciting finale. The closest elements that approach the spectacular are the highly athletic steps of the male soloists who lead the dances.

After seeing Greek dancing for many years at the churches and Greek nightclubs in Los Angeles, where immigrant Greeks and their descendants happily danced the same five dances (*syrto*, fast *hasapiko*, slow *hasapiko, kalamatiano, and tsamiko*) at almost every event, the performance of the Dora Stratou Greek Dances Theatre in the ancient theater was a revelation. The children and young people of the Greek immigrant community always wore the same costumes for performances. For decades, to represent the Greek immigrant community, the young men wore fustanellas (shirts with the many-gored and pleated skirts associated with the palace guard, the Evzones), and the young women and girls wore an approximation of the Queen Amalia costume, inevitably made of cheap red-velvet jackets and fading sky-blue taffeta skirts. I was totally unprepared for the choreographic, musical, and sartorial riches that the Dora Stratou Greek Dances Theatre (named for its founder, the late Dora Stratou) presented with its dancers and musicians. They showed a colorful array of choreographic, costuming, and musical wares, like a jewelry store salesman with his dazzling goods, for which I was an eager customer. This was another step along my path of discovery.

Forty years later, I approached the Dora Stratou Greek Dances Theatre offices in the Plaka district of Athens. The tall ochre-colored building in the shadow of the Acropolis, Dr. Alkis Raftis informed me proudly, is the largest building in the Plaka. The Plaka, the former Albanian quarter and the only area of Athens untouched by the fell hand of modernist development, is a tourist Mecca. It is a charming collection of winding streets and century-old buildings, sidewalk cafés, touristy curio shops, street performers, strolling crowds, and lively tavernas with grapevine-covered arbors that are nightly filled with the sounds of Greek music and tacky folk dance floor shows.

In the company offices one sees a Dora Stratou Greek Dances Theatre unimagined by the viewer, seated in the theater on Philopappou Hill on the opposite side of the Acropolis and still in its shadow. As one enters the ground floor, dust is everywhere. Workmen are reconstructing, renovating, and improving, and have been doing so for seemingly years according to the staff. One goes up the exceedingly narrow steps, and on the next floor the wardrobe staff is bent over the unending work of keeping the twenty-five hundred precious, authentic, and irreplaceable costumes repaired and in readiness for the company's appearances. Those narrow steps have prevented the Ministry of Culture and other interested parties from seizing the building from the company, especially since alterations to buildings in the Plaka, now a national architectural heritage, are prohibited.

At this particular moment in time the wardrobe staff is engaged in the onerous task of preparing two dozen costumes from the company's rich collection to pack and take to San Jose, California. They will take them to a convention where people of Greek heritage are holding a folk dance festival for their youth. The wardrobe staff will select a number of young women from that convention to model the costumes so that the attendees at the convention have the unique opportunity to see the costumes up close.

On the next floor Maria (one of three of the same name on the staff) prepares a package to send to a group of Greek dancers in one of the many immigrant communities in Australia. They have requested books and videos of the company's performances to help them learn how to dance and dress more correctly. These time-consuming efforts are among the myriad educational outreach programs of the Dora Stratou Greek Dances Theatre. Weekly packages are sent worldwide, to wherever immigrant communities seek information about their cultural heritage. At a second desk in the same office, George Mavropoulos, the lead dancer and a perfectionist who has performed with the company for more than thirty years and serves as the closest position to that of what would be called an artistic director in other dance companies, intently studies a tape of a recent performance. He looks for errors, sloppy styling, and mediocre playing by the orchestra—anything that detracts from an ideal, authentic, and professional performance. He will address these problems at the next rehearsal.

On the top floor Adiamanta Angelis, the company secretary, checks the email that comes from around the world, makes appointments, deals with the numerous visitors, including the odd American sifting through the company's library, and feeds a stray pigeon at the window, all with almost superhuman polite deftness. Angeliki Christifilopoulou sits at a second desk. She is a tall, well-groomed, fast-talking businesswoman who arranges for publicity releases to local periodicals, a job that she has held for more than twenty years.

In the executive office, the dapper and distinguished-looking professor of management science, Dr. Alkis Raftis, President of the

Board, draws papers from files as he prepares to do battle—yet once again in regard to the company's assets—with the government, a particular ministry, or a competing cultural organization. This time a governmental committee for the planned Archeological Park from the Ministry of Culture is coming to tell him officially that the company amphitheater on Philopappou Hill sits on a valuable archeological site and that the company must be removed elsewhere—a potential disaster for the company that has been housed there for decades. It is the largest and third oldest company in Greece. Dr. Raftis has been forewarned, but this does not make these series of assaults any easier. This is by no means the first time that such claims have been put forward, for virtually every inch of space in Athens, indeed all of Greece, sits on some kind of valuable historical site. Property owners, out of frustration and under cover of darkness, hide any evidence of historical activity from their property rather than face years of waiting for some archeological team to begin the painstaking sifting of their soil.

By the end of this typical workday at the offices of the dance company, the battle has been won, if temporarily, and the committee, in view of the status of the venerable Dora Stratou Greek Dances Theatre, has decided it is more prudent, for now, to dig elsewhere. Athens does not lack places in which to dig for archeological treasures.

The story of the Dora Stratou Greek Dances Theatre has many strands. Constructed and formed within the Greece of a particular era, the early 1950s, the shaping of the dance company, like those of the other state folk ensembles this study analyzes, took place in the specific social, ethnic, political, and economic conditions of post–World War II Greece. Like the colonialist construct of Egypt, the context of the Dora Stratou Greek Dance Theatre contains myriad binaries. "A historian of China, Charlotte Furth, has made the point that not all binarism arises from the imperial project of orientalism, but that binarism may prove useful for describing the consequences of that project" (Herzfeld 1997, 15). It is the story of two companies, two directors, city and village, Greek islands and the Greek mainland, Communists and conservatives, past and present, Ancient Greece and Byzantium, and Ottoman colonialism and postcolonialism.

The "Period Eye" and "Unmarked"

Two scholars, in different contexts, have suggested ways in which cultural performances can be profitably viewed. Anthropologist Clifford Geertz, expanding on the notion of the "period eye" proposed by art historian Michael Baxandall, analyzes how painters in the Renaissance created works that were filled with culturally specific symbolism and elements, including the omission of specific elements, that their patrons could "read." Because these patrons inhabited the same cultural and historical space as the painter, they brought with them the same culturally acquired knowledge that enabled them to understand the meanings in these works of art. Thus, the painter was able to create a world of images that were closed to those who come from other times and places and do not possess that specialized knowledge. "The period eye . . . is the equipment that a fifteenth-century painter's public [that is, other painters and 'the patronizing classes'] brought to complex visual stimulations like pictures" (Geertz 1983, 102–103). It was a "visual activity that one has to learn to read, just as one has to learn to read a text from a different culture" (ibid., 108). Art historians and other scholars study long years to acquire that specialized knowledge, as do dance historians.

The second part of the idea I am presenting comes from postmodernist theory that problematizes cultural representations, such as dance performances. Peggy Phelan, a scholar in performance studies, questions the representation of the "real." In her book *Unmarked*, Phelan "attempts to find a theory value for that which is not 'really' there" (1993, 1). In other words, "unmarked" stands for what is not represented. I utilize Phelan's concept of the unmarked to refer to the gaps and absences found (or not found or seen) in the performances of the national state folk dance ensembles. To some degree, gaps and absences are a crucial element in the analyses of the performances of all the companies that appear on the world stages. It is within these gaps, not embodied in the performances of the national dance ensembles, that some of the most telling discourses of the nation-state are embedded. I find that these gaps and absences become especially critical in the performances of the Greek and Turkish state folk dance ensembles, and by extension the social, ethnic, and historic contexts in which they were formed, constructed, and developed. As Phelan observes, "Representation follows two laws: it always conveys more than it intends; and it is never totalizing. The 'excess' meaning conveyed by representation creates a supplement that makes multiple and resistant readings possible" (1993, 2).

In the nationalist discourses of Greece and Turkey, embodied in performances of their respective state folk dance companies, these multiple readings are crucial. But, as Michael Herzfeld points out, "Nationalism is directly predicated on resemblance, whether biogenetic or cultural. . . . Most nationalists fear variant cultural readings—

minority, self-determination, youth nonconformism, cultural dissidence—that might undermine their universalist claims" (1997, 27–28).

In order to present some of these "multiple and resistant" readings, I am constructing a lens that is a combination of the "period eye" and the "unmarked." The "period eye" is the special body of knowledge required to make a full reading of the performances of these companies and the contexts in which they appear, while the "unmarked" provides the critical viewer with the capacity to see gaps and absences found in performances. This lens enables the observer to view what is represented and then fill the gaps and absences with the "period," or what we can call the "specialized" eye.

At first glance the viewer, like my younger self, is impressed and even overwhelmed at the sheer volume of villages and regions; some eighty are represented in the repertoire of the Dora Stratou Greek Dances Theatre. It was probably the first national folk dance ensemble to be founded outside of the Second World, as the Soviet bloc was known. A closer scrutiny, through the lens of the period eye, will permit the viewer to see the gaps and absences within the field of representation.

The Burden of History

To say that the burden of history (or better, histories) weighs heavily on Greece is nearly a cliché; after all, every nation has a history. Greece, however, has many layers of history, and each period represents and symbolizes different values. No nation in Europe can match the depth of history found in the archeology of Greece. Whereas the Serbs, the Croats, the Bulgarians, and the Rumanians have one history, the Greeks have multiple histories. Alkis Raftis observes that "Greek identity must be understood in terms of the fortress mentality in which this small nation feels the urge to protect its boundaries, mental and ethnic" (personal interview, February 16, 2000).

The defining element in the history of modern Greece begins in 1830 with the establishment of the fledgling Kingdom of Greece after five hundred years under the colonial rule of the Ottoman Empire. The struggle for independence began in the 1820s and lasted nearly a decade. The fire of revolution was ignited by the winds of nationalism blowing in from Western Europe throughout the Balkans following the French Revolution. A major impetus for nationalism was the idea of the glory of Ancient Greece brought by young Greek students who completed their education in Paris and other European capitals.

"Although not colonized by the Great Powers of Europe during the nineteenth century, the Greeks have adopted their classicist (as equivalent to orientalist) vision of themselves as direct descendants and embodiment of the Ancient Greeks" (Raftis, personal communication, July 7, 2000).

As I asserted in the previous chapter, the Ottoman Empire was in every sense of the word an imperialist colonial enterprise. Because Greece was a colony, scholars often forget that it is part of Europe. The Ottoman dynasty conquered and dominated a vast territory and then proceeded to exploit it. Like the British Empire, in the beginning the Ottoman colonial project was a largely military enterprise, and the considerable monies that flowed through the Ottoman treasury in the form of taxes and booty supported the monarchy, the bureaucracy, the upper clergy, and the military. Through this enormous wealth a nomadic society was transformed into a sophisticated imperial state, a rival to any in Europe for several centuries. By the nineteenth century the Ottoman Empire was Great Britain's third most important source of exports.

While it is beyond the scope of this book to provide a complete history of the Ottoman Empire, I will highlight those aspects that were crucial in shaping the current nation-state of Greece. It is the Ottoman Empire and its domination of Greece for more than four hundred years that define the way in which modern Greece has shaped its identity, if only by its gaps. The legacy of Ottoman domination has left what I characterize as a negative imprint. Every attempt by the Greek elite to excise all traces of Ottoman rule and influence has led to an extraordinary attempt that dominates intellectual and social life.

It is fashionable in academic circles, and certainly in the popular mind of those who are aware of it, to dismiss the Ottoman Empire as the "Sick Man of Europe" run by the "Terrible Turk." These were the terms coined by the European powers, which not only regarded the Ottoman Empire as weak, but also provided the excuse they needed to dismember it. Greece was one of the beneficiaries of this gradual dismemberment.

There is a misconception that the terms "Turk" and "Ottoman" are synonymous. In fact, the term "Turk" to the Ottoman elite meant country bumpkin or illiterate peasant. The Ottoman elite were Muslims: the royal family (a huge group when one considers the number of wives and children in the harem), the elite bureaucracy, military, Islamic clergy, and intelligentsia. Although the official Ottoman language was based on Turkish, it was in fact an elite literary mixture of Turkish, Persian, and Arabic elements and cultural concepts known and understood only by the elite of Istanbul and a few provincial individuals. "Ottoman culture, i.e., the high culture of the Ottoman Empire, was produced and consumed exclusively by educated Ottoman, Arabic, and Persian-speaking Muslims" (Todorova 1996, 57). The Muslim peasantry, both Turkish and Arabic (as well as the fewer numbers of Albanian, Slavic, and Kurdish Muslims) was almost as excluded from participation in the state as the Christian *raya*. Turkish commoners could not understand the official and literary language of the Ottoman court and government.

One of the major misrepresentations of the Ottoman Empire is the image of blood-thirsty Muslim soldiers, scimitars in hand, bent on converting their hapless Christian subjects through massacre and the sword. In fact, the Ottoman authorities had no interest in converting their Christian subjects. As second-class non-Muslims they paid more taxes than Muslim subjects, and the Ottoman authorities were far more interested in taxes than conversion.

Historian L. Carl Brown observes, "In actual fact few major political systems have been so consistently ignored or misrepresented, not just in the West but in the many different states sharing an Ottoman past" (1996, 5). The misrepresentation of the Ottoman Empire as weak and decadent flies in the face of the fact that the empire lasted six centuries, much longer than the British Empire. During most of that time, especially in its first four centuries, the Ottoman Empire was a highly successful, efficiently run state. In the Ottoman Empire, given the multiethnic and multilingual population that comprised it, the rulers developed a state policy that was far more tolerant of religious diversity than any of its European contemporaries. Further, that very diversity required the development of a unique system to contain and make use of its diversity. That system was the millet system, whereby each individual was assigned to his or her millet (ethnic division) determined by religious affiliation. Ironically, according to many historians of Ottoman and Greek history, this afforded the Greek Orthodox Church far more independence and freedom than it ever experienced under Byzantine suzerainty.

Through the millet system, in which each religious body was afforded representation to the central government in Istanbul, intracommunal justice was administered by communal officials (Greeks, Armenians, Jews, etc.) who also collected taxes to be handed over to the central government. This provided a great deal of autonomy to each community within the confines of the overall Ottoman State. It was after the Treaty of Karlovac (Karlowitz) in 1699, which marked the occasion of the Hapsburgs halting the advance of the Ottoman juggernaut at the gates of Vienna, that the first cracks in the Ottoman structure appeared. Throughout the next two centuries the central government in Constantinople, its weaknesses exposed, slowly lost its grip on the outlying provinces.

In the beginning, the Balkan lands were given as temporary fiefs to the Sultan's cavalry (*spahi*). "The system was not a harsh one so far as the Greek peasant was concerned, for the spahi had his fief only for his life whereas the peasant's tenure was hereditary and inalienable" (Woodhouse 1998, 101). These provinces eventually fell into the hands of the Janissaries (*yenicheri*), the elite military class, that spun out of control of the central government in Constantinople. They proceeded to brutally extort the local population by raising the taxes and financial obligations to such an extent that entire populations fled, signaling a breakdown of law and order. The formation of the Janissaries proceeded from the custom of collecting young male children from the Christian populations in the Balkans. This system, called the "devshirme," was locally known as the "blood tax." The devshirme brought young Christian children to Constantinople where they were converted to Muslims and trained as soldiers and administrators, some of whom rose to the highest positions in the Ottoman government. Since the children were separated from their parents at an early age, they owed their entire allegiance to the Sultan, thus preventing the development of a hereditary feudal aristocracy based on military obligations to the monarchy. The devshirme system, too, caused peasant flight.

For centuries entire ethnic groups throughout the Balkans were replaced by new populations, creating an ethnic patchwork that reverberates in today's headlines. "Between 1333 and 1355, Albanians as well as Serbs flooded into Greek territory to settle" (Woodhouse 1998, 85), a pattern that continued throughout the Ottoman period. Albanians, Serbs, Macedonians, and Vlachs (a Rumanian-speaking nomadic ethnic group, and today a code word for unlettered peasant) constituted the majority population in several areas of Greece, and the Albanians formed a majority in the area around Athens at the founding of the Greek state. Travelers describe Greek speakers as a minority in many areas. Woodhouse adds, "It is a striking fact that the leading defenders of Greek liberty at this time [1830] were largely non-Greek" (ibid., 139). These, however, due to the fact that they were Orthodox in religion, were rapidly Hellenized. The process of Hellenization was not forced—the minority groups, except the Muslims, were among the most enthusiastic supporters of the Greek state. Alkis Raftis states that "In many areas, nine out of ten villages have new Greek names. In Attica 90 percent of the villages were Albanian. But the Arvanitis are Albanian Greeks. (Albanians from Albania are called Alvanos.) They as well as the Vlachs are fanatical about their Greekness. They always say, 'We are Albanian-speaking Greeks'" (personal interview, February 17, 2000).

But Hugh Poulton disagrees that Hellenization was a process that occurred without government pressure:

> The process of Hellenisation of the Orthodox population through the millet system had a great effect on the Albanians in the south and the process has continued throughout the twentieth century. In the first quarter of the century, there were many Albanian-speaking citizens in areas of Greece like Attica, Boetia, southern Euboea (Evvoia) and Hydra, while the Plaka district in Athens close to the Acropolis was the city's Albanian quarter, with its own law courts using the Albanian language. Such people have tended to become hellenised due to the millet heritage, magnified by Greece's continuing denial of any national minorities within its borders, and a resolute state directed assimilation policy. (Poulton and Vickers 1997, 142)

A major gap in Greek life, and in the programs of the Dora Stratou Greek Dance Theatre, is any inclusion or mention of the dances and music of ethnic minorities. In Greece minorities do not exist officially, and their presence is a source of uneasiness on a number of levels. They are officially absent, a point to which I will presently return.[2]

The millet system, based on a Muslim elite dominating a large Christian population in the Balkans, excluded any possibility of including them as first-class citizens. Nor did the Ottoman government, until the end, seriously attempt to create a modern state based on equality for all. "That the Ottoman Empire did not create an integrated society is beyond doubt; what some Balkan historians seem unable to understand is that the empire did not strive to achieve such integration" (Todorova 1996, 48).

Thus, the combination of Western ideas of nationalism and the concurrent weakening of the central Ottoman Empire provided the Greeks with the opportunity to seek independence. "The capriciousness of Ottoman rule and the weakness of the idea of the rule of law helped to shape the underlying values of Greek society and to determine attitudes to the state and authority that have persisted into the present" (Clogg 1992, 3). The Christian population longed for its own state, for Christians could never achieve full citizenship in the confines of the Ottoman Empire in which they were the colonized population and a subject people. As Maria Todorova observes:

> This interpretation ... rests on the not-so-erroneous perception of segregation of the local Christian population within the empire. For all the objections to romanticized heartbreaking assessments of Christian plight under the infidel Turk, a tendency that has been long and rightly criticized, the Ottoman Empire was, first and foremost, an Islamic state with a strict religious hierarchy where the non-Muslims occupied, without any doubt, the back seats. The strict division on religious lines prevented integration of this population, except in cases of conversions. (1996, 47)

Todorova adds that the "struggles for national emancipation and the creation of nation-states were thought of not only as radical breaks with the past, but the negation of this past" (1996, 48). This brought about the attempt to dismantle every vestige of the Ottoman presence. In Greece cityscapes, visible traces were erased and replaced with buildings that recalled and emulated Ancient Greece or Paris, and clothing, at least for the urban elite of the court, followed Western European models, with a "Greek" touch.[3] This was part of a process of creating a new state. "In Greece the Bavarian regency immediately launched an elaborate program of educational, judicial, bureaucratic, economic, military, and religious reforms on a society ... [in which] there was almost no continuity of political elites in the Balkans, at least of elites that had participated in the Ottoman political process" (Todorova 1996, 56).

The case of the Greeks was different from that of other Balkan peoples, such as the Serbs and Bulgarians, because of the way in which Western Europeans regarded Greece as the fount of Western culture. In the beginning the Greeks themselves were overwhelmingly unaware of their own historical past. The new Greek state's process of acquiring territory was completed in small increments during the period 1820–1922. In this process they were supported by public opinion in the West, which, inflamed by the death of Lord Byron and other romantic adventurers, held the Greeks as the heroic descendants of the glories of Classical Greece. Philhellenic committees formed throughout Europe and the young United States to raise money for the revolt, fueled by the excessive force used by the Ottoman military in the repression of Greek revolutionaries. The nationalists quickly grasped the value of this position. Clogg states that

> a vital factor in stimulating in the Greeks themselves, or at least in the nationalist intelligentsia, [was] a consciousness that they were the heirs to a heritage that was universally admired. Such an awareness had

scarcely existed during the centuries of Ottoman rule and this "sense of the past," imported from western Europe, was a major constituent in the development of the Greek national movement. (1992, 1)

But this position turned into a double-edged sword as time passed. As Europeans gradually came to realize that the Greeks of the nineteenth and early twentieth centuries were not the intellectual descendants of Periclean Athens that they had envisioned, their enthusiasm for an independent Greek state waned.

Greece [became] at once the spiritual ancestor and the political pariah of the European Union. . . . In pursuit of Western ways of modernization, mainland Greeks neglected their more recent Byzantine heritage and sought to restore the secular ideals of the distant pre-Christian past. Moreover, native Greeks . . . projected a very unfavorable image as narrow-minded, parochial, and unsophisticated people. (Gianulli, qtd. in Herzfeld 1997, 18–19)

Thus, among the gaps and absences, not only do ethnic minorities not appear, but we must also search in vain for any traces of the Ottoman period in Greece. The millennium-long Byzantine past was also largely sidelined by this obsession with the classical past, and only slightly rehabilitated with the arrival of well-educated Greek refugees from Turkey after 1923. Thus, the Byzantine past creates another, perhaps partial, gap.[4] Due to the Western admiration for Ancient Greece, the first Greek nationalists (and most of those succeeding the first) "looked exclusively to the classical past" (Clogg 1992, 2). The most important result of this "progonoplexia," or excessive worship of the ancestors, was a complete denial of any Ottoman associations and a willful ignorance of the Byzantine past. "If the nascent intelligentsia of the independence period looked upon the classical past with a reverence that matched their contempt for Byzantium, it had no time at all for the heritage of 400 years of Ottoman rule" (Clogg 1992, 3).[5]

The Great Powers—Great Britain, France, Austria-Hungary, Prussia, and Russia—were at first reluctant to allow the formation of new national states because of the fear that the European balance of power would be altered. Each of the new states of Serbia, Greece, and Bulgaria became clients of one of the major European players. Alkis Raftis stated that "Greece was never able to achieve any military victories over the Ottomans on its own; it was Great Britain that always stepped in and forced the Ottoman Empire to cede territory to the new Greek state. In this way the English controlled the political situation" (personal interview, February 16, 2000). The new state "nonetheless was to contain fewer than one-third of the Greek inhabitants of the Ottoman Empire" (Clogg 1992, 45).

Because the majority of the Greek population was still under Ottoman control, the government and intelligentsia created the "Great Idea," the concept that any Greek state, with its future capital to be established in Constantinople, must include all Greek inhabitants. The Great Idea was to dominate Greek politics for the period 1830–1923 and led to the notion that Greece had a manifest destiny to occupy all of those territories, which included large areas of Anatolia in present-day Turkey where Greeks formed a majority of the population. The attempt to carry out the Great Idea was to have disastrous effects on Greece and, as we will see, had a direct impact on the life of Dora Stratou.

The struggle with the Ottoman Empire continued into the first decades of the twentieth century. The period was marked by constant forays into the Ottoman-held territories in the north with clandestine government support for bands of irregulars fighting a guerrilla war with the Ottomans. These skirmishes most often ended in humiliating defeat for the Greeks. In 1869, the Great Powers forced the Ottomans to cede Thessaly in Central Greece to the Greeks, which also acquired the Ionian Islands in 1864. As a result of the Balkan Wars of 1912–1913, Greece gained control over the northern areas of the mainland—Epirus, Macedonia, and Western Thrace—and some of the islands at the cost of deep enmity and strife with both Bulgaria and Turkey that lasted well into the post-World War II era.

With support and direction from the Great Powers, and in pursuit of the Great Idea, Greece invaded the Ottoman territories in Anatolia in 1918, at the close of World War I. The allies pulled out and the Greek army, overstretched, was driven out of Turkey in a disastrous defeat by forces under the command of Mustafa Kemal (Ataturk), father of the Turkish Republic. When the armistice was drawn up in the Treaty of Lausanne in 1923, it was agreed that Turkey and Greece would exchange populations: 1.1 million Greeks living in the new Republic of Turkey were exchanged for 350,000 Turks living in Greece. This exchange was based on religion rather than language, so that large Turkish-speaking Greek Orthodox people were exchanged for Greek-speaking Muslims. This population exchange benefited Greece in the long run since most of the new refugees were settled in the north, which Greece had acquired after the Balkan Wars, and in which, until the repatriation, they formed a minority. The Great Idea died in the ashes of the conflagration and retreat from Smyrna (Izmir).

A good example of this was the situation in the latter part of the nineteenth century when Greeks from the independent but desperately impoverished initial Greek state migrated in large numbers to the Ottoman Empire to take advantage of the Tanzimat reforms—so much so that it was only in the nineteenth century after the foundation of modern Greece, that Greeks began to dominate the west coast of Anatolia. (Poulton 1997, 25–26)

After 1923, in a fragile economy of six million, the addition of over one million refugees, some of whom could not speak Greek, added to the already crushing economic problems. Many of the new refugees, who encountered considerable prejudice from mainland Greeks, could not find employment, and the worldwide depression of the late 1920s only added to the misery.

The 1940s were perhaps the darkest decade in modern Greek history. The first half was characterized by the brutal Nazi occupation, during which hundreds of thousands of Greeks perished from famine, direct conflict with the Germans, and German reprisals against the resistance forces. During this period the national resistance, led by the Communists, rose. "By 1949 as much as 40 per cent of the rank and file of the democratic army was composed of Slav Macedonians" (Clogg 1992, 141).

The end of the war did not see the end of Greece's woes. A civil war raged for the next four years between the Communist-led Greek resistance and the monarchy and military elite, newly returned from exile. It was more cruel and unrelenting than the Nazi occupation. This civil war had the devastating effect of emptying the villages as the terrified populations became victims of battles, massacres, and reprisals between the two rival sides and fled to the cities. Alkis Raftis observes that village life and the communal values it represented in Greece were destroyed in this "cultural holocaust" (personal interview, February 16, 2000).

The government finally won the deadly civil war at the end of 1949, with leadership and support from Great Britain and the United States, who feared a Communist takeover. The resistance was brutally crushed with thousands of its members fleeing into Bulgaria and Yugoslavia or imprisoned for years. National reconciliation was never total. After a decade those who were imprisoned were set free, while those who fled to the Communist countries to the north were allowed to return, except for the Slavic Macedonians who, even though they held Greek citizenship when they left, after more than five decades are still denied the right to return.

Dance in the Field

In brief, Greek traditional dances are characterized by regional diversity within the relatively small territory of the Greek mainland and islands. In an excellent article in the *International Encyclopedia of Dance,* Alkis Raftis identifies at least twenty distinct major regional subcultures, each having at least ten unique dances. This diversity, according to Raftis, was created through geographical isolation of both island and mainland regions because of historic and geographic conditions and was compounded by the introduction in 1923 of large populations, who brought their dance and music traditions, from various areas of the former Ottoman Empire, now in present-day Turkey: Smyrna (Izmir), Eastern Thrace (including Constantinople), Cappadoccia in Central Anatolia, and the Black Sea region (Raftis 1998, 296–301).

In brief, in rural areas line and circle dances in which the dancers are linked by a variety of handholds predominate throughout Greece, with the popular couple dance, *ballos,* found on many islands. Solo dances, which Raftis considers of Anatolian origin, are rare. In the line and circle dancers, as in many regions of the Balkans, the leader of the dance is the most important individual, often the most gifted dancer. He (less often she) performs special improvised figures, often highly athletic and requiring enormous skill.[6]

There is also a rich urban tradition known as *rebetika* centered and developed in the social nether regions of nineteenth-century Ottoman urban society, just like jazz and the blues or the Argentine tango. The tradition continued after the population exchange of 1923 in Athens and Piraeus, where the unemployed, outcast, and criminal classes gathered to listen to music, smoke hashish, and drink. In contrast to the rural tradition of large communal groups, solo, couple, and line dances for two to four men predominated (Raftis 1987, 1998; Petrides 1975a). This urban tradition, now much changed through sanitizing to make it acceptable to middle-class urban dwellers after the success of the films *Never on Sunday* and *Zorba,* continues in a watered-down form as a tourist attraction in the *tavernas* of the Plaka and other Greek tourist resorts, as well as Greek nightclubs in Europe and North America.

This rich urban tradition forms one of the gaps in the Dora Stratou repertoire, which promotes and features only dances from the rural tradition. This preoccupation with the rural and peasant dances by urban-dwellers and nationalists reflects the theoretical research concerns and political imperatives of European and Middle Eastern dance ethnography over the past two centuries.

Greece: Dora Stratou Greek Dances Theatre 179

Dora Stratou Greek Dances Theatre. *Dance from Kato Panagia, Asia Minor.* COURTESY GREEK DANCES THEATRE.

Dora Stratou, Founder of the Greek Dances Theatre

As a result of the military debacle in Turkey in 1922, the Greek government and public sought scapegoats to blame for the national catastrophe. In a widely publicized trial, severely criticized in the West, six men were executed for high treason. One of them, Nikolas Stratos (Dora Stratou's father), had served as prime minister for only a few days in the cabinet under whose watch the Treaty of Lausanne was signed.

Dora Stratou had been born into a wealthy and politically powerful family in 1903. Her mother was the daughter of the famous playwright, Dimitrios Koromilas. She learned foreign languages and studied piano with Dimitri Mitropoulos, who later became a world-famous orchestra director. She followed concerts of classical music and theatrical performances that remained a passion throughout her life. When her father was executed, the family's wealth was confiscated and together with her mother and brother, Andreas, Dora went into exile in Paris, New York, and Berlin. After a life of wealth and comfort, the family found itself on the threshold of poverty. Dora underwent a psychological trauma from the shock of her father's execution and the public humiliation that followed in its wake.

The family returned to Greece in 1932. Andreas had studied law and was elected to parliament and eventually was appointed to the cabinet. Dora began to mix with a new crowd of intellectual men of the interwar period and became deeply involved as a volunteer in theater, assisting renowned theater director Karolos Kuhn.

The turning point in her life came when the Yugoslav national folk ensemble came to Athens in 1952.[7] Those performances created a sensation among the Greeks, who until that time had never seen spectacularized folk dancing. Their experience of folk dance performances were small, select salon affairs organized by the Women's Lyceum, a socialite club with branches throughout Greece.[8] During and after World War II, they regularly organized small performances to show off young society ladies in attractive Queen Amalia costumes (Alkis Raftis, personal interview, February 10, 2000). Several intellectuals and members of the public, led by George Megas, a university professor, began to vigorously lobby for the establishment of a permanent professional ensemble with a rich wardrobe of costumes to represent Greece. Dora Stratou asked to assist in the project, and soon the Dora Stratou Greek Dances Society (later Theatre) was created; the company was formed in 1952. She had found her niche: "Greek dance was an orphan," she said, and she adopted it (Alkis Raftis, personal interview, February 14, 2000).

Due to her connections she was able to attract countless friendly artists and intellectuals to support her project and serve on her board. At fifty years of age she embarked on a new life. She began to send members of the new company to collect songs and dances, costumes and jewelry in the countryside. She received enough government and private funding to buy the finest authentic village costumes and jewelry and to select top dancers and musicians, thus creating the most professional ensemble ever to be seen in Greece. The company toured twenty-one countries and throughout Greece to great acclaim.

In 1970 Dora Stratou received the most important international distinction: the World Theater Award of the International Theater Institute. She was also awarded by the Academy of Athens and received a huge grant, in the millions of dollars, from the Ford Foundation. With this funding she purchased the priceless jewelry and twenty-five hundred costumes, representing over eighty regions, that form the basis of the company's wardrobe, as well as musical instruments. The grant also enabled her to record some fifty records of the company's musical repertoire. She also authored three books in which she attempted to develop links between the dances of Ancient Greece with those of contemporary villages. After thirty years, in 1983, she retired due to ill health and died in 1988 (Raftis 1999).

The behind-the-scenes facts of Dora Stratou's life and her philosophy and drive to create the Greek State Folk Ensemble were the determining factors in the company's appearance during the past half-century. In the beginning she had planned to create a spectacle resembling the highly choreographed Moiseyev–influenced company from Yugoslavia. Alkis Raftis said that "there were two factors that fortunately prevented this: first, I credit Roderyk Lange, the dean of European folk dance research. He convinced Dora Stratou that Greek folk dances would never lend themselves to the kind of spectacle as [did] dances from the Slavic countries. Second, Dora Stratou did not want a choreographer whose name would be featured with her own and vying with her for the spotlight. This dance theater was to be her life's contribution to Greece and Greek theater" (personal interview, February 2, 2000).

Thus the unique system that characterizes the Dora Stratou Greek Dances Theatre was developed. Within this system there is no choreographer and no artistic director per se. Lead dancers, self-appointed on the basis of length of service, lead each regional section represented in the program. In case of disputes between these leaders, Dora Stratou mediated and made the final decision concerning performances, and she always retained the final word in any issue concerning the company. "She was known as a charismatic leader who wrapped herself in the myth of research but was in fact unable to conduct research herself. She was rumored to have said to company members, 'Go get the dances; go get the costumes'" (Raftis, personal interview, February 10, 2000). Former Stratou dancer Athan Karras stated, "People have the mistaken idea that Dora Stratou was the Anna Pavlova of Greece. She could not even dance" (personal interview, April 27, 2000).

The system established under her direction still prevails in the company. George Mavropoulos, as the most senior dancer, decides on the personnel and their disposition in each number, the selection of regions to be represented in a performance, the duration of each dance within a regional grouping, and other details of the performance. Mavropoulos says:

> While the dances are not choreographed, the company must still be aware of the audience. For example, in the couple dances the pairs are arranged vertically so that the audience can see them better. I arrange the dances into sequences to represent a region well. I select the dancers for each suite based on their skills in the particular regional style. I

prefer shorter dancers for the *ballos*. I also decide on the length of a dance, three to three and a half minutes is the best length, but I don't "cut the dances in pieces." It must follow village practice. I like to start the program easy to bring the audience into the mood. I create a varied program, and I try to see it through the eyes of the audience. Programs depend on the dancers we have. We are not Moiseyev with highly trained professional dancers. We start with dancers who are beginners and generally have little connection with villages. It takes much dedication to be a dancer in the company with our schedule and the amount of dances to be learned, but we always manage to find good young dancers. The most important ingredient in our performances is the relationship among the performers. (Personal interview, February 7, 2000)

I asked Mavropoulos how the dancers know when to change figures. He said that "they must follow the music and learn from the older dancers. If the musicians make a mistake, just as in the village, the dancers must then depend on following the lead dancer who might call *'opa'* or wave a scarf to signal any changes" (personal interview, February 9, 2000).

Dr. Alkis Raftis, as the current board president and the individual who directs the ethnographic research conducted by ethnographers and company members, gives final input regarding the correctness of the music and dances. There is a constant striving for an ever-elusive authenticity. This authenticity, or "fidelity" as he terms it, is elusive because the company members are urban dancers attempting to emulate the rural dancers of half a century ago. Also, they must master a number of regional styles, which prevents the total mastery of any single style. Whenever possible villagers from a particular region are invited to dance with the company. He envisions the Dora Stratou company "as an instrument to record and represent village life in the best possible way. It is to serve and defend village culture" (personal interview, February 6, 2000).

Two informants, who asked to remain anonymous, stated that while Dora Stratou indeed created and shaped the company, she also had a dark side:

She was authoritative and vulgar and ran the company with an iron hand. She knew nothing of folklore and could not dance. She used the threat of firing company members at a time when unemployment was so high in Greece that no one dared cross her. While touring in Switzerland, ten company members defected. Stratou was so enraged she

Dora Stratou Greek Dance Theatre. *Dance from Episkopi Imathias.* COURTESY GREEK DANCES THEATRE.

called the Swiss authorities and had the unfortunate members deported. (Personal interviews, February 2000)

According to Alkis Raftis,

> Whatever mistakes she made, the company was to serve as her contribution to Greek society and we follow the system that was established under her direction. She wrote three books trying to connect contemporary folk dances with those of Ancient Greece. She was in a long line of individuals who tried to make that connection. While scholars scoffed at her books, in fact due to the worship of Ancient Greece at that time, it made good sense. Villages had become equated with everything negative, so linking the dances with the ancient past was a successful strategy in garnering government support. Claiming links and direct similarity to Ancient Greek dances may seem silly now, and it was a notion that I have opposed for many years, but in her time it was the only means of keeping the company alive. (Personal interview, February 16, 2000)

Given the impossibility and futile efforts of assigning historical origins to every aspect of folk life from music and dance to embroidery designs and cuts of clothing, it is the efforts of the Greek establishment to do so that must draw one's attention.

The Torch Passes: Alkis Raftis

When Alkis Raftis took over the leadership of the Dora Stratou Greek Dances Theatre in 1987, the ensemble was in deep trouble on a number of levels. It was more than a million dollars in debt, there were no financial records kept during the preceding thirty years outside of vague notes used as receipts, and company morale had plummeted. Raftis spent the next decade rebuilding the company's finances and morale. The offices were unused during Stratou's tenure, and everyone was idle during the seven months when the company was not performing. Now it is a beehive of activity, and the company's educational programs occupy the fallow period of the year when the company is not performing.

Alkis Raftis likes the company's performance philosophy and the way the company performs. Every attempt is made, although according to Raftis never to be fully achieved, to follow and emulate as closely as possible village practices and styling. He states clearly that a complete replication is not possible. He makes the distinction between what he terms "traditional dancing," that which the villagers did in their own natural environment, and "folk dancing," which is what the Dora Stratou company and all other performing folk dance companies do. Folk dancing is performed by urban individuals who attempt to emulate traditional dancing, but they can never achieve the actual tradition that serves as their model.

He calls the Dora Stratou Greek Dances Theatre a "living museum" on a number of levels. It is devoted to the use of dance to evoke a golden age of village life in Greece, just prior to World War II. Raftis characterizes this period as a time when dancing was an organic part of village life. The dances reflect the closeness, warmth, family solidarity, and security that he thinks characterized village existence until World War II. In Raftis's view, contemporary urban dwellers, living in an alienated environment, have much to learn and adapt from the life of those villagers. He opposes the idea of a museum that is a passive place where the dead hand of history is on display. His museum is proactive, like the best museums. In his view productive museums educate. He founded and runs extensive cultural outreach projects and educational programs that form a vital part of the company's activities. He ardently oversees and carefully nurtures an intensive research program in which he has sent a legion of capable researchers, particularly natives of a specific region, to document all aspects of the life that the dances in the repertoire represent. These activities include conferences, classes, workshops, and publications. He says that his own contributions to the performances have been minor, mostly corrections brought about by the material found during his research.

The impact of the Dora Stratou Greek Dances Theatre on performing companies in Greece has been enormous. Raftis claims that there are four thousand performing companies in Greece (1999, 296), and most of them, including those of the prestigious groups of the Lyceum of Greek Women, follow the Stratou model of performance (personal communication, April 30, 2000).

Repertoire

The company repertoire represents eighty regions of Greece. These were constituted during the tenure of Dora Stratou—products of her time. There are curious gaps, such as very few dances from the Dodecanese Islands, which Alkis Raftis shakes his head over. "I do not understand the reason for this lack; perhaps Dora Stratou did not like their dances for some reason" (personal interview, February 6, 2000).

Raftis also states flatly that "there has never been minority representation in the repertoire. Dora Stratou avoided any non-Greek-speaking ethnic groups' dances" (personal interview, February 7, 2000). In his research projects, Raftis supports the continuance of tradition not only among Greeks, but also among a wide variety of largely submerged minority cultures. He brings minority groups to participate in workshops and festivals. This is a singular act of bravery in a nation where a few years ago a group of Greeks whose families had come from Cappadoccia (in present-day Turkey) were dragged off the stage for singing in Turkish. He is enthusiastic about bringing a group of Muslims from Thrace and Western Greece who practice Sufi rituals to perform in Athens in the future. He hopes that through such efforts the Greek public will come to accept minorities in their midst and value their cultural contributions to the national life.

The repertoire reflects, to the best of the company's collective ability, the dancing of fifty years ago when it was a living tradition. With current funding there is no possibility of adding new works to the repertoire in the near future.

Dancers and Dance Training

The ensemble has fifty dancers, twenty-five men and twenty-five women. New dancers come from all over Greece to join the company. They begin rehearsals in January with some of the senior dancers. At this time they are not taught in any formal way, but only to attempt to dance like the senior dancers as closely as they are able. Sometimes they will ask an older dancer to show them in detail a particularly difficult step, but there is no formal class setting such as one finds in the Ballet Folklorico or the Turkish State Folk Dance Ensemble. By April when the full company gathers to rehearse, the selection is made to fill any vacant positions. The performing season lasts from May through September (the tourist season) and the dancers perform every day with only one day a week break during this period.

One of Raftis's strategies to rebuild the morale of the company was to create the closeness of village life among his dancers and musicians through a bonding process. The aim is for the company members to reproduce a village in miniature. Marriages take place among the members, and family members of the performers are encouraged to volunteer at various company tasks and attend rehearsals. Often several generations of a family perform in the musical and dance groups. Raftis feels strongly that this closeness is reflected on the stage and brings to the audience something of the joy and depth that characterized village life before World War II. In this way Dora Stratou company performances have a unique element that transcends other types of professional dance performances.

There is great stress placed on seniority, which generally bequeaths the aura of knowledge. Senior members lead the dances and acquire the respect that confers the right to criticize. The leading of dances by senior dancers is an element of performance that reflects village tradition, where the dance leader is always the most important figure in the dance and performs special improvised figures. For the women seniority means the perquisite of choosing the best costumes and jewelry. Unlike other companies, such as Ballet Folklorico where the emphasis is on youthful dancers, the senior members of the Dora Stratou Greek Dances Theatre are the most valued members of the company. They are secure in the knowledge that as in the village, they will not be displaced by younger, more athletic dancers, a not uncommon practice in other professional dance ensembles.

Music

As with all other aspects of performance, the greatest fidelity to original village music is the company's goal. George Mavropoulos stated, "One of my greatest concerns is that the music must be alive and have soul. I cannot dance when the music is poor or without feeling. It is a constant problem to prevent the musicians from taking shortcuts or interpolating modern elements into the music" (personal interview, February 7, 2000). The musicians usually master several instruments, and only authentic instruments are employed in performances.

It is in the lyrics that non-Greek identity was first erased from the company repertoire. Alkis Raftis said, "Many dances have vocal accompaniment. Imagine when it was discovered that many of the songs were in Turkish, Albanian, Bulgarian, and Vlach (Rumanian) languages. In my research I found all these facts about old songs in non-Greek languages. A dilemma: How to deal with this. The Theatre would be doomed! It was decided to replace all of those songs with instrumental music" (personal interview, February 18, 2000).

Costumes

As has been mentioned, the Dora Stratou Greek Dances Theatre uses only authentic village costumes. According to Raftis, "One of the signs of the passing of old village life was when the older women in the village sold precious heirlooms to the Dora Stratou Theatre when they realized that their daughters, granddaughters, and nieces had no more interest in the old costumes." The company's costume holdings amount to a collection of museum quality and it takes constant upkeep to make certain that the costumes are kept in top shape. There are publications by the company (Raftis 1993) featuring photographs of the costumes. In addition, as part of their educational activities, the company has produced a video series on how to tie the intricate headpieces, one of the most difficult aspects of learning how to wear the traditional clothing correctly.

Finances

The company receives state support through the Ministry of Culture and the Greek National Tourism Organization as well as through gate receipts from the performances. In addition, the company has the use of a building for its offices and wardrobe as well as the spectacular outdoor theater on Philopappou Hill. One of the most frustrating aspects of administering the company is working with the government. Every year a battle is enjoined in order to have the scarce allotted funds transferred to the company's account in a timely manner. "On the surface, politicians declare their love for folk art and that they will save the Dora Stratou Theatre, but then no money is ever forthcoming" (Raftis, personal interview, February 10, 2000).

The Greek Diaspora

As I mentioned earlier, due to the chronic impoverished state of Greece, emigration had been high. Many immigrants came to the United States from the Peloponnese in southern mainland Greece due to the widespread destruction of the vineyards from plant disease. More than a million people in the United States claim Greek ancestry, while large numbers of immigrants are also to be found in Canada and Australia as well as Western Europe. In the United States and other countries such as Australia, dance functioned as one of the main forms of ethnic expression for the Greek communities in their new lands (Bottomley 1987). Because the Greeks, like so many other immigrants, came from many different regions at different times, they did not perform specific regional dances from specific villages and regions. In order to duplicate Old World dances, one must have a critical mass of individuals knowledgeable in a particular dance tradition. As a result, the Greeks began to dance a few dances known to the earliest immigrants, such as the *syrto, karslimas, tsamiko, hasapiko serviko,* and *kalamatiano.* These few dances are "largely those originating in the southern mainland, the Peloponnese, the first area liberated from the Turks—which were imposed throughout the country. These dances are mostly known as the pan-Hellenic dances" (Loutzaki 1992, 71) and formed the major dance expressions for decades. Immigrant orchestras had a large repertoire of songs to accompany these dances to play at Greek family and church dance events (Sam Chianis, personal interview, February 21, 2000). In large port cities such as Los Angeles, San Francisco, and New York, where Greek sailors regularly called, tavernas catering to them and recent immigrants (men only for many years), had different orchestras playing the rebetika/taverna repertoire of *zeybekikos, tsifte-telli, karslimas,* and *hasapikos.* Vilma Matchette, long-time observer of the Greek immigrant community in California, notes that "the taverna dances were done in the 1940s but in the homes of Anatolian Greeks. They did not come into the general repertoire of the Greek community until the film *Never on Sunday* and later *Zorba*" (personal communication, April 26, 2000).

In the early 1960s non-Greek folk dancers and individuals brought by Greek friends began to participate in Greek community dance events. One of the first books on Greek dances for folk dancers, *Folk Dances of the Greeks* (Petrides and Petrides 1961), largely reflects this repertoire. By the 1960s a few Greek Americans and folk dancers began to discover the diversity of regional folk dances, many through the performances of the Dora Stratou Greek Dances Theatre in Athens. Instructors such as Rickey Holden, Mary Vouras, George and Vilma Matchette, and Athan Karras—a charismatic teacher who had performed in the Dora Stratou company during 1954–1955—began to hold classes to show the wider repertoire of Greek dances. In the early 1960s Karras produced and directed two performances in the Bay Area that greatly influenced the Greek community as well as recreational folk dancers. Performance groups, largely non-Greek, began to perform some of these regional dances outside of the older repertoire.

Within the Greek community itself, however, most individuals clung to the older representation of dances and costumes. Unlike the Mexican-American community of the American Southwest, the Greek community was not galvanized within a short time by a brief tour of the Dora Stratou company in 1953. As Athan Karras said, "The Greeks here clung to those costumes because of their urban and royal representations. They regarded the regional costumes as *vlachi* [a code word for bumpkin or peasant]. In the 1950s I was bodily thrown out of a Greek church for teaching other dances, and the priest said I was trying to turn their youth into a bunch of vlachi" (personal interview, April 27, 2000). A few Greek Americans who were excited by the discovery of this diversity in Greek culture tried to educate others in the community through writing articles and holding workshops. But even as late as the early 1980s they found it hard going convincing their fellow community members that dances and costumes outside of the older repertoire were "truly Greek" (Kathy Politopoulos, personal interviews, May 15-17, 1994).

In the 1980s, Peter Preovolos, inspired by the performances that Athan Karras had directed, began the Folk Dance Festival for Greek Youth (FDF). The Greek Orthodox Church in California, in an effort to inspire ethnic pride in its youth, quickly joined in the project; they hold an annual festival of Greek folk dance competitions with experts, both Greek and non-Greek, in the fields of dance and costumes to judge and award prizes. This movement has inspired interest throughout the Greek-American community and is growing (Bloland 1992). The Dora Stratou Greek Dances Theatre is now a center for providing educational materials and advice to these groups.

Alkis Raftis is aware of about one thousand Greek dance groups outside of Greece. He was an honored guest at the annual Greek Youth Folk Dance Festival in Seattle in 1995. He expressed amazement at the amount and sophistication of Greek folk dance activity in the diaspora (personal interview, February 17, 2000). The company's performances, via live audiences and videotapes, provide a model for these diaspora communities, as well as non-Greek performing groups that are interested in Greek folk dances.

The Dora Stratou Greek Dances Theatre is a unique folk ensemble among the world's professional folk dance companies. It is a professional state-supported institution, and yet it is the only national company that has no choreographers, no artistic director, no stars, and no artists. As Raftis states, "Artists belong to a city; a village has only artisans, at best. Artists are supposed to have inspiration and creativity, while craftsmen simply possess the techniques of their craft" (2000, 5). In its performances the ensemble attempts to follow village models, and yet small adjustments for theatrical purposes must be made. For example, a dance that can last a half-hour in the village must be reduced to a few minutes for stage purposes. The neat male-female alternation of the line dances are not an actual reflection of village practices. The company performs several dances from a specific region in the style of a suite, and they follow one another in a manner alien to most villages where the dancers would take a rest between longer dance selections. They are better rehearsed than any village would ever be, and there are no poor or mediocre dancers such as one would encounter in a village. Also gone are the elderly and the children, although many of the finest performers in the company are middle-aged. In many ways a typical Dora Stratou Greek Dances Theatre performance is a distillation of the finest dance and musical artistry to be found in a dozen village settings, all presented in a single evening's performance.

This company is the closest to original village performances on the scale that I presented in chapter one. In many ways, the Dora Stratou Greek Dances Theatre performances are closer to some of the dancing in the field than some dancing seen in villages today. This is due to the fact that village groups in many areas of the world borrow and introduce theatrical elements from national companies to make their dance performances "more interesting," while the Stratou company omits any spectacularization that it consider false.

The main audiences for Dora Stratou Greek Dances Theatre performances are tourists who are more interested in the authentic folk dances of Greece than the Greeks. "The elite are interested only in Western art forms. They regard peasant dances as beneath them. The newspapers do not review either our performances or the company's publications" (Alkis Raftis, personal interview, February 15, 2000). As in many countries, it would seem that the population for whom this "living museum" was intended ignores its riches.

Among the many fields of representation in Greece, one of the most important is Greek concern with how Greece is represented to foreigners. The Ministry of Tourism endorses the Dora Stratou Greek Dances Theatre as the official mode of representation of Greece to the outside world. The touristy dance groups in the tavernas of the Plaka "are also seen as marginal to the traditional dances performed, for example, by the Lyceum Club of Greek Women or the Theatre of Dora Stratou, which, in the official state discourse, represent Greek national dance (personal communication, from the Ministry of Tourism)" (Gore and Koutsouba 1992, 31).

Although the company's performance styles and format were set during Dora Stratou's period, the company is in a subtle way now very much the creation, or perhaps recreation, of Alkis Raftis (Raftis 2000). It reflects his philosophy of the "living museum" and of always striving to attain performances faithfully reflective of the golden age of village life in Greece. Raftis epitomizes his fundamental difference with Stratou in one sentence: "She cared for theater but not for villages; I care for villages but not for theater" (personal interview, February 6, 2000). While this statement appears as a stark contrast in directorial and philosophical styles, it has had no impact in the manner of company performances or what the public sees.

Thus, while the repertoire has been little altered, the change of directors from Dora Stratou to Alkis Raftis has greatly changed the philosophical perspective and atmosphere in which the company operates. The company has evolved from the naked passion and ambition of a powerful woman bent on making her mark in Greek society to love of Greek peasant culture and behavior by a scholar who saved a drowning venture.

8

Turkish State Folk Dance Ensemble: The Last of the Great Ensembles

As I entered the spacious, well-lighted rehearsal hall of the Turkish State Folk Dance Ensemble *(Turk Devlet Halk Danslari Toplugu)* in the massive Ataturk Cultural Center in the heart of Ankara, a wave of nostalgia swept over me. I felt that the end of this journey of discovery had come full circle. Groups of men and women in rehearsal clothes, familiar to anyone in the world of professional and amateur folk dance companies, stood chatting and warming up as musicians tuned their instruments. I had walked into an environment that I had known and operated in for more than forty years and that stretched across four continents and hundreds of dance companies. I had come halfway across the world to a strange city, but the rehearsal hall might have been around the block from my own house. The gleaming, well-kept wooden floors, the barre, and the mirrors all proclaimed a prosperous dance environment. The dancers, apart from new faces, were as familiar as those in my own company and those whom I had encountered in Cairo, Zagreb, Sofia, New Orleans, Minneapolis, and Mexico City.

Today's rehearsal was a little out of the ordinary for the ensemble. In addition to the fifteen-piece orchestra of folk instruments that normally accompany the ensemble's performances, a small military band of thirty musicians directed by Col. Albay Metin Arbak, the conductor of the state military band of the Turkish Army, was set up in the corner of the large hall to rehearse with the dance ensemble. The two ensembles had joined forces, temporarily, to prepare for the celebration of the birthday of the famous Turkish composer, Cemal Erkin. In fact, the performance was being readied for celebrating Turkishness and Turkish culture, the raison d'être of the Turkish State Folk Dance Ensemble. The music was a symphonic suite arranged for a combination of military or concert band and folk instruments. One of the ensemble's resident choreographers, Senasi Pala, had created a choreography to give movement to the music. The musical themes and steps and movements were Turkish, but conceptually the arrangement and the choreographic and musical structure of the piece were thoroughly Western. In this manner the choreography and the musical arrangement were compatible with the notions of Turkish modernity as set forth by Kemal Ataturk (1881–1938), the founding father and first president of the Turkish Republic, and Ziya Gokalp (1876–1924), the principal ideologue of Turkish nationalism. In their view the core of the solution for the myriad economic and social problems confronting the new state of Turkey was to embrace the West, while remaining Turkish.

Ethnomusicologist Martin Stokes states that for music "this was to be achieved through a synthesis of Turkish folk music and the musical techniques of Western civilization" (1992, 33). I would extend that observation to include dance.

Several times the company ran through the choreography, a work incorporating steps and movements from a variety of regions covering all of the major Turkish choreographic regions, well-known to observers of Turkish folk dancing. In this way the work comprised a suite, a choreographic form that incorporates a wide variety of possible dances, movements, and steps from a particular region. The suite I observed included dances drawn from the major ethnographic regions of the entire national territory of the Turkish state.

My genial host, Mustafa Turan, founder and artistic director of the Turkish State Folk Dance Ensemble since its official inception in 1975, is a stylishly dressed, highly personable man in his late fifties and the only individual in the field of Turkish folk dance to be named State Artist of Turkey. He was born in Elazig in Eastern Turkey and attended the University of Ankara where he took his degree in journalism. He has been dancing and involved in folk dance companies, both as dancer and researcher, since the age of eight years.

As the rehearsal progressed, he and the director of the military band, speaking in undertones that accompanied the music, kindly provided me with the factual material that made meaningful the rehearsal that was unfolding before my eyes. Although the conversations were in Turkish, nothing about the rehearsal was unfamiliar except the piece itself. I soon understood that in keeping with the modernity promoted by the Turkish state, this work constituted an "advancement" on the choreographies that form the bulk of the repertoire of the Turkish State Folk Dance Ensemble. That repertoire is built primarily on suites of regional dances that come from the entire territory of Turkey. This new choreography was designed to provide an overview of Turkish dance within a few minutes, a sort of synthesis of the company's regular repertoire.

Later I attended a performance of the company's regular repertoire, an engaging evening consisting primarily of regional folk dances, professionally prepared and performed by this excellent company of seventy-five performers. The evening passed in a blaze of primary colors in front of the ensemble's one stage decoration, a large circular hanging medallion with decorative Turkish folk motifs that serves as the company logo suspended from the back curtain above the dancers.

The men's dances from Trabazon, on the Black Sea, represents a typical choreography of the company's more traditional repertoire. In this series of dances, seamlessly performed in a single line by a group of nine men dressed in white shirts with black headscarves, vests, full seated pants, soft long boots, and chains and fancy metal-and-leather belts appended to the chest and waist, the formation of the line never altered except to move forward or backward, and to squat. The dancers in this choreography performed a highly polished version of the dance in the field with dozens of intricate foot patterns, twists of the torso, and shoulder shaking that resulted in a shimmering series of precise quivers of the body in an overwhelmingly masculine style.

The women's performance of the *Ciftetelli* stands in polar contrast. In this large-scale dance, sophisticated choreographic procedures rely heavily on formal geometric figures rather than a variety of steps. Shaking their shoulder demurely throughout the piece, the women open the choreography in lines facing the front of the stage. At a leisurely pace they form two concentric circles moving counterclockwise around the stage. As each pair reaches the back of the stage they move down the center and split into two halves, forming a large semicircle, and sit as a soloist in a contrasting color of costume appears in center stage and steps through the space where the semicircle of dancers meet. This version is not a true belly dance. In spite of the gentle shaking of the shoulders and lifts of the hip, the midriffs are covered and the dance thoroughly sanitized; the soloist and corps draw their movements as much from ballet as the earthy, professional versions of the *ciftetelli*. The soloist points her toes and lifts her leg high in balletic poses never seen in the original dance, which is a solo-improvised dance. The corps rises and with the soloist continues to perform the geometric figures that give the dance its choreographic interest. The company orchestra changes tempo and melody several times during the dance.

As I left the rehearsal hall and passed along the long walkway back to the street a half a mile away, I saw several poor people bent over picking greens for food from the huge untended grounds surrounding the monumental Ataturk Cultural Center. As I turned and looked at

196 CHOREOGRAPHIC POLITICS

Turkish State Folk Dance Ensemble. *Ciftetelli*. COURTESY MUSTAFA TURAN.

the huge white pyramidal modern building, set in the midst of a vast field with walkways that were falling into decay, it symbolized for me the Kemalist modernist dream for Turkey.[1] Kemalism is the term, named for Mustafa Kemal, later Kemal Ataturk ("father of Turkey") that signifies the guiding principles upon which the Turkish state has operated since its founding in 1923. The dream, like the building and the surrounding grounds, was both unfinished and flawed. It was a dream realized by many, but one that was still out of reach for a significant portion of the population, occupying extensive shanty towns *(gecekondu)* that stretch for miles around Istanbul, Ankara, and countless villages, especially in the eastern half of the country. Kemalism and its successes and failures form a crucial part of the national discourse, and Kemalism proceeds from the nationalist structure created by individuals of the pioneering elite of the infant Turkish state, created in 1923 from the ashes of the Ottoman Empire. Thus, in order to understand the structure and repertoire of the Turkish State Folk

Dance Ensemble, it will be useful to look closely at Turkish nationalism, or Turkism, which the company embodies on a variety of levels.

Theories of Nationalism

The field of nationalism is clamorous with competing theoretical frameworks and models. Unfortunately, few of them can fully account for the very unique and specific way in which Turkish nationalism was created. Most of the theoretical works on nationalism attempt universal frameworks with unifying elements such as literacy and industrialism in which to cast the phenomenon of nationalism, often based on Western European models. This permits theoretical gaps to occur that evade empirical evidence for states such as Turkey, where the population was less than 10 percent literate and virtually no industrial activity occurred at the time that the state came into existence and nationalism was created and developed.

By far the most widespread theory, or perhaps better expressed as a collection of theories, is what Anthony D. Smith calls the "modernist theory" of nationalism.[2] Nationalist scholars such as Gellner (1983), Anderson (1991), Brass (1991), and Hobsbawm (1990, 1994), among others, represent this modernist group. Smith observes that "the differences between their analyses are, in fact, less important than their shared basic commitment to 'modernism'" (1995, 165, n.13).

Briefly, modernist theory argues that nations and nationalism are modern phenomena created in the nineteenth and early twentieth centuries. These writers, generally, treat nations and nationalisms as "products of the specifically modern conditions of capitalism, industrialism, bureaucracy, mass communications and secularism" (Smith 1995, 29). However, Turkey, as I stated above, was overwhelmingly agrarian and illiterate.

Ernest Gellner, a major figure in nationalist studies, claims that nationalism arose from the needs of industrialized societies to create a labor force that was well educated and prepared to serve the needs of the burgeoning economy. The state, which used nationalism as its cement, was the only organization with sufficient size and resources to create a modern state education system. In order to create such a system, what Gellner terms a "high culture" of standardized language for purposes of communication had to be developed. The work force had to be highly educated, mobile, egalitarian, and interchangeable, and only a modern state had the organizational apparatus to create an effective system suitable to the needs of industry. He states,

"Nationalism is rooted in a *certain kind* of division of labour, one which is complex and persistently, cumulatively changing. High productivity, as Adam Smith insisted so much, requires a complex and refined division of labour" (Gellner 1983, 24; emphasis in original).

Another aspect of modernist theories is that it is elite groups that create and spread nationalism among other elements of the population through the state educational system, the media, literature, and other communication systems. Combining several of these ideas together in a recent work on nationalism, Paul R. Brass states that

> Two central arguments run through the volume. The first is that ethnicity and national are not "givens," but social and political constructions. They are creations of elites, who draw upon, distort, and sometimes fabricate materials from the cultures of the groups they wish to represent in order to protect their well-being or existence or to gain political and economic advantage for their groups as well as for themselves. The second argument is that ethnicity and nationalism are modern phenomena inseparably connected with the activities of the modern centralizing state. (1991, 8)

As Gellner states, "Contrary to popular and even scholarly belief, nationalism does not have any very deep roots in the human psyche" (1983, 33). I wish to discuss several aspects of these statements and show how these models fail to account for the elements of nationalism that exist in two neighboring nations. For example, Turkish nationalism does not have deep roots, while Iranian identity, the basis for Iranian nationalism, has very deep roots.

I find three aspects of modernist theories to be problematic for the understanding of the phenomena of nationalism in Turkey and Iran. Anthony D. Smith points out two of these aspects. The first is that Gellner and other authors ignore historical evidence of nationalist, or perhaps protonationalist, sentiments before the French Revolution, the date usually cited by scholars who espouse modernist theories as the beginning of nationalism (Smith 1995, 39). While I recognize that nationalism is a dynamic process and that modern nationalism in Turkey and Iran today is not what it was in the 1960s or 1970s, and certainly not at the turn of the twentieth century, I disagree with Brass that ethnic identity is a modern phenomenon. In the Iranian case, but not the Turkish case, as I will demonstrate, a powerful national and "patriotic" sentiment existed from which modern nationalism grew.

The second problem concerns the antecedents of nationalism. Many of these writers treat nationalism as if it were an "invented tradition," in Hobsbawm's terms (Hobsbawm and Ranger 1983). But the case of Yugoslavia demonstrates how impossible it is to attempt to create a new nationalism where nationalist sentiment and identity did not previously exist. However much Tito attempted to create a new idealistic Yugoslav nationalism and Yugoslav identity, he failed because neither the elite nor the general population was sufficiently committed to this invented tradition. Rather, the general population and the majority of its elites clung to their earlier identities and accompanying antagonisms of Croat, Serb, Slovene, and Muslim others. Uganda and Rwanda, among other countries in Africa, manifest similar ethnic dysfunction. Nationalism does not spring like Minerva from the head of Zeus in some magical fashion. In contrast to Brass's statement quoted earlier, I see nationalism as proceeding from some very real preexisting sense of ethnic identity.

The third problem that I find with virtually all of the writers in the field of nationalism is the emphasis they place on standardized languages and literacy as an aspect of nationalism. Oral tradition, as folklorists are able to demonstrate, is often as powerful a communication tool as the written word in various societies and in different historical periods. As was true of many medieval and Renaissance individuals for whom memory was the "palace of the mind," nonliterate and illiterate people in a wide spectrum of societies are capable of memorizing and reciting entire histories. The presence of an oral tradition spread by professional bards can have a powerful influence on the development of nationalism.

Eickelman points out another interesting aspect, that "Islam is one of the basic 'bricks' in Gellner's political thought." Like many other theorists, Gellner "preferred the single, society, to the plural, societies, in writing about Islam because he regarded Islam as a faith as imposing 'essential' constraints on the conduct and thought of those committed to it" (1998, 258). However, closer examination reveals many Islams throughout the Middle East and other parts of the Islamic world that stretches from the Atlantic Ocean to Indonesia. More to the point, it is a reductionist and orientalist stance to characterize Muslim societies as if they are all alike, and within that sameness that every member of those societies is equally committed to the tenets of religion. I agree with Craig Calhoun who states, "We cannot really stop thinking at least partially in categories—and therefore in at least something rather like an essentialist manner" (1994, 19). What I am suggesting is that it is not useful to think in a grand "Islamic" category that conceals the nuances of ethnic and social divisions, politics, and history that characterize that term.

Two neighboring contemporary states with overwhelmingly Muslim populations, Turkey and Iran, both have strong nationalist sentiments and movements. They have taken separate paths in their respective nationalisms, with highly different results. These results are manifest in the performances of their respective national folk dance companies. To demonstrate how different the nationalist paths of these two states are, I will compare and contrast the nationalist elements and development in each. While Gellner's theory of nationalism, as well as those of others in the modernist camp, correctly characterize several aspects of Turkish and Iranian nationalism, they also contain serious shortcomings and flaws when applied to these specific nationalisms. Although this book is not concerned with addressing all of the possible elements of nationalist theory, I will comment on those aspects that pertain to Turkish and Iranian nationalism.

In the studies of the various nationalisms in the Middle East, perhaps the most egregious and justifiably criticized theoretical model is the one created by Samuel Huntington, which posits a sweeping regionally and religiously based model of the world.[3] Within this model, among eight other general categories, he proposes a category of "culture-Arab," "religion-Islam," and "region-Middle East, North Africa" (Huntington 1990; see also Davison 1998, 23). Any student of Middle Eastern history and politics is aware that nationalism in the Middle East has taken several diverse paths and was created or developed in different ways. Even the casual observer can quickly see the difference between what I call "created" states such as Jordan, Iraq, Tajikistan, and Kuwait, successor states of the Ottoman Empire or the former Soviet Union, and historical states such as Iran. The created states have no history as independent states or regions, and they differ radically in their creation by the Russian, French, and English colonial powers.[4] Nationalism in these states is truly a created tradition, while, by contrast, Iranian nationalism proceeded from a long historical sense of ethnic identity.

Iranian Nationalism

In the case of Iran, prior to the advent of modern nationalism, a powerful sense of ethnic identity existed that is manifest in the poetic recitation of the national epic. The characteristics of Iranian identity are abundantly manifest in Ferdowsi's *Shahnameh*, the epic history, completed in A.D. 1010, of Iran from creation until the Arab conquest in A.D. 650. Ferdowsi gathered and set in his own unique poetic style tales that had been staples for bards during at least the Sasanian period (A.D. 224–634), if not before. It has been spread both in the written and oral form by bards who recite this history in vivid story-telling sessions. The dramatic recitation of the *Shahnameh* known in Persian as *shah-nameh khani* often takes two to three years. It formed one of the major entertainments in male gatherings in castles and coffeehouses throughout the Persian-speaking world. Men returned night after night to hear the beloved stories, with which everyone was familiar, told by storytellers of immense histrionic ability. "'It was and is sung before battle, recited in villages, tribes, coffee houses, community centers'" (Issa Sadiq, qtd. in Cottam 1979, 27). This practice still occurs in California in the Iranian-American community where storytellers continue to celebrate Iranian patriotism through the telling of these tales. This demonstrates how powerful the nationalist sentiments of Iranian identity are.

Scholars who come from societies in which the written word is paramount often have difficulty in understanding the power of oral tradition. Individuals in oral traditions are often capable of memorizing prodigious amounts of information. Roy Mottahedeh, who clearly holds the bias of the supremacy of the written word over the oral, suggests that this Iranian identity may only have been shared by the elite. He stresses "that we are talking only about educated Iranians who could record their opinions, not about peasants whose feelings of group identity are lost to history" (1976, 181). In contrast, I suggest that the longstanding oral story-telling tradition of *naqqali* and *shah-nameh khani* appealed to large audiences of individuals who could not read and write but, nevertheless, were intimately familiar with the *Shahnameh*, often memorizing it.[5] "Many Iranians who cannot sign their names can quote at length from this great literature" (Cottam 1979, 28). But, one can identify this articulation of Iranian identity through the bardic tradition that spans more than a thousand years. In part this meant attachment to and the protection of "Eranshahr," the land of Iran. The images of the glory and honor of the royal leaders of Iran were so powerful that subsequent non-Iranian (usually Turkish) dynasties that ruled Iranian lands adopted the *Shahnameh* as an icon and attempted to cast themselves as a continuation of its historical tradition.

Thus, in the Iranian world the pre-Islamic Iranian identity was embedded in an Islamic identity and the two were often in tension. The Pahlavis followed this tradition of identifying with the glories of pre-Islamic Iran through the wide use of pre-Islamic symbols, culminating in the coronation of Shah Mohammad Reza Pahlavi at Persepolis, the capital of the Aechamenid Empire. The Pahlavis were perceived by the ulema as elevating the pre-Islamic values encoded in the *Shahnameh* above Islamic ones, and this constituted one of the reasons for the Islamic Revolution of 1979.

This literary expression of Iranian identity was by no means confined to Ferdowsi. Subsequent poets such as Rumi, who refers to *parsiya-ye mara*, "my Persianess" (Shiva 1995, 58), and Hafez, among others, also contrast their Iranian identities to those of Turks and Arabs (Hafez 1994, 75).

A second early and less familiar literary phenomenon that sparked an articulation of Iranian identity occurred after the Islamic conquest. Known as the *shu'ubiyah* controversy, this consisted of a hostile literary exchange that lasted through the first three centuries after Islam (A.D. 650–950). During this period the Iranians had been treated as a second-class group by the Arabs (Zarinkub 1975). In the *shu'ubiyah* certain Iranian individuals, particularly recent converts (*mawwal*) to Islam, who resented their inferior status vis-à-vis the Arabs, began a literary polemic glorifying and articulating their unique Iranian heritage in contrast to the Arabs' tribal origins.

The recognition of a specific Iranian identity, at least by some elements of the population, dates back to at least the beginning of the first millennium. Bruce Lincoln cites a passage from the Middle Persian (Sasanian era) apocalyptic epic, the *Jamasp Namag:* "All Iran falls to the hand of the enemy, and Iranian and non-Iranian mix together such that non-Iranian-ness is indistinguishable from Iranian-ness, and Iranian becomes like non-Iranian" (1989, 43). Richard W. Cottam states that "the roots of nationalism, of course, extend into the extraordinarily rich Iranian civilization down to and beyond the Achemenid period (550–330 B.C.)" (1979, 11).

The veneration and recognition of their long history is expressed in the programs and performances of the Iranian National Folk Dance Company, which, among its regional representation of folk dances, included several historical reconstructions of dances from different periods. I am not concerned here with the accuracy or success of these reconstructions, but with the impetus that caused them to be created.

I have laid out this evidence for a sense of Iranian identity to delineate its great historical depth in contrast with that of Turkey, which I cover in the next section. The importance of this identity formation in the case of Iran is crucial in the way that the modern nation-state regards what constitutes "Iranian." This nationalist construction dictates the relationship between the Persians who are the core *ethnie* (the French term for an ethnic group used in studies of nationalism), who comprise no more than 50 percent of the population of Iran, and the non-Persians. The other half of the population consists of a myriad of linguistic and religious minorities, all of whom are considered Iranian by the state. This includes Azerbaijanis, Turkoman, Qashqa'i, and other Turkic-speaking groups; Iranian-language groups such as the Kurds, Baluchis, Gilakis, and Mazanderanis; Arabs along the Persian Gulf and the province of Khuzistan; and Armenians, Assyrians, Zoroastrians, and Jews.[6]

In spite of this diversity, the vast majority of the entire population, whatever an individual's background, take great pride in the Persian language and Persian literature. "The educated Iranian's great pride in the Persian language does much to offset the problem of diversity" (Cottam 1979, 32).

The performances of the Iranian State Folk Dance Company, the Mahalli Dancers (disbanded in 1979 after the Islamic Revolution), revealed this cultural diversity in its programming. Dance suites, and the dances within them, were given such labels as *Dances from Kurdish Tribes* and *Turkoman Folklore*, indicating specific non-Persian ethnic groups, as well as *Dances from Bojnurd* and *Folk Dances from Jiroft*, reflecting specific locations. Thus, the program identifies various ethnic groups in the nation as well as regions, and whatever their background—Persian, Baluchi, Armenian, Jew, Kurd—all are considered "Iranian." The Turkish case (as well as the Greek case that I considered in the previous chapter) is very different. The former Mahalli Dancers of Iran, in line with government policy, represented a spectrum of rainbow diversity.

Turkish Nationalism

Turkish nationalism contrasts with Iranian nationalism in a crucial fashion. Turkish nationalism has no deep roots. No widespread national epic on the scale of the *Shahnameh* exists in Turkey. As I pointed out in the previous chapter on Greece, the very term "Turk" throughout most of the history of the Ottoman Empire had the negative and derogatory connotation of a rustic or country bumpkin; it was not a term of esteem like "Iranian." According to most historians of Turkish history, Turkish identity barely existed, even among the elite, until after the year 1908. Bernard Lewis, one of the leading scholars of Turkish history, notes: "The old Turkish civilizations were too thoroughly obliterated by Islam for any real revival of ancient Turkish culture to be possible" (1968, 10). Further, he states, "There is only sporadic evidence of any sense of Turkish national identity. The first Turkish converts to Islam . . . identified themselves completely with their new faith, and seem to have forgotten their separate Turkish past with astonishing rapidity and completeness" (ibid., 330–31).

Prior to 1908, the House of Osman and the Ottoman state commanded the loyalty of the elite, while among the masses the primary identity was that of Muslim, an identity that they shared with other ethnic groups in the empire—Arabs, Kurds, Albanians, and Bosnians, among others. The Ottoman Empire fostered this complete identity with Islam with its loyalty to the sultan in his dual role as caliph and sultan. Lewis observes that "its people thought of themselves first and foremost as Muslim. Both Ottoman and Turk are . . . terms of comparatively recent usage, and the Ottoman Turks had identified themselves with Islam—submerged their identity in Islam—to a greater extent than perhaps any other Islamic people" (1968, 130).

Early in the twentieth century, a few Turkish writers, particularly Zia Gokalp, the intellectual architect of Turkish nationalism, began to formulate the characteristics of a new Turkish nationalism. This new Turkish identity was largely created and produced between the period of 1908, the time of the coming to power of the Young Turks, and 1923, the year of the founding of the Turkish Republic. According to Stephan Astourian, "The self-identification of most Turkish-speaking Muslim Ottomans as Turks occurred in great part between 1908 and 1914" (1998, 38). However, I think closer examination reveals a much later date when a significant number of the population regarded themselves primarily as Turks rather than Muslims. "Thus along with building the Turkish nation-state, the Turkish nation as such had to be created. People had to be given a new collective identity, and they had to be persuaded to accept it" (Kramer 2000, 5). This creation and development of a new Turkish national identity, as well as its acceptance on a mass level, took a longer time than Astourian suggests.

Beginning in 1923, nationalism became a tool of the state, which, as I will show, utilized and engineered folk music, dance, and costumes to promote a unified Turkish identity. Turkish nationalism, until relatively recently, remained one of Gellner's classic examples of a nationalism constructed and disseminated by the nation's elite, which I discussed earlier. "Turkish nationalism is an extreme example of a situation in which the masses remained silent partners and the modernizing elite did not attempt to accommodate popular resentment. Anatolian peasants were at the passive end of the spectrum. The masses in Turkey generally remained passive recipients of the nationalist message propounded by the elites" (Keyder 1997, 43).

However, in contrast to the modernist theory proposed by Gellner and other scholars, Turkish nationalism was not created to serve the needs of a newly industrialized society: Turkey was overwhelmingly agrarian until the 1960s at least. Turkish nationalism was created to rally the population to protect the threatened Anatolian Turkish-speaking heartland territory of the former Ottoman Empire from further erosion rather than to provide an industrialized state with a working force. As occurs in many cases, war and conflict provided the machine to fire a newly created nationalism. In the Balkan Wars of 1912–1913 almost one-third of the Ottoman Empire was lost. A scant four years later, following the World War I, the Ottoman territories of the Middle East were forever lost, leaving only Anatolia and a small area in Thrace to the Turkish-speaking Muslim population. Much of this area was highly contested, with Armenians in Eastern Anatolia and large Greek populations in the West claiming territory.

The nationalist movement in Turkey developed, in part, as a reaction to the nationalist movements in the Balkans, which resulted in the founding of the Ottoman successor states of Serbia, Bulgaria, Greece, Rumania, and Albania and the consequent loss of huge amounts of territory of the Ottoman Empire. The disintegration of the Ottoman state, particularly after 1912, increasingly eroded the confidence of the elite group the "Young Turks," who tried to save the Ottoman Empire. After 1918, when the European powers attempted to dismember Turkey and claim large parts of Ottoman territory for themselves and client states such as Greece and Armenia, the nationalist movement picked up energy through what I call a "fortress" mentality, galvanized by Ataturk and his colleagues. The sultan and his government, in their willingness to concede every territorial loss to the victorious allies through the Treaty of Sevres (1920), disgraced himself irretrievably in the eyes of many of his people and paved the way for Kemal Ataturk's creation of the Turkish republic and the new Turkish nationalism.

Had the Treaty of Sevres been implemented, Turkey would have been reduced to the northwest corner of Anatolia. Kemal Ataturk utilized a nationalist battle cry, with Islamic overtones, to repulse the Greek, Italian, French, and English forces that had invaded the former Ottoman lands still in government hands after World War I. However, for the mass of the population this was conceived of as a Muslim-infidel struggle. Ataturk was given the honorific title of "Ghazi," an Islamic warrior for the faith, which, for all his secularist thinking, he used until his death.

Anthropologist Paul Stirling notes that during his study of Turkish village life in the early 1950s, "The War of Independence [1919–1922] created for the first time a Turkish nation-state, demanding a new loyalty. Many villagers even today speak of this war as a religious conflict, a victory of Islam over infidels" (1965, 268).

The sinister side of this fortress mentality took the form of a xenophobic mistrust of all those who were not considered Turkish. Ultimately, Turkish was equated with a Muslim identity, as it is today. This "us or them" Turkish nationalism resulted in the Armenian genocide of 1915–1916, resulting the deaths of one million souls, and the expulsion of more than a million Greeks in 1923.[7] "The repressive and centralist policies of the Young Turks were by no means limited to the Christian subjects of the Empire. In both Rumelia [the portion of Turkey in Europe] and the Asian provinces, they followed a policy of Turkification, and attempted to impose the Turkish language on Arabs, Albanians, and other non-Turkish Muslims" (Lewis 1968, 219).

The War of Independence forced the Turkish elite to form a new state, shorn of its former Ottoman possessions, primarily in Anatolia and a reduced portion of Rumelia. Turkish historian Ergun Ozbudun states:

> While Turkish nationalism was a relative latecomer, the Young Turks first (1908–1918) and then the Kemalists were successful in building a new collective identity around Turkish nationalism to replace the Ottoman-Islamic identity. This was helped by the loss of Arabic-speaking lands of the empire at the end of World War I, the traumatic experience of the Turkish War of Independence (1919–1922), the religious and linguistic homogeneity of the new Turkish republic, the charisma and the prestige of Kemal Ataturk, and perhaps the strong sense of statehood in Turkish political culture alluded to above. Of all the successor states, Turkey has made the easiest transition to nation-state. (1996, 139–40)

Turkey pursued its aims for ethnic homogeneity through the expulsion of the overwhelming majority of Greeks and any Armenians who remained in the country except those in Istanbul, who were given the right to remain under the terms of the Treaty of Lausanne (1922). This treaty marked the end of the War of Independence and provided the terms for the massive population exchanges between Greece and Turkey.

> What touched the masses directly during the Turkish nationalist movement was the expulsion, deportation, massacre, and exchange of the Greek and Armenian subjects of the empire. Indeed, the presence of the Christian population was the only medium through which Muslim

Anatolians had experienced the otherwise abstract notion of peripheralization in their daily lives. Rather than being popular, however, the events culminating in the expulsion and disappearance of some nine-tenths of the Christian population (around one-sixth of the total population in Anatolia) were laden with embarrassment and shame, covered up in official discourse as much as in the national psyche. (Keyder 1997, 43–44)

Nationalism is a jealous mistress, promising security and comfort. Today another form of nationalism has raised its head in Turkey in the form of Kurdish nationalism. Like all rival ethnic identities in Turkey, Kurdish identity is denied. This denial contrasts dramatically with Iranian nationalism, which recognizes all its ethnic groups as legitimately Iranian. The fact that there is a province of Kurdistan in Iran while references to Kurds are illegal in Turkey illustrates the difference. As Poulton observes,

There is no mention of the Kurds as a separate people or of the Kurdish language being spoken as the mother tongue of a sizeable percentage of the population. On the contrary, the traditional Kemalist line is continued, to the effect that the Turkish nation ... is a monolith without ethnic minorities and comprises the entire population of the republic. (Poulton 1997, 217)

In 1923, the problem of the Kurds, who formed at least 10 percent of the population, was yet in the future because Kurdish nationalism as a political force came about even later than Turkish nationalism. Kurdish nationalism today haunts Turkey and clouds its relations with the West (Barkey and Fuller 1998; Kirisci and Winrow 1997).

Kemalism and Nationalism

Having established those aspects of Turkish nationalism that have an impact on how the Turkish State Folk Dance Ensemble constitutes its programming, the specific aspects of Kemalist state policies will further illuminate how this company constructs its performances.

Kemalism, as I use the term, refers to the etatism of the Turkish government. Kemalism pervaded all aspects of public life, and that includes the use and control of folklore in the service of Turkish nationalism. Kemalism, above all, was a drive for the modernization and Westernization of Turkey. "Turkish modernizers had readily identified modernization with Westernization—with taking a place in the civilization of Europe. Modernity in their conception was a total project: one of embracing and internalizing all the cultural dimensions that made Europe modern" (Keyder 1997, 37). One might then ask how Turkish folkloric forms would find a place in such a modernizing scheme. The answer lies in the form in which Turkish nationalism was created.

> The silence of the masses also permitted the construction of an imaginary "popular" by the elite. Redefinition of the "popular" (via folklore and history) is a common feature of all nationalisms and is expected to proceed from the assimilation of various decontextualized elements of the mass culture to the totalizing semiotics of the national project. In the Turkish case, this redefinition could take place with more than the usual liberty because the freshly constituted elements of a popular "tradition" were presented to the masses as the authentic (and official) version, without much concern for preexisting versions. The defining vector of this reconstitution was an unsullied ethnic heritage endowed with all the positive virtues of might, unity, state-building acumen, and self-confidence. This trope, designed to boost self-esteem, established a matrix through which all the national symbols—from heroic sculptures to ethnographic detail, from folk music, legends, and heroes to public ceremonies—were defined. Henceforth, popular culture would be yet another realm amenable to social engineering. (Keyder 1997, 45)

Within Keyder's astute observation one can readily see that the Turkish government took an active role in the promulgation of an "official" folkloric expression. This control extended into how dance and costume would appear in the public domain.

The first aspect of Kemalism that strikes all observers of Middle Eastern history and politics is the apparent distancing of the Republic of Turkey from its Ottoman past. "Ataturk laid stress on the fact that the regime they were creating had nothing in common with the former Ottoman state and was a complete break with the corrupt past" (Ahmad 1993, 3). In this manner, Ataturk followed the practices of the other Ottoman successor states such as Greece and Serbia. Ataturk always stressed that he had completely turned his back on the Ottoman past. For this reason Turkey was proclaimed and held up as a successful model of modernization by many observers of the Middle East who contrasted countries such as Iran and the Arab states unfavorably with Turkey. Westerners often applauded changes such as the Hat Act, which symbolized Ataturk's move to modernize the outer appearance of Turkish men with the abolition of the fez and the adoption of Western hats; the Language Reform Act, which abolished the use of the Arabic script and substituted instead a form of the Latin alphabet adapted to Turkish; and the abolition of Islamic institutions such as the caliphate, the office of the *seyholislam*, the Sufi *tarikas*, and the *vakf*.

Certainly in four dramatic ways Turkey was different from the Ottoman Empire. First, the official secularization of the state and the privatization of religious practices were a major departure from the Ottoman state, which acted as a leader in Islam for its Muslim population and even those beyond. "An extreme form of nationalism, with the attendant creation of historical myths, was used as the prime instrument in the building of a new national identity, and as such was intended to take the place of religion in many respects" (Zurcher 1998, 189). Secularization is manifest in the way in which the Turkish State Folk Dance Ensemble performs. In an Islamic context the public performance of music and, even more so, dance is questionable, especially given the fact that unrelated men and women perform on the stage together.

Second, Turkey became a nation with a single core national group. Expressions of other than Turkish ethnicity became, and remain, illegal in contrast to the relatively tolerant practices of the Ottoman Empire. Turkish identity was not emphasized by the Ottoman state.

The third way in which Turkey differed from its Ottoman predecessor was its wholehearted embracing of Western technological, economic, educational, and social models as state policy. And finally, Kemalist state policy was to valorize Anatolian peasant culture, albeit in a carefully engineered fashion. This latter element will be seen in the manner in which the Turkish State Folk Dance Ensemble, and most other folk dance companies, presents itself. The repertoire of the Turkish State Folk Dance Ensemble does not include dances from the Ottoman period, but rather is built around the folk dance expression of the Turkish peasants. The *ciftetelli* is a very popular, widespread solo-improvised dance, which like belly dancing is performed with many articulations of the torso and hips. Professional dancers in the Ottoman period performed it, and today the general population, both men and women, perform it in a domestic version at weddings, parties, and other festivities. The Turkish State Folk Dance Ensemble performs a very chaste choreography of the *Ciftetelli* with a large number of women in pretty, orientalist costumes, suggestive of, but, in true Kemalist fashion, carefully decontextualized from its Ottoman origins. The regional dances of Anatolia, on the other hand, are specifically identified in their programs. Thus, the *ciftetelli,* a choreographic and musical genre, is identified differently from the regional dances.

Historian Feroz Ahmad states that

> The period after 1908 was crucial to the formation of Turkish national consciousness and the mythology of the Kemalist revolution was a vital element in its formation. Turkishness involved pride in the history and traditions of Anatolia ("the cradle of civilization") both of which had to be rediscovered or even manufactured. But Turkishness was also defined in contrast to the rest of the Islamic world, thus the emphasis on secularism. (1993, 78)

Like folklore, history was also reworked and recreated. Ataturk and his colleagues carried these radical reconstructions of history and folklore to an extent that, to modern eyes, borders on the ludicrous. As historian Bernard Lewis states,

> The theory propounded by Kemal and his disciples was, briefly, that the Turks were a white, Aryan people, originating in Central Asia, the cradle of all human civilization. Owing to the progressive desiccation of this area, the Turks had migrated in waves to various parts of Asia and Africa, carrying the arts of civilization with them. Chinese, Indian, and Middle Eastern civilizations had all been founded in this way, the pioneers in the last named being the Sumerians and Hittites, who were both Turkic peoples. Anatolia had thus been a Turkish land since antiquity. This mixture of truth, half-truth, and error was proclaimed as official doctrine, and teams of researchers set to work to "prove" its various propositions. (1968, 359)

This valorization of Turkishness was an important element in the distancing of the Ataturk regime from that of the Ottomans. But recent scholarly reevaluations of the Ottoman period indicate that the break with the Ottoman past might not have been as decisive as Ataturk and his associates claimed. Currently in Turkey there is a renewal of interest in the Ottoman period, which many older people still remember. A spate of books and articles on all aspects of Ottoman life have begun to appear in both Turkey and abroad, and demonstrate the degree of continuity that exists into the present.

> Kemalist historiography, beginning with Kemal's classic account of the Independence War as detailed in his famous speech of October 1927—Nutuk—likes to portray the founding of the republic and the abolition

of the Caliphate as revolutionary measures which owed their inspiration and execution to the "genius" of one man—Mustafa Kemal. (Poulton 1997, 87–88)

Nevertheless, important links with the Ottoman past continued into the republican period and left an important legacy.

The Ottoman Empire had an extensive and elaborate civil and military bureaucracy, highly developed by the standards of its day and certainly by those of most of the third world countries. This was the most direct legacy of the Ottoman state to the Turkish republic. Rustow has calculated that 93 percent of the empire's general staff officers and 85 percent of its civil servants continued their service in Turkey. (Ozbudun 1996, 148)

The changes were both huge and crucial for the Turkish people who lived in urban areas, but "generally these writers overestimated the extent to which Turkish society was changed. The reforms hardly influenced the life of the villagers who made up the great mass of the Turkish population (Zurcher 1998, 202).

The Ottoman Empire concerned itself with two things: the collection of taxes and the maintenance of public order. By contrast, Kemalist policy is concerned with all public aspects of Turkish life. "This project permitted local culture no greater space than that of the folkloric" (Keyder 1997, 37). It is at this point that we enter the world of Turkish folk dance.

Kemalism and Folk Dance and Music

Dance in the Field

Turkey is particularly rich in dance in the field and, due to historical and geographical circumstances, contrasts sharply with Egypt in the amount of regional dances and dance types within its territory. In this way it resembles the dancing traditions of the countries of Eastern Europe that boast a rich tapestry of regional folk dances. In addition, Turkey also has a far less well-known urban dance tradition, rarely shown in the repertoires of the Turkish folk dance companies, including the national dance company, because of its Ottoman associations. Recent intense interest in the Ottoman period may alter that viewpoint.

In brief, among the most important dance genres in the field the largest number of dances consist of those in which the dancers hold hands, arms, or shoulders; in a variety of ways, the dancers are connected to one another. There are dozens and even hundreds of each type of such dances, which depending on the region are generically called *bar, halay, horon,* and *horo.* A second group of dances are those in which the dancers do not touch and often carry scarves, weapons, or wooden spoons. Typical of these dances are the spoon dances of Central Anatolia, the sword and shield dance of Bursa, the dagger dance of the Black Sea area, and the *zeybek* of the Izmir region. Solo-improvised dances such as the *ciftetelli* and couple dances such as *karslima* in the western part of Turkey and the virtuosic solo and couple dances of the Caucasian regions of Erzerum and Kars complete the broad strokes of dance in the field.

The republican government, eager to valorize Anatolian peasant culture as an icon of ethnic identity, very early established institutes

Turkish State Folk Dance Ensemble. *Dances from Elazig.* COURTESY MUSTAFA TURAN.

for the collection of folklore in all categories. That included folk dance. The categorization and collection of this rich trove of dances has occupied Turkish folk dance researchers and scholars for decades. Turkish folk dance scholar Arzu Ozturkmen observes:

> Within the overall picture of folklore studies in Turkey, the development of the so-called "Turkish dances" can be seen as one of the most significant phenomena in the nationalization of Turkish folklore. In Turkey, as in many other countries, folk dances, I believe served the construction of a visual national image, which was projected as the nation's "Sunday clothes" to the nation itself. . . . The folk dance emerged as the unique folklore genre which acquired a widespread popularity, even among those people and institutions which do not necessarily have a formal affiliation with the State. Second, the study of the early history of the folk dance movement illustrated how and why the research-centered trend in Turkish folklore dominated the field until the 1950s, that is until the "imagined" national identity was more or less consolidated. (1992, 83)

One look at Cemil Demirsipahi's *Turk Halk Oyunlari* (1975)—a huge encyclopedic compendium of traditional dances and accompanying musical examples—and the interested reader can begin to comprehend the immense number of dances in the field. To make sense of this rich Turkish dance tradition, researchers have spent much time and effort first recording and collecting, with films and written notes, dance traditions in the field, and then attempting to reduce the vast field research material into conceptual geographic regional or social, functional and contextual categories. Serif Baykurt divides Turkish folk dance into six choreographic/ethnographic regions known by the principal dance genre of the particular region. These regions are reflected in the repertoire of regional dances performed by the Turkish State Folk Dance Ensemble.[8] Metin And (1959, 1976, 1989) categorizes Turkish dance by function and context: social dances, regional folk dances, dancing in religious and sacred contexts, and theatrical dancing.

Generally speaking, the casual visitor to Turkey rarely encounters dance in the field, but rather she or he is more likely to attend the folk dance programs regularly organized by government tourist organizations throughout those areas of Turkey that are heavily visited by tourists. In addition, the performance layer of Turkish dance is experienced in the government-sponsored international tours and appearances of the many amateur companies and the Turkish State Folk Dance Ensemble.

Amateur Folk Troupes

The performances of the amateur companies based in urban areas, as well as the national company, are distant from the field in terms of staging elements. Typical Turkish choreographies for the stage consist of such elements as the shortening of repetitive dance phrases; intricate, geometric floor patterns; and rapid and choreographically sophisticated transitions between individual dances. The dancers of the national and amateur urban ensembles often have no knowledge of the original contexts and meanings of dances in the field. Dance scholar Arzu Ozturkmen observes, "Obviously, the city performers had no direct familiarity with the local culture which generated the various dance genres they have learned. In most cases, they had neither a particular interest, nor the necessary cultural competence to decipher the referential meaning of these dances" (1992, 85).

As I observed in the Chapter 1, there are two layers of folk dance in Turkey, as there are throughout many nations such as Egypt, the former Soviet Union, and Bulgaria. The first genre characterizes the traditional dances performed as an organic aspect of social life among people in both cities and rural areas. These dances "in the field" are performed largely in informal events, or in socially public events such as weddings.

The second genre is performance folk dance; that is, the primary intent of the activity is for public performances. This requires hours of devoted rehearsals and the formation of a group of young dancers for whom this constitutes a pleasurable social activity. In addition, in a Muslim nation such as Turkey, this is one of the only activities that is considered as occurring in a healthy and proper environment in which young men and women may participate together with parental approval. This genre of dance in Turkey constitutes one of the primary social activities for Turkish urban youth and receives considerable moral and financial support by the national and local governments and members of the general population, such as prominent businessmen.

The Ministry of Culture has, through its various folklore research and administrative departments, constructed a national network in which these amateur groups vie with one another in competition performances and appearances that begin locally and culminate in regional and finally national competitions. The winners are sent by the government to perform and compete in international festivals. Turkey has won many first prizes in these competitions, and such opportunities for foreign travel adds to the luster of performing in these amateur companies.[9]

During visits to Istanbul in 1968 and 1976, I observed several of these amateur groups. Hundreds of young men and women were enthusiastic devotees of performing in these amateur dance groups. I found the level of performances of some of the larger companies, which had in excess of a hundred performers, to be of professional performance level and capability.

Interestingly, this early use of Turkish folk dance as an urban phenomenon geared toward performance, and therefore national representation, served the Kemalist governments and preceded the state's similar political use of folk dance in both Nazi Germany and the former Soviet Union. In the Soviet Union and its East European satellites, the formation of these amateur performance groups came largely in the wake of the formation of their respective national folk dance ensembles.

The presence of groups for the performances of folk dances in a choreographed context for amateur dancers contrasts vividly with practices in the United States and other countries where folk dancing primarily constitutes an enjoyable recreational hobby for hundreds of thousands of urban dwellers of all ages. Both of these activities are equally distant from the rural environment and society in which the dances form an organic part of life and thus constitute parallel traditions. In the United States, the government has no interest in such hobbies, but in countries such as Turkey in which folk dance has attained a status of national representation, government support and supervision exists. The state sponsors an entire hierarchical network of competitions for both amateur dance clubs and school groups.

> The Ministry of Youth and Sports directs an annual series of competitions for primary and secondary schools (public and private). Competition teams are organized as of the third grade and continue through high school. The competitions are organized at three levels—city, regional, and national—the whole series of which is spread out over several months....
>
> In many ways, it is the national competition of amateur associations, directed by the government, which rivets the attention of the Turkish folk dance world.... The official goal of the annual competition is to "check" groups that expect to tour outside of the country to see if their presentation appropriately represents the nation.... Technically, any group wishing to perform Turkish folk dance abroad must be approved by the state. (Cefkin 1993, 167, 169–71)

Mustafa Turan serves on the judging committee of these competitions. In this manner both of these genres, the amateur and professional folk dance company performances, constitute multiple layers of parallel traditions with the dances in the field.

The Turkish State Folk Dance Ensemble

Perhaps more than any of the other state-supported dance ensembles profiled in this book, the Turkish State Folk Dance Ensemble embodies the idea of "choreographic politics." Perhaps even more than is the case with the amateur dance companies, every aspect of its production is the result, direct or indirect, of government control and intervention. This government involvement of more than seventy years now appears so "natural" that most individuals in Turkey accept the folk music, dances, and costumes found in stage performances as "authentic."

Indeed, Mustafa Turan takes obvious pride in the authenticity of the performances of the Turkish State Folk Dance Ensemble. "We conduct extensive field research and we also bring the finest dancers from villages to demonstrate proper style to our dancers," he declared in an interview (March 8, 2000). It is clear from the ensemble's performances that his statement is true and that he and the members of the ensemble feel a connection with the peasant dancers, and their dances, in the field.

Choreographers with the state ensemble do considerable research when they prepare a new suite of regional dances. Like LADO, the Turkish State Folk Dance Ensemble pays considerable attention to details of dance style, movements, and steps learned in the field. The overall effect carries a sense of verisimilitude to the viewer precisely because of the attention to the authentic details of music and movement.

Nevertheless, their performances, like those of the amateur troupes, also support the concept of parallel traditions. These performances are "not the village." The performances of the Turkish State Folk Dance Ensemble are artistic and carefully staged presentations parallel to, and yet distant from, village traditions and practices.

In Turkey, Mustafa Turan formed the Turkish State Folk Dance Ensemble, the nation's official professional dance company, in 1972. He spent long hours in preparation for this project in which he deeply believed. "I beat on the doors of government for three years, and I finally succeeded in convincing the government of the value of sponsoring a professional folk dance company," he said in an interview (March 8, 2000). It was officially designated as the Turkish State Folk Dance Ensemble in 1975 and gave its first performance the following

Turkish State Folk Dance Ensemble. *Zeybek from Ege* (the Aegean Region). COURTESY MUSTAFA TURAN.

year. It represents Turkey at home and abroad, appearing in tours throughout the world and at diplomatic events in Turkey. In the spring of 2000, the company traveled to China.

In addition, the reputation of the company has grown to the point that other countries wish to follow its model. Mustafa Turan journeyed to the Sudan in the summer of 2000 and spent a number of months establishing a similar company there based on the organizational principles of the Turkish State Folk Dance Ensemble. This step follows the pattern that I outlined in the Chapter 1 in which new state folk dance companies were established in many countries based on the model of the Moiseyev Dance Company. Now the Turkish State Folk Dance Ensemble has reached a level of excellence that inspires the foundation of new companies in other nations such as the Sudan.

The company numbers ninety individuals—sixty dancers and sixteen orchestra members, as well as choreographers, costumers, wardrobe staff, and support staff. They occupy spacious quarters in the Ataturk Cultural Center in Ankara. An important aspect of the attraction of outstanding dancers and musicians to the company, and underscoring the importance attached to the presence of this company to the Turkish state, is that the dancers and musicians receive pay and benefits equivalent to that of dancers and musicians in the state ballet, opera, and symphony orchestras, which enhances their status as artists. This practice contrasts vividly with the poor pay and working conditions found in Greece and Egypt, where Western art forms and the artists who participate in them receive higher pay and better working conditions than those engaged in traditional music and dance.

Dance scholar Melissa Cefkin states that

> The State Folk Dance Ensemble, thus, embodies and enacts the disciplining agency of the state in many ways. For one, it acts as an official representative of the state when outside the country. Secondly, it operates through the promotion of training and competence, sanctioning its "professional" status and thus advancing Turkey's claims to being a fully modern nation-state. Moreover, it is based on homogenizing principles of organization in that the folk dances it represents are equally weighted in their ability to stand for Turkishness while at the same time it is only the ensemble of them that signifies the nation. (1993, 106–07)

Thus this ensemble sits at the apex of hundreds of long established, professional-level amateur companies throughout Turkey.

Repertoire

Unlike the amateur companies in Eastern Europe, which are modeled after the repertoire and performance levels of the respective national company, the opposite obtains in Turkey. The repertoire and performances of the Turkish State Folk Dance Ensemble are of the highest technical level due to the presence of professional choreographers and dancers who possess the highest possible level of dance skills in this specific genre. Nevertheless, the performances are aesthetically and conceptually informed by the decades-long tradition of the amateur companies that preceded its founding. Although it followed as an extensive development of amateur dance activity that has been one of the most popular youth activities throughout Turkey, it now constitutes the model of high performance that the amateur troupes attempt to emulate.

The concept of the dance repertoire that is seen, with variations, in most of the folk dance clubs and troupes, as well as the state folk

Turkish State Folk Dance Ensemble. *Dances from Artvin.* COURTESY MUSTAFA TURAN.

ensemble, was created through the network of folk dance festivals and competitions from the inception of the republic. "Such nationwide folk dance festivals, and later the folk dance competitions, helped the formation of a certain sense of what the Turkish 'national' dance spectrum was like, in the eye of the audiences in big cities" (Ozturkmen 1992, 84). This spectrum is seen in the repertoire of the Turkish State Folk Dance Ensemble.

The bulk of the repertoire of the Turkish State Folk Dance Ensemble consists of some twenty suites of regional dances. Mustafa Turan commented: "To represent Turkey, it is important to have dances from throughout the national territory" (personal interview, March 8, 2000).

For many years I was aware that representation of the Ottoman period, one rich in urban dances, had been taboo in Turkey. I was told this in interviews with Turkish folk dance company leaders in 1968. However, in my most recent visit to Turkey in the winter of 2000, I also noticed, especially in Istanbul, that many publications about all aspects of the Ottoman period, some of them very elaborate, were prominently displayed in most bookstores. I asked Mustafa Turan about the possible reconstruction of historical urban dances for the Turkish State Folk Dance Ensemble, and how the government would react. He replied charmingly: "Everyone wishes to forget a bad business deal, but no man forgets his mother and father, and for our republic the Ottomans were our parents. I do not forget the Ottoman past" (personal interview, March 8, 2000). He regards the inclusion of the choreography *Ciftetelli* as a step in that direction. This cannot have been an easy step since it was a major departure from the regional dance suites based on village dances. Although the general audiences that I observed loved the work, the company has received sharp criticism for its inclusion. Folk dance researchers and purists decried the addition of the *Ciftetelli* choreography to the repertoire as "appealing to the orientalist images of foreigners" (Baykurt, qtd. in Cefkin 1993, 140).[10]

As an artist, Turan is keen to expand the ensemble's repertoire in new and innovative ways. One new direction he has chosen for the ensemble is to utilize "theme choreographies" based on customs such as weddings, circumcision ceremonies, and harvest celebrations, among, others and construct what are termed by Cefkin as "potpourri" choreographies. The wedding suite, accompanied by a Western orchestra and/or military concert band with the addition of folk instruments, utilizes composed classical music and features dances from throughout Turkey that are associated with weddings. He also plans to have his company perform dances from other countries for a future international festival of dance.

Dancers and Dance Training

As I outlined above, an intricate network of amateur dance companies numbering in the hundreds attracts young people from all over Turkey. These young dancers often learn the dances in the extensive folk dance programs found in elementary and secondary schools throughout Turkey. The Turkish State Folk Dance Ensemble auditions for new dancers when positions open because of dancers leaving the company for various reasons. The company has the pick of the best dancers in Turkey. Cefkin reports that "in 1989, approximately 1,700 people entered the auditions competing for sixteen positions"—a choreographer's dream! She also reports that Mustafa Turan profiled the requirements for the company. "Candidates must be between eighteen and twenty-three years old and should be "tall, have a medium complexion (not too light or too dark), have no facial scars, not wear eyeglasses, have a good arch in the foot, and have good posture. They also must prove a good ear for music, though prior dance experience is not necessary" (Cefkin 1993, 105).

Perhaps times had changed a decade later, for when I interviewed Mustafa Turan he stated that there were no special requirements regarding looks, and indeed a wide range of body types, heights, skin complexions, and ages were seen among the dancers. "We do not do the tall-short thing," he said in reference to the well-known practice in Eastern European dance companies, such as the Moiseyev Dance Company, of maintaining a tall and short corps to perform separate repertoires (personal interview, March 8, 2000).

In addition to relatively high salaries, touring opportunities, and other perquisites, the dancers and musicians receive excellent benefits. They can retire on full pension after twenty years. Several of the dancers appeared to be in their late thirties and early forties, emphasizing the comfortable working environment of the ensemble. With such excellent working conditions and the popularity of folk dancing in Turkey, it is small wonder that thousands of candidates apply to compete for openings. It is also a benefit to the company that new dancers who are selected are already extensively trained in the individual dances and styles and therefore ready to learn the specific choreographies of the state company.

Music

The Turkish State Folk Dance Ensemble largely uses authentic instruments for its regional repertoire. Its musicians are highly trained and familiar with many local regional styles. Like the musicians of LADO, the sixteen musicians are extremely versatile and able to play multiple instruments.

The dancers sing to accompany certain of the line dances. They do not have LADO's vocal power, but the singing adds an extra dimension to the performance.

Costumes

The costumes, like the dances, are a result of Kemalist social engineering. When I first encountered the folk costumes of Turkish folk dance companies, I was struck by the uniformity they displayed. They were more like uniforms than clothing worn by rural populations at festive or other events.

> After the Clothing Reform was made between 1925–1934 under the leadership of Ataturk, the tradition of dancing folk dances on the occasion of religious feasts, national holidays, at weddings and on joyful occasions continued. When the dance groups appeared, large groups of people would select one of the traditional costumes for themselves that had been worn before the Clothing Reform. When choosing these costumes, with the costumes worn to weddings in the lead, the costumes of merchants, soldiers, civil servants, religious leaders, the class of men learned in religion and the members of the palace were made use of as well. Today, the costumes worn by the folk dance groups are these and have become fixed. Even the slightest discrepancy is the cause of criticism. Every province, in fact every county, has designated a separate costume for its folk dance group. (Ozel et al. 1992, 43)

The idea that "in public-cultural centers each group chose a special costume for themselves" does not ring true in a country in which all decisions descended from above (Turkish State Folk Dance Ensemble n.d., 2). Although this is the official story, it is difficult to imagine a costume-by-committee arrangement like the one described in the government's publication about folk costumes.

Like the dances, the costumes have been carefully choreographed to conform to the government's notion of the proper representation of Turkishness.

Finances

The Turkish State Folk Dance Ensemble is totally supported by the government. Turkey, as I stated above, invests an enormous amount of money in folk dance activities. Ankara is not a major tourist center, and thus tourism does not constitute an important source of support for the ensemble, as was the case for the Greek national company and Ballet Folklorico.

The Turkish State Folk Dance Ensemble gives meaning to the central idea of this study, which is that performances by national state folk dance companies embody and participate in the national discourse. In Turkey, folk dance, both amateur and professional, embodies and participates in the official concepts of what constitutes Turkishness. The repertoire and the descriptive program notes omit any mention of Kurdish or Ottoman identity.

Unlike other nations that I have described in which urban elites regard their national ensembles as quaint and suitable for tourists, the performances of the Turkish State Folk Dance Ensemble resonate with Turks. Its performances are largely attended by Turks, for many of whom folk dancing constitutes a passion.

9

Conclusion: The Power of Representation

Throughout this study I have attempted to develop several themes for which performances of folk, traditional, or world (as it is now fashionable to call it) dance by large state folk dance ensembles provides a unique lens for analysis. Scholars of dance have largely ignored the performances of the many state-sponsored folk dance ensembles because their performances are considered to be "unauthentic," "theatrical," "slick," and "glitzy." These performances form the intersection between popular culture in regard to their sources and high art in their formal choreographic formats, which has placed the genre beyond the interests of scholars of Western theater dance on the one hand, and dance ethnologists on the other. Therefore, few serious studies of these performances exist. I have demonstrated that these performances are revealing of crucial elements of political, social, ethnic, and class issues that resonate in the national discourses of their respective nation-states.

In this study I principally focused on issues of representation, for representation is a form of power: the power of describing others either verbally or choreographically. Choreographic strategies of representation foreground some of the most deeply felt and unspoken aspects of national discourses in which professional folk dance performances provide a singular socially and culturally constructed document for analysis. The discussion in the individual chapters above analyzes and describes how state folk dance ensembles utilize specific choreographic strategies to represent entire nation-states in specific fashions. Representation requires conscious decisions regarding who will be represented and how they will be represented, as well as decisions, marked by absences, that will determine who will not be represented.

No project of representation can ever be total, allowing for alternative readings of the folk dance ensemble's performances. Representation is usually achieved through the inclusion and exclusion of certain

Conclusion: The Power of Representation 225

elements of the population. The exclusion of certain elements of the national population, or worse, negative portrayals such as the Serbian state folk ensemble's portrayals of Gypsies described in Chapter 1, provides vital insights for analyzing national discourses of nationalism and ethnicity. Excluded groups that are often glimpsed only in the gaps and empty spaces in the repertoire can include unpopular minority ethnic or religious groups, urban populations, and upper or lower social classes, among others. A rare but telling example of exclusion is provided by the all-male state folk dance ensemble of Saudi Arabia, which excludes women from its field of representation.

These companies were formed within specific contexts of the discourses of ethnicity, religion, gender, class, race, nationalism, and colonialism. Because dance is embodied, through analyses of these performances unspoken aspects of these discourses—such as the way in which Gypsies are perceived in Serbian society or the absence of Saudi women—can be identified and deconstructed.

In short, it is necessary to any analysis of these large national folk dance ensembles to accept the idea that they are political institutions: these companies are a reflection of the political and social realities and national discourses of the nation that is on display and fulfill a crucial role in a nation's strategies of representation. So powerful were the choreographic displays and images of the Moiseyev Dance Company—performances that reached audiences numbered in the millions in Europe and the United States in the late 1950s and 1960s—that the U.S. Department of State held several meetings of leading American dance figures to attempt to mount a challenge to the highly popular Soviet dance company (see Prevots 1998). The images that Moiseyev created of the Soviet Union were so powerful and positive that the American government became alarmed that their carefully constructed negative Cold War images of the "Russians Are Coming" and the "Evil Empire" were rapidly melting under the warm and fuzzy appearances of wholesome young dancing Russians in charming native costumes. The appearances of the Moiseyev Dance Company became a political instrument without politicians. For the first time, the U.S. government confronted the true power of folk dance and its representational potential. It was a problem that the American dance experts selected by the State Department, who were largely ignorant of the myriad possibilities of ethnic representation available through folk and traditional dance throughout the United States, and with their narrow focus exclusively fixed on ballet and modern dance, never solved.

In order to provide a basis for this type of analysis in which I was able to scrutinize and read the performances of large state-sponsored dance ensembles, without carrying the weighty cultural and scholarly baggage of issues of "authenticity," I developed the concept of "parallel traditions." With the concept of parallel traditions I established the idea that the performances of folk or traditional dances on the stage constitute a separate genre of Western theater dance, even when performed by non-Western folk dance companies, because they all utilize the format established by Moiseyev. In this manner a researcher need not make invidious comparisons of the relative merits and value of dance in the field versus staged folk dance based on issues of authenticity, but rather can treat each of the genres as a separate analytical category, each with its own characteristics.

Briefly, the genre of staged folk dance operates in a parallel space to folk and traditional dances "in the field." That is, the staged performances of professional state folk dance ensembles make constant reference through claims of authenticity to those dances that occur in the physical and social environments in which individuals perform dances that are native to them. These references are visually and aurally emphasized through choreographic strategies that attempt to recall and refer to village practices in dance, instrumental and vocal music, and costuming as well as in program notes and publicity releases that stress the amount of research the choreography of the staged version of the dances requires.

The crucial difference between dances on the stage and dances in the field is that dances in the field, particularly for social occasions, which are the dances that choreographers from the national companies heavily draw upon as source materials and inspiration, are largely unrehearsed and spontaneous.[1] That having been said, the second half of the twentieth century saw an immense growth in the tourist industry worldwide for which colorfully garbed natives performing appropriately colorful native dances became a desirable attraction. Around the world—from hula dancers throwing leis around the necks of visitors in the Honolulu airport to the ersatz Egyptian "villagers" at the Cairo Hilton—folk dance forms a chosen site for the creation of "national" images and an "authentic" native experience for tourists.

In addition, as I alluded to in the study, governments everywhere, following the lead of the Socialist bloc, began organizing festivals featuring folk music and dance. These festivals, often huge events, performed the important political act of demonstrating mass support for the regime through the appearance of hundreds, sometimes thousands, of colorfully costumed dancers.[2] These political and touristic demands caused an upsurge in dancers from the field preparing staged and theatricalized versions of their own social and ritual dances.[3]

Conclusion: The Power of Representation

Thus, the concept of parallel traditions permits a deeper analysis of dance in the field as well as makes space for more penetrating studies of professional and amateur folk dance ensembles, their creative theatricalized products, and their audiences.

By contrast, dance on the stage, even though containing possible elements of improvisation and spontaneity, are invariably staged and largely conceived, shaped, and choreographed by a single individual. They are rehearsed and performed by individuals who are generally not native to the traditions they portray, and the artistic rosters of most of the state ensembles are populated with dancers who are urban dwellers and have learned these largely rural-based choreographies and stagings through a formal style taught in a studio setting. The individual Turkish, Croatian, or Mexican professional dancer of the national dance ensemble most often comes from a large city, and the rural dances of the countryside that he or she learns constitute, more often than not, an alien tradition.

Why was folk dance, especially this new theatricalized spectacle of folk dance, so powerful in its ability to create images? Other forms of theater dance, such as ballet and modern dance, have the capacity to carry overtly political messages. Ballet as a separate theatrical genre began as a means of glorifying the royal persona of Louis XIV. Dozens of tractor ballets glorifying the sanctity and value of work, like those found in the former USSR created during the Stalin era (but never shown in the West), and the *White-haired Girl, Red Detachment of Women,* and other well-known political, agitprop creations of the Chinese People's Republic, constitute examples of explicitly politically based choreography.

Modern dance makers have also created works with specifically political content. These genres are not, however, inherently political in nature. Their chief creators have developed these genres into forms of high elite art, and they are so regarded throughout most of the world. These genres do not and cannot claim to represent the large masses of people in nation-states. The large numbers of audience members who avidly watch performances of the national folk dance ensembles as a popular entertainment rarely attend performances of ballet and modern dance, which typically attract smaller audiences.

The development of "folk" and "traditional" dance as a separate genre, while not explicitly a political act, is implicitly so. In this genre, the content of the choreography is rarely explicitly political: a village wedding, a charming local ritual, or a suite of spirited dances to celebrate the wine harvest. What could be more innocent? The power of these performances does not lie in their specific content, but rather in their potential capacity to represent, describe, and embody the essentialized identities of millions of inhabitants of a specific nation-state in the course of an evening performance.

During the project of creating a repertoire for purposes of representation, national and regional stereotypes are created or enlarged through choreographies that are designed to inscribe positive national images. This creation of national stereotypes, often featured in the signature pieces of the respective ensembles, enables the audience members to apprehend these bigger-than-life images through visual spectacle, as the Moiseyev Dance Company demonstrated so stunningly in its early tours around the world.

It is obvious that each of the major ensembles visually differs from one another, at least insofar as their performance formats and in ethnically specific areas such as costumes, music, and dance movements, and also in the individual elements and styles of choreography that are the idiosyncratic contributions of the company's choreographers.[4] These ensembles fall into two broad categories: those that represent a single nationality such as the Croatian, Turkish, Greek, and Egyptian state companies, and those from multiethnic nation-states that attempt to portray a "rainbow diversity" such as the former state dance company of Iran and the companies of Mexico, the Philippines, and the former Soviet Union, which officially celebrate cultural and ethnic diversity. The Croatian state ensemble, LADO, while it was a part of Yugoslavia, fell into the latter category; however, following the point that I stressed above, namely that these companies are shaped and formed within specific political and social environments and that these can change, LADO currently performs exclusively Croatian material.

Apart from these differences, state folk dance ensembles also have several characteristics that they hold in common.

First, each one of these ensembles was founded by a charismatic leader. Interestingly, this individual is not always a choreographer or even a dancer in the sense of having the basic professional performing skills required for the company members of the ensembles he or she leads. What each of these charismatic leaders had or has in common is a vision and a driving force to fulfill the mission of the company—a mission and a vision that they have largely created or shaped. Each of these men and women held a fervent belief that traditional/folk dance and music was the most positive and effective vehicle for the representation of his or her nation-state.

Most of these leaders repeatedly state that they believe in intensive research, through which they make claims that they have identified and embody in their choreographic representations the true national character of their respective nations. Choreographers such as Igor Moiseyev, Mahmoud Reda, and Amalia Hernandez claimed to have the ability to distill the "national" or "regional" character of the peoples that they represented through the essentialization found in their choreographies. They were able to show the "happy" or "industrious" natives of their nation on the world stage. Claims are sometimes made that the national spirit resides in the choreographer's own person, resulting in statements such as the one referring to Amalia Hernandez and "the Mexico that she *is*" (Terry 1969, emphasis mine).

Second, these ensembles are designed to reach wide audiences. It is important at this point to refute the old cliché that dance is the international language.[5] Dance is *not* the international language. Each folk and traditional dance tradition is as culturally specific as language, and learned in the same way. Just as individuals have different levels of command of a specific language, their native language or a foreign one, the same can be said of dance. I emphasize this point because each of these ensembles plays to multiple audiences with multiple levels of capabilities of apprehending their performances. Thus, the constant flow of cultural references emanating from these performances is received differently by individuals in their audience who depend on their specific cultural competency. Broadly, these audiences can consist of elite educated individuals in the capital city, other urban individuals, or rural peoples in the home country, in addition to international audiences that vary as to ethnic background. These sometimes include diaspora members of multiple generations from the nation-state represented by a dance ensemble. Immigrant communities in the United States and Western Europe such as Mexicans, Croatians, and Greeks often constitute culturally competent enthusiasts. When the ensembles travel abroad, they frequently perform before large audiences who have never experienced the specific dance traditions being represented. Within all of these groups, individual audience members bring different levels of understanding to the performances.

The full study and analysis of audiences and their reactions and readings of folk dance performances lies beyond the scope of this study, and yet it opens important areas of inquiry for future study. On a practical level, if a state-sponsored folk ensemble does not connect with important elements of the audience, during times of economic downturn or changes in political fortunes the company can be shut down, as occurred in Iran after the Islamic Revolution, when the Mahalli Dancers were not perceived as carrying out a mission in the national interest. The Iranian troupe, rather than being identified with the nation-state, was perceived as being identified specifically with the Shah's regime. Audience reactions and readings of dance performances inform the analyst as to the efficacy and reception of the ensemble's performances among the various layers of attendees.

Most of these ensembles have been successful in reaching at least some of their audiences. As we have seen, Igor Moiseyev was spectacularly successful in reaching international audiences. The Turkish State Folk Dance Ensemble resonates strongly with its home audiences. The Dora Stratou Greek Dances Theatre does not resonate with its home audience in Athens but is very popular with tourists. The former Iranian State Folk Dance Ensemble, the Mahalli Dancers, was also largely unable to connect with audiences at home. The reasons for this are multiple and form a fruitful area of analysis. Engaging different audiences with nationalist messages is a fluctuating, ever-changing project. A repertoire that engaged and attracted the public to performances in the 1960s may not resonate one or two generations later, or conversely, changing political fortunes might rekindle interest at any time.

I suggest that currently one of the principal reasons that many state folk ensembles do not successfully reach their elite home audiences is due to the peasant references of their repertoire. Sophisticated inhabitants of Tehran, Cairo, and Athens are often more interested in attempting to lead lives that parallel those of cities in Western Europe and the United States and do not wish to be reminded of the large, and in their eyes, backward peasantry that makes up the majority of the population of their respective nation-states. They feel that this parallel existence, and their status as sophisticated, urbane individuals is better fulfilled attending avant-garde performances of modern dance or ballet and symphony concerts as they imagine that their opposites in London and New York do.

When observing the performances of a national state folk dance ensemble, it is possible for the culturally competent observer to analyze the different levels of audience reactions as a means of understanding which elements of the audience apprehend the variety of cultural references that make up a specific company's performance. Individuals of non-Mexican background are often startled at the degree of enthusiasm and participation that Amalia Hernandez's choreographies elicit from Mexican-American audience members, who are very vocal in their responses.

One of the most important audiences for these companies is the large diaspora living in the West, described describe in some detail in the study. Diaspora audiences are sometimes the most avid consumers

Conclusion: The Power of Representation 231

of folk dance performances. Clearly, however, not all of these companies have large diaspora audiences. For example, although there is a large Turkish immigrant population in Germany, their numbers are negligible elsewhere in the West in contrast to the numerous numbers of Greek and Croatian immigrants found throughout many areas of the West. Mexican-American audiences are among the Ballet Folklorico's most devoted fans, forming a major portion of the audiences in the frequent appearances of that company to the United States. Diaspora attendance helps the financial health of several of these ensembles. Appearances by the national folk dance ensemble also serve as a means by which the mother country remains in contact with its diaspora communities.

The impact of these companies on the diaspora communities has been immense. The very strategies that ethnic communities in the United States and elsewhere utilize to represent themselves has changed over the past five decades and now often includes dance performances that clearly reflect the repertoires of their respective national companies. In the United States we have seen this in the proliferation of ballet folklorico groups in communities with large Mexican-American populations.

Throughout this study I have referred often to the element of nationalism as one of the dominant factors in both the founding and the continuing support of these expensive organizations. Their respective governments find their performances an important source of displaying the nation; they are frequently called upon to perform before visiting heads of state and accompany their own leaders on important state visits. The theories of nationalism presented in this study demonstrate how these ensembles embody a particular nationalism through the use of cultural references that are read by the culturally competent individuals in the audience, but are sometimes missed by those who are unfamiliar with those specific elements of representation. The Soviet bloc and the former Yugoslavia regarded the innocence of folk dancing as a safe outlet for the nationalistic feelings that they tried, unsuccessfully, to suppress on a political level. Ultimately, the Croatians, Lithuanians, and Slovaks, among others, wanted political independence rather than choreographic representation. All of these governments were and are enthusiastic about the popular receptions that these ensembles receive during their international tours and frequently send them abroad.

Of all of the fields of representation, nationalism and ethnic pride stand out as the most important factors that ensure the continuance of these companies.

Even among the intellectuals and elite that I referred to above, who personally disdain attending the performances, I heard several times in all of the countries in which I conducted research that their nation "needed" the national folk dance ensemble to properly represent the nation. These same intellectuals do not, however, hesitate to take foreign guests to these performances and evince pride in the way that their nation is displayed by the spectacularized representations of the national folk dance company. Many of these intellectuals, as well as the majority of the urban population, largely accept the company's claims to authentic representation. They want to believe that their rural compatriots dress neatly and dance in a spectacular fashion, although the reality in the field is often far different. This notion proceeds from the widely held notion that I discussed above, that the peasant, who is typically the most represented figure in the repertoire of most of these ensembles, is the most representative element of the population. Rousseau's idea of the peasant as "noble savage" still holds wide currency among many urban dwellers who deeply believe that the peasant embodies the purest, most authentic spirit and ethos of the nation and that their dances are a basic primordial representation.

Thus, through spectacular choreographic representation, displaying their respective nation's folk dances, the national state folk dance ensembles have assembled the most positive, colorful, and stereotypical elements of the nation's folklore, and through their choreographic displays serve their respective nation's representational priorities. Those representational priorities formed the core of this study. More importantly, through a deeper, more careful analysis of the "unmarked," the gaps and spaces of the unrepresented, the careful observer is able to catch tantalizing glimpses of important discourses of political, ethnic, gender, and class issues that are left unspoken when the nation is symbolically dressed in its Sunday clothes and putting its best foot forward.

Notes

Introduction: Ethnicity and Nationalism (pp. 1–12)

1. Baroque dance historian Wendy Hilton notes: "In seventeenth-century court ballet, Louis XIV was usually the central figure of the performance, his roles reflecting his deification; the King's most famous identification was with the Greek sun-god Apollo, a role he danced many times" (1981, 7).

2. Sally Ann Ness came to a similar analysis in her study of a Philippine ballet, *Igorot*. "Given ballet's global popularity and prestige, the art form is an ideal vehicle for objectifications of nationalist identity that seek to achieve approval and affirmation at international and cosmopolitan venues. The ballet dancer's body, a masterwork of self-improved, controlled technical sophistication, represents dramatically nationalistic desires to achieve the autonomous conditions of modern excellence on a much larger collective scale. The dancing bodies of national ballet companies are not simply metaphors for a nationalistic fantasy but are, in fact, living proof of the 'advances' made by individual citizens inhabiting the nation-state" (1997, 98).

3. Excellent studies by Nash (1989) and Hutchinson and Smith (1996) are available for those interested in reading more on the topic of ethnicity and nationalism.

4. The former Yugoslavia had three professional ensembles: KOLO from Serbia, LADO from Croatia, and Tanec from Macedonia, as well as many highly skilled semiprofessional dance companies. All of the professional ensembles and many of the semiprofessional companies called themselves the Yugoslav State Folk Ensemble or the Yugoslav Folk Ballet when touring abroad. This created confusion for scholars who attempted to follow the careers of these various state ensembles. Further confusing the picture, another company, Frula, styling itself as an official state company of the former Yugoslavia, made up of professional dancers mostly from the KOLO ensemble and other Serbian companies, formed a company in Germany and toured widely through the United States and other parts of the world. Its repertoire was closer to a nightclub act, aimed at spectacle at the expense of the use of authentic elements.

5. See, for example, Buckland (1999a).

6. The KOLO ensemble depicted the Gypsies of the Vojvodina area (north central Serbia). The company also has a Gypsy dance, *duj duj* (a type

of cocek, a dance genre of solo-improvised dance and a form of belly dance) from Vranje in South Serbia, that does not display the very different Muslim Gypsies offensively. The Croatian ensemble LADO also performs a version of *duj duj*, which aesthetically fails because the choreography has the feel of a sorority slumber party rather than successfully conveying the potentially sensual elements that characterize this dance, probably of Turkish origin.

7. Further evidence of such official anti-Turkish state policies by the Bulgarian government came to a head immediately after the fall of the Communist state: all Turks were required to Bulgarianize their names. Hundreds of thousands of them were expelled into Turkey, creating enormous economic difficulties with a state that was providing a safe haven for thousands of Bosnian Muslims.

8. The study of private companies also merits a full-length study. Although from time-to-time I will mention such companies since they influence of state companies upon them was tremendous, but, in general, an in-depth analysis of such companies is beyond the scope of this study as I have defined it.

9. Strictly-speaking, there is no dance that one can characterize as "Persian," that is to say a dance form that is performed exclusively by Persian speakers in contrast to other ethnic groups in Iran or Afghanistan. The (unknown) author of the program notes for the concert was referring to the solo-improvised dance tradition found throughout the Iranian world (in which I include Georgia, Azerbaijan, Armenia, Afghanistan, Iran, Turkmenia, Tajikistan, and Uzbekistan), which has been utilized by professional dancers of many ethnic backgrounds for centuries. In the second half of the twentieth century, and perhaps earlier, the rich movement tradition of this dance genre was choreographed for groups of dancers performing in synchronized stagings. This dance genre is most often associated with urban aesthetic expression, although it is also found in rural areas. The rural areas are more generally characterized by regionally specific group dance traditions (Shay 1999a).

10. Recent visits of the Moiseyev Dance Company (1996 and 1999) and the Georgian State Folk Company (1998) suggest that, regarding these companies and their repertoires, little has changed from the performances given prior to 1989. On the other hand, LADO omitted all non-Croatian material, including the Ivancan suite, *Na Baniji bubanj bije*, that had premiered only two years before at great expense in time and money. Even though the suite was set in Croatia, its Serbian references had to be purged.

1. Parallel Traditions: State Folk Dance Ensembles and Folk Dance in the Field (pp. 13–37)

1. These scholarly attitudes are strikingly underscored and supported by the appearance of *Dance in the Field: Theory, Methods and Issues in Dance Ethnography* (Buckland 1999b), a collection of seventeen essays by dance ethnologists that was published after the completion of the original article

upon which this chapter is based that I wrote for *Dance Research Journal* (Shay 1999b).

2. This situation is beginning to change. With the collapse of the former Soviet Union and the change of governments throughout most of the Soviet bloc, scholars from the region are producing articles in Eastern European languages on what Rumanian dance scholar Anca Giurchescu calls "the use and abuse of folk dance" (personal communication, February 25, 1998). These observations are often filled with bitterness at having been forced to participate in what many of these scholars feel was government-sponsored misuse of folklore. (See especially Giurchescu 1992; Petrovic 1997; Zemtsovsky and Kunanbaeva 1997; and Ilieva 1992.) These observations are, however, generally confined to the activities that occurred in a specific nation. To date there have been no analytical surveys of the phenomenon of state dance companies on a wider basis.

3. A fine and detailed study of the kinds of contrasts I am discussing is provided by Andriy Nahachewsky (1995) for Ukrainian dance in Canada. See also Jones (1999), Koutsouba (1999), and Gore (1999).

4. Another genre of folk dance, which merits a full study, is the recreational folk dance movement of the United States of the period 1940–1999 in which thousands of Americans were taught a large repertoire of European folk dances by teachers of varying degrees of expertise. Occasional novelty dances from Japan, Africa, or the Middle East were taught, as well as a number of highly stylized Mexican dances that were also found in the repertoires of the folk dance clubs, as shown in the records of dances taught at folk dance camps. I am grateful to Isabelle Persh for giving me a gift of many decades of these records, which include the dances taught with their full instructions and who taught them. These same sources show that the overwhelming repertoire was composed of dances of European origin. These latter were popular for their patterned quality and reflected the distant origins of the largely middle-class European backgrounds of the American dancers. The focus for the average recreational folk dancer was to learn many dances from many contrasting regions. The result was that recreational folk dance hobbyists, while learning many dance forms, movements, and steps, rarely acquired the stylistic characteristics manifest by dancers in "the field." (There were notable exceptions to this. A few individuals so "internalized" a new dance tradition, for example Greek or Hungarian, that they sometimes also acquired a native command not only of the dance tradition, but also of the language and other aspects of their "adopted" culture. A few individuals even changed their names and moved to the country of their specific interest.) The dances learned by recreational folk dancers were generally of a three-minute duration, due to the constraints of existing recordings, whereas in the field such a dance, accompanied by native musicians, might last many times that long and never be performed in the exact same way twice. The instructions for these were "standardized" by committees especially selected by such organizations as the California Folk Dance Federation so that, theoretically, wherever folk dance hobbyists chose to dance, they could be assured that the dances they learned would be performed in exactly the same way in every venue visited. (So large was this organization that it had northern and southern components, each with its own publications.) In spite of these efforts, complaints circulated that the people in such

and such a club did not dance in the "proper" way. The "proper" way did not indicate how the dance might have been performed in the field, but whether it was according to the standardized instructions. Such insistence on standardization stands in stark contrast to the movement practices found in the field where people largely dance with spontaneity and a degree of improvisation that would be impossible to teach in classroom/studio settings in which most recreational folk dancing was taught.

The 1960s ushered in a nostalgic attempt to create communal ties, and the folk dance movement reflected this social movement. Young people poured into folk dance clubs, particularly those that featured dances from the Balkans with their communal line and circle dances. The old folk dance hobbyists, who preferred dancing in heterosexual couples and wearing "folk dance garb," which marked them and reflected distinct and dated notions of gender roles, avoided participating in the communal dances, creating a generational split in the folk dance movement. See Quigley (1992) for a description of a similar phenomenon for the square dance movement.

5. Andriy Nahachewsky points out that many individuals in the field also learn from professional teachers and perform dances from neighboring regions, and even sometimes outside the nation-state (personal communication, March 1998.) This certainly tallies with my observations, i.e., the repertoire of the Uzbek state company, Bakhor, included dances of Egypt, India, and Vietnam as well as those of neighboring republics.

A second point is that presentations from the field seen in festivals often feature dances that were popular generations ago and that no longer exist "natively" with the generation that currently performs it. This was the case for dances from Medimurje, Croatia, in the *Smotra Folklora*, an annual folklore festival held in Zagreb. The dances had to be resuscitated for purposes of performing old, traditional dances required by the folklore experts sitting on the Smotra committee rather than the polkas and waltzes that had been in vogue for at least a century.

In a telling essay in *Dance in the Field*, Egil Bakka, Norwegian dance ethnographer and self-confessed "folk dance enthusiast and neo-traditionalist" (1999, 71), describes in detail how he "rescued" old Norwegian folk dances and taught them to younger generations "to ensure that our dances are never lost forever" (ibid., 80)—a process he characterizes as "the restocking of fish in a river where the species had died out" (ibid.,78).

6. While I was traveling and conducting research in Central Asia and Azerbaijan, the professional dance companies and training schools *(koreografski instituti)* that hosted me, my dancers, and other guests would perform their formal dance routines and then, following the presentation, would come into the audience and encourage everyone to dance. At this point they all reverted to performing the social dance native to the entire urban Iranian culture sphere, solo-improvised dance (Shay 1999a).

7. That gain could be considerable for the community. For example, Professor Ankica Petrovic stated that she served on committees that selected groups to appear in the Smotra Folklora, a prestigious annual festival held in Zagreb, Croatia, and attended by thousands of spectators and tourists. Participant groups, in addition to the honor of appearing in the festival, sometimes received important perquisites for their village, such as electrification

and paved roads. Committee members often made suggestions or ordered village groups to shorten their presentation or to dance in semicircles rather than closed circles in order for the audience see better and be more interested (personal communication, November 3, 1997).

8. Those changes made for public performance can vary widely. For instance, when the villagers of the Khorasan province of Iran appeared in dances in an exhibit in the capital city, Tehran, to acquaint the city dwellers with these dances, some of the dances appeared better rehearsed, while other groups from the same region simply performed as they would have in their own village. All of the other aspects of the dance—formations, steps, figures, music, and costumes—were not altered and were the same as the vernacular tradition (see videocassettes *Dances of Khorasan* and *Raqs-ha-ye mahalli-ye Iran*).

9. As an artistic director of a dance company that represents various cultures and ethnicities, I am sometimes approached by audience members about inclusion of dances of their ethnicity in our repertoire. For example, Assyrians question me as to why I have not included their dances. The answer to such a question, as I will point out in Chapter 2, is often lack of finances, lack of sufficient research materials, problems with finding proper music, etc. However, it is important to stress that the pleas for inclusion in our repertoire by individuals representing a wide variety of ethnicities from the areas that my nonofficial company, the AVAZ International Dance Theatre, represents, are constant. The pressure for inclusion in a state-sponsored company must be even more acute.

10. Knowledgeable observers of the Reda Troupe of Egypt concur with this assessment. Lois Al-Faruqi, scholar of dances from the Islamic world, commented: "In the Middle East, recent attempts at programmatic dance by companies like Firqah Rida [sic] of Egypt are obvious attempts to imitate an alien tradition (European dance) rather than one native to Egypt" (1987, 6).

Morroe Berger, former director of the Program in Near Eastern Studies at Princeton University observed:

> As the fame of belly dance spread to the Western world, it became something of an embarrassment to the cultural and political custodians of the East, who began to consider themselves above their own popular arts. . . . This is because the government encourages instead the performance of a sort of folkloric dance that only vaguely resembles the belly dance. (1966, 43)

11. Interestingly, there exists a lively urban and historical dance tradition in the various cities of Croatia, and perhaps Ljevakovic would not have missed such a promising aesthetic opportunity had folklore scholarship in the period in which he was creating been more inclusive. As I mentioned above, post-Ljevakovic LADO has begun to include at least one urban-based work, *Stari Splitski Plesovi* (Old Split Dances), in the repertoire.

12. A full discussion of the topic of theories and practices of nationalism and the development of nation-states is beyond the scope of this study. For those who are interested, see the following works: Brubaker (1996), Calhoun (1995), Eley and Suny (1996), Gellner (1983), Hall (1998), and Smith (1986).

13. This process is not over. For example, in Georgia, the various groups

such as Abkhaz and Ossets wish further subdivision; various areas of Uzbekistan are contested by Tajiks and Kirghiz; the Albanians of Kosovo wish to separate from Serbia; and the Croatians of Hercegovina wish to join the Republic of Croatia.

14. Ljevakovic's view of the peasantry was unique. In contrast, Nevenka Sokcic, one of the earliest dancers with LADO, the Croatian state ensemble, recalls that when the peasants from the villages around Zagreb came to collect the laundry, her mother would send her and her brother and sister from the room so as not to see the uncouth peasants (personal interview, October 16, 1999). Nor are Americans free of such stereotypical images of rural populations. The "Ma and Pa Kettle" series of films and the "Beverly Hillbillies" television series utilize these images for the basis of their "humor."

2. Anatomy of a Dance Company (pp. 38–56)

1. Many unimaginative suggestions for the creation of a national folk dance ensemble for the United States were put forth. As an example of how American dance artists were unable to shake off their prejudice of presenting folk dance in a ballet format, Prevots details how Agnes DeMille wanted to create a "folk ballet." De Mille wanted to call it the American Lyric Ballet, which would feature music by composers such as Aaron Copland, dances by ballet choreographers such as Michael Kidd, and movie choreographers such as Gower Champion and Bob Fosse (Prevots 1998, 117–18).

2. The china poblana as seen in the Ballet Folklorico's *Jalisco* choreography has only the sketchiest relation to the actual china poblana costume, both historically and in its current stylized state. This style of dress was worn throughout most towns and cities of Mexico and California during most of the nineteenth century. It was not a regional folk dress. It consisted of a chemise (sometimes daggeted), a skirt in which a different fabric constituted the upper one-third of the garment and a (usually) darker fabric made up the lower portion. The fabric used varied with the means of the wearer but ranged from cheap calicos and cottons to expensive silks, sometimes garnished with gold trim and metal sequins. A rebozo was often worn with the ensemble, both as a shawl and as head covering. In the twentieth century as the china poblana went out of fashion as everyday wear, it began to assume the symbolic aspect of a "national" costume for Mexico and became associated with the state of Jalisco and the city of Guadalajara. Beautiful young ladies wearing this costume were used to advertise Mexican products such as beer and tortillas. Waitresses in restaurants serving Mexican food often wore, and still wear, this costume. The Mexican-American population in Southern California used this dress for many decades as festive wear. In its new guise as a festive costume, the skirts became garnished with increasing amounts of sequins and adorned with the emblem of the eagle and snake found on the Mexican flag. The richest examples of these costumes became too heavy to dance in, so the Ballet Folklorico opted for a simple, lightweight version of the dress. The company did not, however, opt to return to the simpler historical dress of the nineteenth century. Several examples of this earlier dress are found in the Los Angeles County Museum of

Natural History as well as in numerous contemporary lithographs and photographs. See Shay and Matchette (1987).

After the first visits of Ballet Folklorico, the icon of the china poblana for Mexican Americans, at least, was substituted to some degree by the norteno costume with its full skirts. Since the 1970s it has become more common to see dancing children in norteno clothing in the news stories that accompany the annual *cinco de mayo* and other festivities. The charro image for the male still retains its hold on the popular imagination as a visual icon of "Mexicanness."

The jarabe was also more widespread as a popular dance in the nineteenth century. It was performed in Early California as an improvised dance to several different melodies and might be better characterized as a style or complex of dance figures like the waltz (Shay 1982).

3. There are many devoted practitioners of belly dancing in the West. It is hobby for thousands of individuals. The majority of these enthusiasts favor more delicate terms for belly dancing such a *danse du ventre* and *danse orientale*.

4. An example of such attitudes is found in the Moroccan segment of the six-part television series "Dancing" (Program 3). While a group of men enthusiastically perform all of the movements of a domestic belly dancing, with far more energy than the professional female dancers whom they largely ignore, a male Moroccan sociologist, clearly embarrassed by such dancing, intones that it is "unmanly." In his judgement, he clearly ignores the fact that the solo-improvised dance tradition in the Arab world, popularly known as belly dancing in the West, is equally popular among both men and women. The notion that such movements are "feminine" has been appropriated from European notions of what movements are "proper" for each gender.

5. It is beyond the scope of this study to enumerate all of the reasons why historical iconographic materials can be used for an actual reconstruction of how dances and movement practices appeared in various periods. I refer the reader to Fermor (1987), Lawler (1964), Marti and Kurath (1964), and Shay (1999a).

6. For example, the Moiseyev Dance Company, in its last two tours (1996 and 1999) substituted the large live orchestra with recordings for most of the performances, one exception being the *Old City Quadrille*, because the musicians also dance. Ballet Folklorico used to travel with a full chorus but has abandoned the practice in the past several tours. Obviously these attempts at downsizing are for financial reasons. Ballet Folklorico again brought a chorus for its September 1999 performances in Pasadena, California (Pasles 1997).

7. See Silverman (1997, 61), who observed that this type of decision is not "a political decision, but politics itself."

8. For example, if a young girl in the district of Baranja, Croatia (before the breakup of the former Yugoslavia, at least), wore her hair in a certain style, one could tell if she was in mourning. Yet a different hairstyle was adopted if she were in semimourning (*sitne bole* or little woes). The semimourning hairstyle would be worn, for example, if her brother had gone into the army. As another example, as late as the 1990s the length of fringe around the apron in parts of Bosnia informed the knowledgeable if the wearer was Catholic, Orthodox, or Muslim. See Gusic (1955).

240 Notes

9. The Moiseyev Dance Company's *Gopak* finale, the Mahalli Dancers' Qashqa'i tribal dance, and the Ballet Folklorico's *Tarima de Tixtla*, among several other dances, illustrate these alterations.

10. One of the saddest memories of my professional career was the purchase I made, facilitated by a friend from LADO, of a set of Slavonian costumes made of homemade silk and gold bullion embroidery that were destroyed by the crew of ship, who tore the silk dresses to shreds by removing the gold embroidery in order to steal it. I still remember how I first saw the shredded remnants being pulled out of packing boxes, and how I sat next to them weeping at the loss of two years of financial and emotional investment, the destruction of precious human labor, and years of dreaming.

11. See especially Madcz (1983), Zemtsovsky and Kunanbaeva (1997), Gutkin (1997), Petrovic (1997), Silverman (1997), and Rice (1997).

3. The Moiseyev Dance Company: Ancestor of the Genre (pp. 57–81)

1. A fuller description of the press and public for the first Moiseyev tour in the United States is provided by Naima Prevots (1998), *Dance for Export: Cultural Diplomacy and the Cold War*, Wesleyan University Press, 70–74.

2. It should be mentioned that the Moiseyev Dance Company traveled to Paris and London in 1955, but due to political problems its first tour to the United States was delayed for three more years. Also, the Moiseyev Dance Company was not the first company from Eastern Europe to perform in the West. In 1950 an aggregation of Yugoslavian dance groups performed in London, and in 1956 Tanec, the national dance company of Macedonia, and KOLO of Serbia toured widely through the United States and Canada but did not make the kind of impact that the Moiseyev Dance Company made.

3. The company to which I belonged at the time was the Gandy Dancers, a well-known exhibition and recreational folk dance group in the Folk Dance Federation of California, South, in the 1940s, 1950s, and 1960s. Prevots (1998) mentions a similar party that took place among folk dancers in New York City.

4. For works on ethnicity issues in the former Soviet Union, see Allworth (1971, 1995), Atkin (1992), Bennigsen (1971), Gross (1992), Motyl (1990), Naby (1994), Panarin (1994).

5. A practice found in neighboring Afghanistan right up until the Soviet invasion. An example may be seen in the 1972 film *Afghan Village*, purchasable from the Smithsonian Institution.

6. For a fuller description of Moiseyev's career in ballet, see Isareva (1998).

7. Official company biography found in Cerritos Center for the Performing Arts Program, February 1999, P-5 (Moiseyev Dance Company 1999).

8. Jozo Vlahovic, the amateur company that two years later changed its name to LADO and became the professional ensemble of Croatia, proudly noted that in 1947 it had participated in the immense folk dance festival in Prague and taken second place, "coming right after the professional state dance company of the Soviet Union" (*Yugoslav Folk Dances* 1949). The program cited here accompanied the exhibition of Yugoslavian folk dances in London in 1950, which featured the Serbian State Folk ensemble, KOLO, Jozo

Vlahovic amateur ensemble of Croatia (already LADO at time of the printing of the program), and a group of villagers from Lazaropolje, Macedonia.

9. See Tkachenko (1955) and Karimova (1973, 1975, 1977, 1979) for typical examples.

10. The Neva Russian Dance Company and the Khadra Folk Ensemble in the San Francisco area are examples of companies that utilize character dance and a Moiseyev format.

11. See videocassette listings in the bibliography.

4. Ballet Folklorico: Viva Mexico! (pp. 82–107)

1. The Ballet Folklorico de Mexico is also called Ballet Folklorico of Mexico in the United States. In the past few years it has been officially named Ballet Folklorico de Mexico de Amalia Hernandez. Similarly, certain dance suites such as *Veracruz* and *Jalisco* have undergone name changes. *Veracruz* has been variously named *Fiesta en Veracruz, Mocambo,* and *Fiesta en Tlacotalpan.* These changes of name often follow the introduction of new elements into the work, but the general outline of the choreography remains the same. Likewise, *Jalisco* has been named *Guadalajara, Christmas in Jalisco,* and *Fiesta in Jalisco.*

2. See Dallala and Martinez (1998, 396) for examples.

3. I am grateful to Gema Sandoval for a discussion of this topic.

4. In a curious statement, Bayanihan, the Philippine national dance company, then known as the Dance Company of the Philippine Women's University, which first performed in 1956, claims that "Bayanihan has inspired other countries to exploit their own folk material for international theater presentation. Among these is Mexico whose international folkloric ballet company, formed after Bayanihan's first performance [1959–1960] there, now gives the Company lively competition" (*Bayanihan* 1987, 6). No acknowledgment of Bayanihan's claim in inspiring the Ballet Folklorico appears in any of the Ballet Folklorico's programs or publicity, which indicate 1952 as the founding year.

5. Cristiani (1994) gives a full history of the company's performances.

6. For a description of dance in the field see Sevilla (1998).

7. This practice may have resulted from the *Los Angeles Time*'s policy of reviewing only new works.

5. LADO, Ensemble of Folk Dances and Songs of Croatia: Proper Peasants (pp. 108–125)

1. I subtitled the chapter "Proper Peasants" after a classical anthropological study of a Hungarian village using the same title by Edit Fel and Tamas Hofer (1969). In this study the peasants attempted to portray themselves as a people of deep gravity, dignity, and honor, hard working and demonstrating a constant sense of serious purpose. These are positive and noble demeanors that Zvonko Ljevakovic utilized to characterize the Croatian peasants in LADO choreographies.

2. Like many dance companies from the former Yugoslavia, LADO has used multiple names: LADO, Ensemble of Folk Dances and Songs of Croatia; State Folk Ensemble of Folk Dances and Songs; LADO, Folk Dance Ensemble Zagreb, Croatia; Folklore Ensemble of Croatia "LADO" Zagreb; LADO, The Ensemble of Croatian Folk Song and Dance; Folk Ensemble of Croatia, LADO; Folk Dance Ensemble of Croatia; and LADO, National Dance Ensemble of Yugoslavia. These are some of the names gleaned from programs listed in the bibliography.

3. These new and administrative political boundaries were different from its previous several incarnations in the former Hapsburg Empire when Hungary dominated most Croatian territory—the kingdom of Serbs, Croats, and Slovenes—and then the kingdom of Yugoslavia that lasted until World War II. For the most part these remain the boundaries of the newly constituted Republic of Croatia.

4. Dubinskas (1983) details the identification of Croatian nationality and nationalist sentiment with the performance of Croatian peasant expressive culture, especially singing.

5. At an early age, Nevenka Sokcic, who came from a prosperous upper-middle-class family, found herself an enemy of the state because of her background. The Communist Party, when it first came to power, labeled her identity characteristics as "bourgeois bastard." She said, "You can not imagine how shameful it was for a young girl to carry around such an identification card for all to see. One day when we had to hand our cards to the office to apply for passports, I felt terrible." Her feelings of loyalty toward LADO for her twenty-five-year career in the company were increased when the first managing director, a very strong woman and member of the party, called her into the company office. "Ljevakovic was there, and in front of me she silently tore up the card. 'We'll apply for a new one—with different characteristics. No one will ever know'" (personal interview, October 15, 1999).

6. I accompanied LADO as a tour manager and interpreter for several weeks of the 1992 tour of North America.

7. In the *Baranjska Zetva* (Harvest from Baranja) a man in a highly decorative Hungarian coat comes on the stage and looks at the laboring peasants. To knowledgeable eyes, with his clothing and arrogant walk he represents the Hungarian aristocracy that politically and economically dominated Central and Northern Croatia prior to World War I, and sometimes beyond. He is not presented in a negative light, but clearly he represents a symbol of power.

8. Along with two other members of AMAN, a company I founded and directed for fifteen years, we were privileged to attend those classes for several weeks in April and May of 1968. They were taught by Nevenka Sokcic.

9. Other state ensembles also feature vocal music. Bayanihan dancers occasionally sing, as do the dancers in the ensembles of the Hungarian State Folk Ensemble, KOLO of Serbia, Tanec of Macedonia, and, rarely, Bakhor of Uzbekistan. More commonly, when vocal music is a feature of the company, a separate chorus exists. Ballet Folklorico, Mazowse of Poland, the Bulgarian State Ensemble of Folk Songs and Dances (the Philip Koutev Ensemble), the Pirin Ensemble of Bulgarian Macedonia, and the Hungarian State Folk Ensemble all maintained separate choruses. Of those, the Hun-

garian State Folk Ensemble, until the past decade, maintained a large chorus that sang in classical Western style with elaborate choral arrangements by such renowned composers as Kodaly and Bartok, while the dancers in the ensemble sang in a traditional style. Ballet Folklorico followed the practice of utilizing traditional vocal styles by soloists in the various regional musical groups and a chorus that sang in Western classical style. The Bulgarian state folk ensemble performed with a female chorus of forty-four voices. The choral arrangements were elaborate but sung in a traditional vocal style, rather than Western-trained vocal style.

10. For example, Mazowse and Moiseyev utilize large symphony orchestras; the KOLO ensemble of Serbia largely employs a small chamber orchestra of strings, flutes, and oboes and a tamburica ensemble for the pieces from North Serbia, or Bakhor; and the Uzbek ensemble uses a largely classical Uzbek ensemble of ten men who play instruments from the *shash maqam* tradition. The Bulgarian state folk ensemble developed a large orchestra based on traditional instruments. The Rumanian and Hungarian state folk ensembles use large violin-dominated Gypsylike orchestras.

11. These songs were often performed with new lyrics composed to old traditional songs, a not uncommon practice in many parts of the world.

6. Egypt: Bazaar of Dance (pp. 126–162)

1. The fluid character of the company personnel was reflected in the three subsequent performances that I attended in which the number of instrumentalists and dancers varied.

2. These finger cymbals are called *saqat darwishi* (dervish cymbals) to distinguish them from the smaller and lighter *saqat sharqi* (oriental) favored by performers of oriental dance (belly dance).

3. The viewer of this little-known dance is reminded that contemporary flamenco, in this viewer's opinion, has most likely developed from the aesthetics of art and architecture from the Islamic world, most specifically North Africa music and dance traditions, Andalusian regional folk dances, and Spanish theatrical dance. It would be remiss not to note how much this dance holds in common with contemporary flamenco practices, especially the rhythms, poses, and attitudes; carriage of the upper torso, hands, and arms; and spins and turns.

4. According to long-time observer of the Cairo dance scene Morocco (Carolina Varga Dinicu), who travels at least once a year to Egypt, the two tannoura (skirt) performers that we observed were what she terms "secular" dancers. There is also a true dervish, "sacred" in Morocco's terms, performer who sometimes appears with the company. Since I was unable to observe the "sacred" performer I am unable to comment on any differences in the performances. One of the two tannoura performers accompanied the 1995 Festival of the Nile tour of the United States and created a critical sensation with his performance, which lasted nearly thirty minutes.

5. Ironically, this same stance is taken by some Islamist groups who according to Morocco "are attempting to place an artificial puritanical concept of morality on the country that is at variance with the requirements of

actual Islamic religious practice and custom. They tried to ban weddings because of dancing and intimidate people in Imbaba by threats of violence, but the people held them anyway" (personal interview, January 25, 2000). Such threats are omnipresent. When I asked a proprietor of a video store in the traditional bazaar for a dance video, he told me that he no longer carries them because of threats from Islamist groups (personal interview, January 27, 2000).

6. There may be other state-supported folkloric ensembles in Cairo, but my inquiries did not yield any others. According to Mahmoud Reda, regional ensembles exist in cities throughout Egypt that are modeled after the Reda Troupe. "The artists throughout Egypt follow me. They think that my work is authentic" (Reda, personal interview, January 10, 2000).

There is a children's ensemble, which is also housed in the Balloon Theatre, but its repertoire is contemporary and outside of the purview of this study. Its performances represents a modernist view of contemporary Egyptian childhood in a repertoire that is a combination of "Romper Room" and Disneyland without any connection to actual childhood existence in Egypt. This ensemble is ripe for analysis by an interested dance scholar.

7. Farida Fahmy, Mahmoud Reda's sister-in-law who was for many years the lead dancer in the Reda Troupe, and subsequently its artistic director for some years, wrote her master's thesis (Fahmy 1987) on the topic of Mahmoud Reda's choreographic creations and the history of the company.

8. According to Fahmy (1987, 60), this work had at least two shorter versions.

9. *Ya 'ain, ya leil* means "oh eye, oh night" and is the refrain commonly used by vocalists during performances of the improvised musical passages in classical and popular music known as *mawwal*.

10. For the reader who is interested in the details of the founding process of the Reda Troupe see Fahmy (1987).

11. During my stay in Egypt I attended two parties and two weddings, and all of the men who danced in the city performed solo-improvised dances using the same movement vocabulary, and in the countryside men danced both the solo-improvised dance form and dances with long staves (*tahtib*) and short sticks and canes (*'asa*). In the village wedding celebration a man stood at the edge of the dancing space (a dirt area cleared for the purpose) and had a basket containing scarves. These he would tie around the pelvis of each man or boy who rose to dance in order to emphasize the pelvic movements that would have been lost under the galabiyas (robes) that many of them wore.

During one of the parties, a long-time (twenty-five years) European resident expressed his surprise that heterosexual men danced like women and that no one could explain why. I told him that his was a common Western notion of the kinds of movements that were considered appropriate to Western men and women and that these attitudes had been adopted by elite Westernized individuals in Egyptian society. Nevertheless, while some of these Westernized individuals disparaged such performances (see Shay 1999b), their own bodily imperatives responded to the powerful call of the music in a culturally appropriate way learned from childhood—that is, each of the men in the room performed the movements of solo-improvised dancing.

12. For purposes of brevity I have paraphrased Fahmy's evaluation of Reda's work using short quotes from her thesis.

13. I was told at the Balloon Theatre that the Reda Troupe was going to perform the production, *ginniyat al-bahr*, but it never materialized. Reda's relation with the theater seemed distant and wary and he expressed disappointment in its reception. The last performance of it in the fall had only three audience members in a theater that seats at least three thousand. He retired from his position as active director of his company in 1991. Farida Fahmy directed it for some time but now designs costumes for productions, and a series of other individuals have directed the company since Reda left.

14. See Franken (1996) for detailed descriptions of the plots.

15. Professional performers of belly dance, or solo-improvised dance, both male and female have always been considered professional sex workers. In the case of women, it is not the movements or the sensuality that bring the air of disgrace but rather the fact that a woman is dancing and revealed in front of men not properly related to her, thus bringing dishonor to the men in her family. Some Islamic clergy consider such performances as arousing unlawful sexual passion in male observers, thus causing *fitna* (social chaos). The topic of belly dancers and their problems in commanding respect in Egypt is a constant source of many articles, by both Egyptians and non-Egyptians, usually belly dancers themselves, who attempt to create an aura of respectability around a dance form that has always been considered dishonorable and its performers to be sexually available. For recent examples see Berger (1966), Buonaventura (1996), and Dabbous and Fam (1999).

16. In attempting to make a comparison with other professions, I found that a young scholar at the National Museum, who worked in the library, made 145 pounds (equivalent to a little more than forty-eight U.S. dollars). The Egyptian government employs many individuals who would otherwise have no income, and the salaries are very low. Mahmoud Reda said that during the time he was undersecretrary of state with the Ministry of Culture, he received three hundred pounds a month.

17. Most knowledgeable observers such as Morocco (Carolina Varga Dinicu) agree that dancing, particularly professional performances of belly dancing, have fallen on hard times. This is reflected as well in slashed budgets for the state companies and is partly due to the threat of Islamist resurgence to which the government feels obliged to make gestures of Islamic piety; thus, Mubarak can blame the riots on belly dancers and drummers from the slums, as well as on the state's own economic problems.

Making the performances of state-supported companies regular stops on tourist itineraries rather than highly expensive belly dance shows, often featuring foreign dancers, on Nile cruise boats could easily solve this problem. There is little to do in the evening in Cairo, and tourists would love to see the performances of the state-supported dance companies. This would provide year-round employment for the company artists.

18. In a performance I attended, the National Folk Troup did in fact use native *mizmar* players in three of its numbers. I also heard the orchestra members on the trumpet and piccolo warming up with passages from Verdi's *Aida*. The Western theater orchestra played the bulk of the program.

19. See, for example, the videocassettes *"Reda Troup" Egyptian Folklore* and *Funun Sh'Abiah Misriyah*.

20. Reported in 1979 by the ABC news program "20/20." See also Sellers-Young (1992) for an excellent overview of this community.

7. Greece: Dora Stratou Greek Dances Theatre, A Living Museum (pp. 163–192)

1. Several variations of the company name appear in programs: Dora Stratou Greek Dances Theatre, Greek Dances—"Dora Stratou" Theatre, Greek Dances Theatre Dora Stratou, and Dora Stratou Theatre Greek Dances.

2. One area in which minorities are not absent is in the reports of crime in the newspapers. If the suspect is Albanian, Gypsy, or Rumanian, this is duly noted in the description. Greek criminals are not identified by ethnicity.

3. For example, the Greek royal family, themselves imported from Bavaria, created court clothing, incorporating elements of Western styling, an elite version of traditional clothing that came to be known as the "Amalia," after the first queen.

4. This disparity of attention between the different historical periods can be seen in the museums in Athens and other parts of Greece. Museums devoted to the classical past and that of the modern Greek state, both in size and number, dwarf the single, relatively small museum of Byzantine art in Athens. There is, of course, no museum devoted to the Ottoman period; there are only museums devoted to the post-Ottoman period portraying the valiant struggle of the Greek nation against the Ottomans.

5. This avoidance of any mention of Ottoman presence or influence in Greek life pervades most areas of national life. It has marred scholarship in a number of areas such as the research of folklore, national costumes, music, and dance, where ancient origins are sought to legitimate all aspects of material and intellectual culture as "pure."

6. See also Holden and Vouras (1965) and Petrides (1975b).

7. This ensemble was most probably the KOLO ensemble of Serbia but might have also included LADO and a group of Macedonian villagers from Galicnik (see *Yugoslav Folk Dances* 1949). This aggregation numbering some hundred individuals had toured successfully in London and other Western European cities in the previous season.

8. It is beyond the scope of this chapter to go into detail concerning the Lyceum of Greek Women, which has sponsored folk dance performances since 1910 and have branches in most cities and towns throughout Greece as well as Boston and Atlanta. Because of its social position, the Lyceum of Greek Women has considerable numbers of supporters in the Greek establishment. Under the influence of the performances of the Dora Stratou company, with which it had considerable competition, it has broadened its scope to include regional dances from all over Greece. The Lyceum of Greek Women also sponsors lectures and exhibitions on many aspects of Greek folk traditions. Alkis Raftis, personal interviews, February 10 and 14, 2000; personal communication, Vilma Matchette, April 26, 2000.

8. Turkish State Folk Dance Ensemble: The Last of the Great Ensembles (pp. 193–223)

1. "Ataturkism" is the following of Kemal Ataturk's philosophy of how Turkey should be administered and developed into a modern state. It is sometimes called "Kemalism" in English.

2. The field of nationalism has had an enormous recent burgeoning of studies. It is beyond the scope of this study to go into detail, but the interested reader may consult a number of excellent works in addition to those cited in the text. A collection of essays on Ernest Gellner's theory is to be found in John Hall (1998). Two important basic readers on the topic are: *Nationalism* (Hutchinson and Smith 1992) and *Ethnicity* (Hutchinson and Smith 1996).

3. In 1995 I attended a National Endowment for the Humanities seminar, "Rethinking the Middle East and Central Asia," organized by Professor Dale F. Eickelman at Dartmouth College. The members of the seminar discussed the Huntington model at length. I am grateful to Professor Eickelman and the members of the seminar for the valuable insights that they provided.

4. Hugh Kostanick, UCLA professor of political geography, as early as 1956 warned his students to beware of the "naturalness" of any states that have any straight lines for borders.

5. My partner, Khosrow Jamali (Jamal) states that his father was unable to read and write, but had memorized the Koran and the *Shahnameh* in their entirety as well as a large body of poetry by such famous poets as Hafez and Sa'adi. His father was from Kurdistan and was by no means exceptional in his neighborhood (personal interview, May 21, 2000).

6. Large numbers, if not the majority, of the religious minorities migrated when the Islamic Republic was formed in 1979.

7. The question of the Armenian genocide is a highly contested area in both the scholarly world and in Turkish relations with Europe and the United States. The Turkish government has vigorously denied and continues to deny accusations of genocidal intent. It is beyond the scope of this book to go deeply into this dark issue. I recommend to those that are interested in this issue to read a series of essays in *Remembrance and Denial: The Case of the Armenian Genocide* (Hovannisian 1998).

8. Baykurt's six primary areas of choreographic and musical folkloric types are: The Aegean in the west where the *zeybek* is the principal form; the Thracian region from the portion of Turkey in Europe in which the two principal dance forms are the *horo* and the *karslima*; the Black Sea region in which the *horon* is the main dance form; the southeast, i.e., Kurdish districts, in which the *halay*, a genre of line dances, is widely performed; Kars-Erzerum, i.e., the Caucasian style of couple dances and the line dances known as *bar*; and central and south central Anatolia where the principal dance form is spoon dances (1996, 49–51). See also And (1959, 1976, 1998).

9. For the interested reader, Melissa Cefkin (1993) has admirably detailed this process in her dissertation.

10. This chapter does not have the scope to enter into what ethnomusicologist Martin Stokes (1992) calls the "arabesk debate." Arabesk is a highly

popular genre of music that is perceived to copy Egyptian musical styles. It took on highly political overtones during the 1970s and 1980s as the musical emblem of the urban lower classes and became a highly passionate cause célèbre during that period. Turkish officials and Kemalists decry the music as non-Turkish. Dance ethnologist Serif Baykurt stated that in the national company's *Ciftetelli* choreography, "the State Folk Dance Ensemble is involved in arabesk kinds of dancing" (qtd. in Cefkin 1993, 140).

9. Conclusion: The Power of Representation (pp. 224–232)

1. Dances for ritual purposes are often rigorously rehearsed by native populations, particularly if, as among the Pueblo Indians, for example, exact and correct performances are required for the efficacy of the ritual. According to dance scholars Samuel Marti and Gertrude Kurath, "This policy was also expressed in the rigidity of Aztec ceremonial dances and music, formalized to such an extent that the slightest deviation or mistake was immediately detected and the culprit severely punished" (1964, 15). Among the Kwakiutl, anthropologist Franz Boas noted, "In former years the Fool dancers and the grizzly Bears are said to have killed a dancer who made a mistake. Nowadays the punishment is merely performed symbolically, for the Fool dancers carry lances with tips that slide into the handle, with which they pretend to kill the offender" (1972, 13).

For the solemn attitudes with which ritual and ceremonial dances are regarded among several Native American (both North and South American Indians) ethnic groups, the reader may refer to Boas (1972), Marti and Kurath (1964), and Heth (1992).

2. The Moscow Youth Festivals, held in the mid-1950s, drew hundreds of thousands of young people worldwide, as well as a extensive coverage by *Life Magazine*. The U.S. government deplored the event as propaganda and harassed the American participants as "pinkos," when in fact participants were often more interested in the colorful folk dance and music. It was at these festivals that the Moiseyev and other Eastern European national ensembles made appearances and sparked the idea for founding companies throughout the Third World.

3. For discussions of this phenomenon in specific cultural contexts, see Dubinskas (1983) for Croatia and Sweet (1985, 45–64) for the Tewa Pueblo Indians.

4. Several of the companies within particular nation-states do, however, visually and aurally resemble one another. For example, the ensembles of the former Soviet Union, such as the several professional and amateur companies of Russia and the Ukraine, do strongly resemble one another through the use of choreographies clearly inspired by Moiseyev and imitating the Moiseyev Dance Company. The Ballet Folklorico de Teatro Nacional is clearly an Amalia Hernandez look-alike, and in the same vein the National Folkl Troup of Egypt is obviously modeled on the successful company and choreographies created by Mahmoud Reda.

5. At a meeting of dance consultants that I attended at the National Endowment for the Arts, during one of the endless discussions of what

constitutes "authentic" traditional dance, one of the consultants, a modern dance choreographer, said, "We can all tell what is authentic." This is a variation of "dance is the international language." I hastened to assure him that his understanding of what constitutes authenticity in Chinese dance would be no greater than his understanding of the Chinese language. The only way to gain such an understanding is to study Chinese dance in some intensive way.

Bibliography

Ahmad, Feroz. 1993. *Making of Modern Turkey.* London and New York: Routledge.
Al-Faruqi, Lois Ibsen. 1987. "Dance as an Expression of Islamic Culture." *Dance Resource Journal* 10(2): 6–17.
Allworth, Edward. 1971. "Restating the Soviet Nationality Question." In *Soviet Nationality Problems,* ed. Edward Allworth. New York: Columbia University Press.
———. 1995. "New Central Asians." In *Central Asia,* ed. Edward Allworth. Durham, N.C.: Duke University Press, 527–72.
And, Metin. 1959. *Dances of Anatolian Turkey.* New York: Dance Perspectives, no. 3.
———. 1976. *Pictorial History of Turkish Dancing.* Ankara: Dost Yayinlari.
———. 1998. "Turkey." *International Encyclopedia of Dance.* Vol. 6. New York: Oxford University Press, 208–13.
Anderson, Benedict. 1991. *Imagined Communities.* Rev. ed. London and New York: Verso.
Appadurai, Arjun. 1990. "Disjuncture and Difference in the Global Cultural Economy." *Public Culture* 2(2) (Spring): 1–23.
Arkin, Lisa C., and Marian Smith. 1997. "National Dance in the Romantic Ballet." In *Rethinking the Sylph: New Perspectives on the Romantic Ballet,* ed. Lynn Garafola. Hanover and London: Wesleyan University Press, 1997.
Armbrust, Walter, ed. 1996. *Mass Culture and Modernism in Egypt.* Cambridge Studies in Social and Cultural Anthropology. Cambridge: Cambridge University Press.
Astourian, Stephan H. 1998. "Modern Turkish Identity and the Armenian Genocide: From Prejudice to Racist Nationalism." In *Remembrance and Denial: The Case of the Armenian Genocide,* ed. Richard Hovannisian. Detroit: Wayne State University Press, 23–49.
Atkin, Muriel. 1992. "Religious, National, and Other Identities in Central Asia." In *Muslims in Central Asia,* ed. Jo-Ann Gross. Durham, N.C.: Duke University Press, 46–72.
Bakka, Egil. 1999. "'Or Shortly They Would Be Lost Forever': Documenting for Revival and Research." In *Dance in the Field,* ed. Theresa J. Buckland. New York: St. Martin's Press, 71–81.
Ballet Folklorico de Mexico. 1963. Souvenir program accompanying phonograph record. Mexico City.
———. 1965. Dance program. Palacio de Bellas Artes, Mexico.
———. 1967. *Artes de Mexico,* numero 88/89, Ano XIV.

———. 1969. Program for January 6. In *Performing Arts, the Music Center Monthly* 3(1): 51–53.
———. 1977–78. Souvenir program. Mexico City, Bellas Artes.
———. 1982. Program. Mexico City, Bellas Artes.
———. 1995a. Program. U.S. Tour.
———. 1995b. Souvenir program. U.S. Tour.
———. 1997. Program. In *Performing Arts* 31(9): P3–P7.
———. 1998. Souvenir program. U.S. tour.
———. 1999. Program. In *Performing Arts, Southern California Edition* 33(9): P1–P13.
Ballet Folklorico de Mexico de Amalia Hernandez. 1999. Souvenir program. U.S. Tour.
———. 2000. Dance program. September 22–23.
Ballet Folklorico of Mexico. 1969. Souvenir program. New York, Sol Hurok Productions.
———. 1974. Program. Shrine Auditorium, Los Angeles, February 8–10, 15–17.
Barbir, Karl K. 1996. "Memory, Heritage, and History: The Ottoman Legacy in the Arab World." In *Imperial Legacy: Ottoman Imprint on the Balkans and the Middle East*, ed. L. Carl Brown. New York: Columbia University Press, 100–14.
Barkey, Henri J., and Graham E. Fuller. 1998. *Turkey's Kurdish Question*. Carnegie Commission on Preventing Deadly Conflict. Lanham, Md.: Rowman & Littlefield.
Bayanihan. 1987. Manila, Bayanihan Folk Arts Center.
Baykurt, Serif. 1996. "Turk Halk Oyunlarinin bolgelere Dagilisi." *Turkiye'de Ilk Halk Oyunlari Semineri* (The Second Seminar on Folk Dances in Turkey), ed. Serif Baykurt. Istanbul: Yapi Kredi Yayinlari.
Beiza'i, Bahram. 1965. *Namayesh dar Iran* (Theatre in Iran). Tehran: Kaivan Press.
Bennigsen, Alexandre. 1971. "Islamic or Local Consciousness Among Soviet Nationalities?" In *Soviet Nationality Problems*, ed. Edward Allworth. New York: Columbia University Press.
Berger, Morroe. 1961. *Curious and Wonderful Gymnastic: "Arab Danse Du Ventre."* New York: Dance Perspectives, no. 10, 4–42.
———. 1966. "Belly Dance." *Horizons* 8(2): 41–49.
Bernheimer, Martin. 1967. "Yugoslavian Dancers End Season at the Greek Theater." *Los Angeles Times*, September 27, sec. 4, p. 14.
Bloland, Sunni. 1992. "16th Annual California Greek Orthodox Youth Folk Dance Festival: A Social and Artistic Extravaganza." *Proceedings. 17th Symposiun of the Study Group on Ethnochoreology*. Nafplion, Greece, July 2–10: 25–28.
Boas, Franz. 1972. "Dance and Music in the Life of the Northwest Coast Indians of North America (Kwakiutl)." In *Function of Dance in Human Society: A Seminar Directed by Franziska Boas*, ed. Franziska Boas. 2d ed. New York: Dance Horizons, 1944, 1972.
Bottomley, Gillian. 1987. "Folk Dance and Representation." Paper for Conference of the International Organization of Folk Art on Folk Dance Today. Larissa, Greece, July 1–5.
Brass, Paul R. 1991. *Ethnicity and Nationalism: Theory and Comparison*. New Delhi/Newberry Park/London: Sage.

Brown, L. Carl. 1996. "Setting: An Introduction." In *Imperial Legacy: Ottoman Imprint on the Balkans and the Middle East*, ed. L. Carl Brown. New York: Columbia University Press, 1–12.
Brubaker, Roger. 1996. *Nationalism Reframed: Nationhood and the National Question in the New Europe.* Cambridge: Cambridge University Press.
Buckland, Theresa J. 1999a. "[Re]Constructing Meanings: The Dance Ethnographer as Keeper of the Truth." In *Dance in the Field*, ed. Theresa J. Buckland. New York: St. Martin's Press, 196–207.
———, ed. 1999b. *Dance in the Field: Theory, Methods and Issues in Dance Ethnography.* New York: St. Martin's Press.
Buonaventura, Wendy. 1996. "Arab World: Steps to Emancipation." *UNESCO Courier* (January): 30–33.
Calhoun, Craig, ed. 1994. *Social Theory and the Politics of Identity.* London: Blackwell.
———. 1995. *Critical Social Theory: Culture, History, and the Challenge of Difference.* London: Blackwell, 1995.
Carriaga, Daniel. 1969. "Ballet Folklorico de Mexico: Controlled Creativity, Styled Authenticity." *Los Angeles Times*, February 1, p. F1.
Cefkin, Melissa. 1993. "Choreographing Culture: Dance, Folklore, and the Politics of Identity in Turkey." Ph.D. diss., Rice University. Ann Arbor: UMI Dissertation Services.
Cheremetievskaya, Natalia. n.d. *La Revelation de la Danse: Ensemble de Danses Folkloriques de l'U.R.S.S. sous la Direction de Moisseev.* Moscow: Novosti.
Chudnovskii, Mikhael A. 1959. *Folk Dance Company of the U.S.S.R.: Igor Moiseyev, Art Director.* Moscow: Foreign Languages Publishing House.
Clogg, Richard. 1992. *Concise History of Greece.* Cambridge: Cambridge University Press.
Cottam, Richard W. 1979. *Nationalism in Iran.* (Updated through 1978). Pittsburgh, Penn.: Pittsburgh University Press.
Cristiani, Gabriela Aguirre. 1994. *Amalia Hernandez' Folkloric Ballet of Mexico.* Mexico City: Fomento Cultural Banamex.
Dabbous, Dalia, and Mariam Fam. 1999. "Vamp Next Door: Philosopher Belly Dancer Dina Exposes Her Contradictions." *Cairo Times* 3(12) (August 5–18): 18–21.
Dallal, Alberto, and Cesar Delgado Martinez. 1998. "Mexico: Dance Companies." *International Encyclopedia of Dance.* Vol. 4. New York: Oxford University Press, 395–98.
Danielson, Virginia. 1997. *Voice of Egypt: Umm Kulthum, Arabic Song, and Egyptian Society in the Twentieth Century.* Cairo: American University Press.
Daniszewski, John. 2000. "Tummy Trouble in Cairo." *Los Angeles Times*, August 2, p. A1.
Davison, Andrew. 1998. *Secularism and Revivalism in Turkey: A Hermeneutic Reconsideration.* New Haven and London: Yale University Press.
Demirsipahi, Cemil. 1975. *Turk Halk Oyunlari.* Ankara: Turkiye Is Bankasi Kultur Yayinlari.
Desmond, Jane. 1997a. "Embodying Differences: Issues in Dance and Cultural Studies." In *Meaning in Motion*, ed. Jane Desmond. Durham and London: Duke University Press, 29–54.

---. 1997b. "Introduction." In *Meaning in Motion*, ed. Jane Desmond. Durham and London: Duke University Press, 1–25.
Don Cossacks Song and Dance Ensemble. n.d. Souvenir program. Russian-English edition.
Dubinskas, Frank A. 1983. "Performing Slavonian Folklore: The Politics of Reminiscence and Recreating the Past (Yugoslavia)." Ph.D. diss., Stanford University. Ann Arbor, MI: UMI Dissertation Services.
Egyptian Gazette. 1995. "Mubarak Talks to the New Yorker Magazine: No Political Prisoners in Jails." January 25, p. 1.
Eickelman, Dale F. 1998. "From Here to Modernity: Ernest Gellner on Nationalism and Islamic Fundamentalism." In *State of the Nation: Ernest Gellner and the Theory of Nationalism*, ed. John Hall. Cambridge: Cambridge University Press, 258–71.
El-Nil Folkloric Troup [sic]. 1995(?). Arab Republic of Egypt, Ministry of Culture. Official Program. Cairo.
Eley, Geoff, and Ronald Grigor Suny, eds. 1996. *Becoming National*. Oxford and New York: Oxford University Press.
Fahmy, Farida. 1987. "Creative Development of Mahmoud Reda: A Contemporary Egyptian Choreographer." Master's thesis, UCLA.
Fel, Edit, and Tamas Hofer. 1969. *Proper Peasants: Traditional Life in a Hungarian Village*. Chicago: Aldine Publishing Company.
Felfoldi, Laszlo. 1999. "Folk Dance Research in Hungary: Relations among Theory, Fieldwork and the Archive." In *Dance in the Field*, ed. Theresa J. Buckland. New York: St. Martin's Press, 55–70.
Fermor, Sharon. 1987. "On the Question of Pictorial 'Evidence' for Fifteenth-Century Dance Technique." *Dance Research*. 5(2) (Autumn): 18–32.
Festival of the Nile (Nile Folkloric Group). 1995. Program. Ambassador Auditorium, April 5.
Fisher, Jennifer. 1995. "Folkloric Look at Mexico's Past, Present." *Los Angeles Times*. September 11, p. 5.
Flores, Oscar. 1993. "La Fiesta Del Cuerpo: Danza Folklorica en Mexico/Cronica." *Memoria de Papel: Cronicas de la Cultura en Mexico*. 3(6) (June): 35–50.
Franken, Marjorie A. 1994. "Revolutionary Images: Farida Fahmy and the Reda Troupe of Egypt." Unpublished paper delivered at Middle Eastern Studies Association (MESA), Phoenix, Arixona, November 20.
---. 1996. "Egyptian Cinema and Television: Dancing and the Female Image." *Visual Anthropology* 8: 267–85.
Geertz, Clifford. 1983. *Local Knowledge: Further Essays in Interpretive Anthropology*. New York: Basic Books.
Gellner, Ernest. 1983. *Nations and Nationalism*. Ithaca, N.Y.: Cornell University Press.
Georgian State Dance Company. 1998. Dance program. *Performing Arts* 32(3) (March): P3–P6.
Gilbert, Paul. 1998. *Philosophy of Nationalism*. Boulder, Colo.: Westview Press.
Giurchescu, Anca. 1992. "The Power and the Dance Symbol and Its Socio-Political Use." *Proceedings. 17th Symposiun of the Study Group on Ethnochoreology*. Nafplion, Greece, July 2–10, pp. 15–23. [Last name is spelled "Giurschescu" on this work.]

———. 1999. "Past and Present in Field Research: A Critical History of Personal Experience." In *Dance in the Field*, ed. Theresa J. Buckland. New York: St. Martin's Press, 41–54.
Gore, Georgiana. 1999. "Textual Fields: Representation in Dance Ethnography." In *Dance in the Field*, ed. Theresa J. Buckland. New York: St. Martin's Press, 208–20.
Gore, Georgiana, and Maria Koutsouba. 1992. "'Airport Art' in a Sociopolitical Perspective: The Case of the Greek Dance Groups of Plaka." *Proceedings. 17th Symposiun of the Study Group on Ethnochoreology.* Nafplion, Greece, July 2–10, pp. 29–34.
Greek Dances Dora Stratou Theatre. n.d. Souvenir program. Athens, Greece.
Gross, Jo-Ann. 1992. "Introduction: Approaches to the Problem of Identity Formation." *Muslims in Central Asia*, ed. Jo-Ann Gross. Durham, N.C.: Duke University Press, 1–23.
Gusic, Marijana. 1955. *Tumac Izlozene Grade*. Etnografski Zagreb: Muzej.
Gusic, Marijana, et al. 1963. *Folklor Naroda Jugoslavije*. Zagreb: Graficki zavod Hrvatske.
Gutkin, Irene. 1997. "Historical Paradoxes of Soviet Folklore and Folkloristics: A Response to Zemtsovsky and Kunanbaeva." In *Folklore and Traditional Music in the Former Soviet Union and Eastern Europe*, ed. James Porter. Los Angeles: UCLA, Department of Ethnomusicology, 32–41.
Hafez, Shams Ad-din Mohammad. 1994. *Hafez be s'ai-ye Sayeh*. Tehran: Tus, 1994/95.
Hall, John, ed. 1998. *State of the Nation: Ernest Gellner and the Theory of Nationalism*. Cambridge: Cambridge University Press.
Herzfeld, Michael. 1997. *Cultural Intimacy: Social Poetics in the Nation State*. London: Routledge.
Heth, Charlotte, ed. 1992. *Native American Dance: Ceremonies and Social Traditions*. Washington, D.C.: National Museum of the American Indian, Smithsonian Institution.
Hilton, Wendy. 1981. *Dance of Court and Theater: The French Noble Style 1690–1725*. Princeton, N.J.: Princeton University Press.
Hobsbawm, Eric. 1990. *Nations and Nationalism since 1780*. Cambridge: Cambridge University Press.
———. 1994. "The National as Invented Tradition." In *Nationalism*, ed. John Hutchinson and Anthony Smith. Oxford and New York: Oxford University Press, 76–82.
Hobsbawm, Eric, and Terrence Ranger, eds. 1983. *Invention of Tradition*. Cambridge: Cambridge University Press.
Hoerburger, Felix. 1968. "Once Again: On the Concept of 'Folk Dance.'" *Journal of the International Folk Music Council* 20 (1968): 30–31.
Holden, Rickey, and Mary Vouras. 1965. *Greek Folk Dances*. Newark, N.J.: Folkraft Press.
Hovannisian, Richard G., ed. 1998. *Remembrance and Denial: The Case of the Armenian Genocide*. Detroit, Mich.: Wayne State University Press.
Huntington, Samuel P. 1990. "Clash of Civilization." *Foreign Affairs* 72(3) (1990): 22–49.
Hutchinson, John, and Anthony D. Smith, eds. 1992. *Nationalism*. Oxford and New York: Oxford University Press.

———. 1996. *Ethnicity*. Oxford and New York: Oxford University Press.
ICM Artists, Ltd. 1997. "Moiseyev Dance Company: Brief History." New York. May 1997.
Ilieva, Anna. 1992. "Bulgarian Folk Dance in the Past 45 Years." *Proceedings. 17th Symposiun of the Study Group on Ethnochoreology*. Nafplion, Greece, July 2–10, pp. 35–38.
Ilupina, Anna, and Yelena Lutskaya. 1966. *Moiseyev's Dance Company*. Moscow: Progress Publishers.
Isareva, Margarita I. 1998. "Moiseyev, Igor." *International Encyclopedia of Dance*. Vol. 4. New York: Oxford University Press, 443–46.
Jones, E. Jean Johnson. 1999. "The Choreographic Notebook: A Dynamic Documentation of the Choreographic Process of Kokuma Dance Theatre, an African-Caribbean Dance Company." In *Dance in the Field*, ed. Theresa J. Buckland. New York: St. Martin's Press, 100–10.
Karimova, R. 1973. *Ferganskii tanets* (Ferghana Dance). Tashkent: Literatura i Iskusstvo.
———. 1975. *Khorezmiskii tanets* (Khorazmian Dance). Tashkent: Literatura i Iskusstvo.
———. 1977. *Bukharskii tanets* (Bukharan Dance). Tashkent: Literatura i Iskusstvo.
———. 1979. *Tantsy Ansambl'a Bakhor* (Dances of the Bakhor Ensemble). Tashkent: Literatura i Iskusstvo.
Kealiinohomoku, Joann Wheeler. 1972. "Folk Dance." In *Folklore and Folklife: an Introduction*, ed. Richard Dorson. Chicago: University of Chicago Press, 381–404.
Keyder, Caglar. 1997. "Whither the Project of Modernity?: Turkey in the 1990s." In *Rethinking Modernity and National Identity in Turkey*, ed. Sibel Bozdogan and Resat Kasaba. Seattle: University of Washington Press, 37–51.
Kirisci, Kemal, and Gareth M. Winrow. 1997. *Kurdish Question and Turkey: An Example of a Trans-state Ethnic Conflict*. London: Frank Cass.
Kisselgoff, Anna. 1991. "Moiseyev Company Visits with Its Legendary Bravura." *New York Times*, September 26, publicity packet.
Koutsouba, Maria. 1999. "'Outsider' in an 'Inside' World, or Dance Ethnography at Home." In *Dance in the Field*, ed. Theresa J. Buckland. New York: St. Martin's Press, 186–95.
Kramer, Heinz. 2000. *Changing Turkey: The Challenge to Europe and the United States*. Washington, D.C.: Brookings Institute.
Krauze, Enrique. 1997. *Mexico: Biography of Power, A History of Modern Mexico, 1810–1996*. Trans. Hank Heifetz. New York: HarperPerennial.
LADO. 1949–1959. Souvenir program marking tenth anniversary.
———. 1949–1969. Souvenir program marking twentieth anniversary.
———. 1949–1979. Souvenir program marking thirtieth anniversary.
———. 1949–1989. Souvenir program marking fortieth anniversary.
LADO U Svijetv/LADO and the World. n.d. Publicity brochure.
Laine, Barry. 1986. "Folk Ballet of Moiseyev: 'People's Art'." *Los Angeles Times*, September 28, p. 60.
Lawler, Lillian. 1964. *Dance in Ancient Greece*. Middletown, Conn.: Wesleyan University Press.
Lewis, Bernard. 1968. *Emergence of Modern Turkey*. 2d ed. London: Oxford University Press.

Libman, Lillian. 1986. Moiseyev Dance Company Souvenir program. New York: McTaggart-Wolk, 1986–1987.
Lincoln, Bruce. 1989. *Discourse and the Construction of Society: Comparative Studies of Myth, Ritual, and Classification.* Oxford and New York: Oxford University Press.
Loutzaki, Irene. 1992. "Dance in 'Political Rhythms'." *Proceedings. 17th Symposiun of the Study Group on Ethnochoreology.* Nafplion, Greece, July 2–10, pp. 65–72.
Madcz, Laszlo. 1983. "Folk Dancing and the Folk Dance Movement." In *Art of Dance in Hungary,* ed. Edit Kaposi and Erno Pesovar. Budapest: Corvina Kiado, 57–108.
Mahalli Dancers of Iran. 1976. Program of tour of the United States.
Marti, Samuel, and Gertrude Prokosch Kurath. 1964. *Dances of Anahuac: The Choreography and Music of Precortesian Dances.* Chicago: Aldine Publishing Co.
Mazo, Margarita. 1998. "Forward." *JVC Video Anthology of World Music and Dance.* Tokyo: Victor Company of Japan, Ltd., vii–xi.
McNeill, William H. 1995. *Keeping Together in Time: Dance and Drill in Human History.* Cambridge: Harvard University Press.
Misiunas, Romuald, and Rein Taagepera. 1993. *Baltic States: Years of Dependence, 1940–1990.* Expanded and enlarged ed. Berkeley: University of California.
Mitchell, Timothy. 1991. *Colonising Egypt.* Berkeley and Los Angeles: University of California Press.
Moiseyev Dance Company. 1986. Souvenir program. New York: ICM Artists, Ltd.
———. 1999. Program. *Performing Arts* 33(2) (February): P1–P5.
Mottahedeh, Roy. 1976. "Shu'ubiyah Controversy and the Social History of Early Islamic Iran." *International Journal of Middle East Studies* 7: 161–82.
Motyl, Alexander J. 1990. *Sovietology, Rationality, Nationality.* New York: Columbia University Press.
Moustafa, Tamir. 2000. "Conflict and Cooperation between the State and Religious Institutions in Contemporary Egypt." *International Journal of Middle East Studies* 32(1) (February): 3–22.
Naby, Eden. 1994. "Emerging Central Asia: Ethnic and Religious Factions." In *Central Asia and the Caucasus after the Soviet Union,* ed. Mohiaddin Mesbahi. Gainesville: University of Florida, 34–55.
Nahachewsky, Andriy. 1992. "National Standards Versus Social Traditions in Ukrainian Dance." *Proceedings. 17th Symposiun of the Study Group on Ethnochoreology.* Nafplion, Greece, July 2–10, pp. 73–81.
———. 1995. "Participatory and Presentational Dance as Ethnochoreological Categories." *Dance Research Journal* 27(1) (Spring): 1–15.
Nash, Manning. 1989. *Cauldron of Ethnicity in the Modern World.* Chicago: University of Chicago.
National Folk Troup [sic]. (*Al-firqat al-qawmiyat al-funun ash-sha'biyah*). n.d. Souvenir program. Ministry of Culture Folk and Show Arts Sector, Cairo, Egypt.
Ness, Sally Ann. 1997. "Originality in the Postcolony: Choreographing the Neoethnic Body of Philippine Dance." *Cultural Anthropolgy* 12(1) (February): 65–108.

Ozbudun, Ergun. 1996. "Continuing Ottoman Legacy and the State Tradition in the Middle East." In *Imperial Legacy: Ottoman Imprint on the Balkans and the Middle East,* ed. L. Carl Brown. New York: Columbia University Press, 133–57.

Ozel, Mehmet, et al. 1992. *Folkloric Turk Kiyafetleri* (Turkish Folkloric Costumes). Ankara: Fine Arts Development Foundation of Turkey.

Ozturkmen, Arzu. 1992. "Folk dance and Nationalism in Turkey." *Proceedings. 17th Symposiun of the Study Group on Ethnochoreology.* Nafplion, Greece, July 2–10, pp. 83–86.

Panarin, Sergei A. 1994. "Ethnohistorical Dynamics of Muslim Societies within Russia and the CIS." In *Central Asia and the Caucasus after the Soviet Union,* ed. Mohiaddin Mesbahi. Gainesville: University of Florida, 17–33.

Pasles, Chris. 1997. "Ballet Folklorico Offers a Program Full of Skill, Flash and Color." *Los Angeles Times,* September 5, p. F14.

Petrides, Ted. 1975a. "Dances of the Rebetes." In *Rebetika: Songs from the Old Greek Underworld,* ed. Katharine Butterworth and Sara Schneider. Athens: Komboloi, 27–33.

———. 1975b. *Greek Folk Dances.* Athens: Lycabettus Press.

Petrides, Ted, and Elfleida Petrides. 1961. *Folk Dances of the Greeks.* New York: Exposition Press.

Petrovic, Ankica. 1997. "Status of Traditional Music in Eastern Europe." In *Folklore and Traditional Music in the Former Soviet Union and Eastern Europe,* ed. James Porter. Los Angeles: UCLA, Department of Ethnomusicology, 49–59.

Phelan, Peggy. 1993. *Unmarked: The Politics of Performance.* London and New York: Routledge.

Porter, James, ed. 1997. *Folklore and Traditional Music in the Former Soviet Union and Eastern Europe.* Los Angeles: UCLA, Department of Ethnomusicology.

Poulton, Hugh. 1997. *Top Hat, Grey Wolf and Crescent: Turkish Nationalism and the Turkish Republic.* London: Hurst & Company.

Poulton, Hugh, and Martha Vickers. 1997. "Kosovo Albanians: Ethnic Confrontation with the Slav State." In *Muslim Identity and the Balkan State,* ed. Hugh Poulton and Suha Taji-Farouki. London: Hurst & Company, 139–69.

Poulton, Hugh, and Suha Taji-Farouki, eds. 1997. *Muslim Identity and the Balkan State.* London: Hurst & Company.

Prevots, Naima. 1998. *Dance for Export: Cultural Diplomacy and the Cold War.* Hanover, N.H., and London: Wesleyan Press.

Quigley, Collin. 1992. "Reflections on the Hearing to 'Designate the Square Dance as the American Folk Dance of the United States'." Cultural Politics and the American Vernacular Form. *Proceedings. 17th Symposiun of the Study Group on Ethnochoreology.* Nafplion, Greece, July 2–10, pp. 87–97.

Raftis, Alkis. 1987. *World of Greek Dance.* London: Finedawn Publishers.

———, ed. 1993. *Forty Greek Costumes from the Dora Stratou Theatre Collection.* Athens: Dora Stratou Theatre, 1993(?).

———. 1998. "Greece: Dance in Modern Greece." *International Encyclopedia of Dance.* Vol. 3. New York: Oxford University Press, 296–301.

———. 1999. "Dora Stratou: 11 chronia meta" (Dora Stratou: 11 years after). Souvenir program, February 8.
———. 2000. "'Parallel Traditions' from Within." Unpublished paper.
Reda Fokloric Troupe. n.d. Souvenir program. Cairo: Ministry of Culture, Egypt, Foreign Press & Information Department.
Reda, Mahmoud. 1968. *Fi Ma'Bad Ar-Raqs* (In the Temple of Dance). Cairo: Dar Al-Ma'Arif.
———. 2000. *Al-raqs haiyati* (Dance Is My Life). Manuscript copy. Cairo: forthcoming.
Rice, Timothy. 1997. "Bulgarian Folkloristics and Ethnomusicology at and after the Fall of Communism." In *Folklore and Traditional Music in the Former Soviet Union and Eastern Europe*, ed. James Porter. Los Angeles: UCLA, Department of Ethnomusicology, 65–77.
Rombos-Levides, Marica. 1992. "Dynamics of Traditional Dance as a Penetrating Force in the Formation of Modern Greek Ideology and Culture." *Proceedings. 17th Symposiun of the Study Group on Ethnochoreology.* Nafplion, Greece, July 2–10, pp. 99–108.
Root, Deborah. 1998. *Cannibal Culture: Art, Appropriation and the Commodification of Difference.* Boulder, Colo.: Westview Press.
Said, Edward. 1978. *Orientalism.* New York: Vintage Books.
Saleh, Magda Ahmed Abdel Ghaffar. 1979. "Documentation of the Ethnic Dance Tradition of Egypt." Unpublished Ph.D. dissertation, New York University. Ann Arbor, Mich.: University Microfilms International.
———. 1998. "Egypt." *International Encyclopedia of Dance.* Vol. 2. New York: Oxford University Press, 481–98.
Segal, Lewis. 1995. "Looking at Postcards: World Dance on Western Stages." In *Looking Out: Perspectives on Dance and Criticism in a Multicultural World*, ed. David Gere et al. New York: Schirmer Books, 41–49.
———. 1997. "Fine-Tuning the Authentic: Ballet Folklorico de Mexico's Versions of Native Dances Are Seen around the World. What's Lost in the Translation?" *Los Angeles Times*, August 31, pp. 4–5, 66–67.
Sellers-Young, Barbara. 1992. "Raks El Sharki: Transculturation of a Folk Form." *Journal of Popular Culture*, 26 (Fall): 141–52.
Sevilla, Amparo. 1998. "Mexico: Traditional Dance." *International Encyclopedia of Dance.* Vol. 4. New York: Oxford University Press, 383–89.
Shay, Anthony. 1982. "Fandangos and Bailes: Dancing and Dance Events in Early California." *Southern California Quarterly* 65(2) (Summer): 99–113.
———. 1986. "Transferring and Transforming Traditional Music and Dance for and to the Stage." Paper given at the 25th Year Anniversary Symposium, Folklore and Mythology Studies: Retrospect and Prospect, UCLA, May 30–31.
———. 1995. "Dance and Non-Dance: Patterned Movement in Iran and Islam." *Iranian Studies* 28(1–2) (Winter/Spring): 61–78.
———. 1998. "Danse du Ventre." *International Encyclopedia of Dance.* Vol. 2. New York: Oxford University Press, 344–46.
———. 1999a. *Choreophobia: Solo Improvised Dance in the Iranian World.* Costa Mesa, Calif.: Mazda Publishers.
———. 1999b. "Parallel Traditions: State Folk Dance Ensembles and Folk Dance in 'The Field'." *Dance Research Journal* 31(1) (Spring): 29–56.

Shay, Anthony, and Vilma Matchette. 1987. "Clothing in Early California." *Folk Dance Scene* 2(6) (October): 5–8.
Shiloah, Amnon. 1995. *Music in the World of Islam: A Sociocultural Study.* Detroit: Wayne University Press.
Shiva, Shahram T. 1995. *Rending the Veil: Literal and Poetic Translations of Rumi.* Prescott, Ariz.: Hohm Press.
Silverman, Carol. 1997. "Comments on the Study and Practice of Ethnomusicology in Eastern Europe." In *Folklore and Traditional Music in the Former Soviet Union and Eastern Europe,* ed. James Porter. Los Angeles: UCLA, Department of Ethnomusicology, 60–64.
Slater, David. 1994. "Exploring Other Zones of the Postmodern." In *Racism, Modernity and Identity on the Western Front,* ed. Ali Rattansi and Sallie Westwood. Cambridge, U.K.: Polity Press, 87–125.
Smith, Anthony D. 1986. *Ethnic Origin of Nations.* Oxford, U.K.: Basil Blackwell.
———. 1995. *Nations and Nationalism in a Global Era.* Cambridge, U.K.: Polity Press.
Soviet Georgian Dancers with Tbilisi Polyphonic Choir. 1977. Souvenir program. CAMI, 1977–1978.
Stirling, Paul. 1965. *Turkish Village.* New York: John Wiley & Sons.
Stokes, Martin. 1992. *Arabesk Debate: Music and Musicians in Modern Turkey.* Oxford, U.K.: Clarendon Press.
Stratou, Dora. 1966. *Greek Dances: Our Living Link with Antiquity.* Athens: n.p.
Strinati, Dominic. 1995. *Introduction to Theories of Popular Culture.* London and New York: Routledge.
Sweet. Jill D. 1985. *Dances of the Tewa Pueblo Indians.* Santa Fe, N.M.: School of American Research Press.
Swift, Mary Grace. 1968. *Art of the Dance in the U.S.S.R.* Notre Dame, Indiana: University of Notre Dame Press.
Terry, Walter. 1969. "Ballet Folklorico of Mexico." In Ballet Folklorico of Mexico souvenir program.
Tkachenko, Tamara. 1954. *Narodny Tanets* (Folk Dance). Moscow: Iskusstvo.
Todorova, Maria. 1996. "Ottoman Legacy in the Balkans." *Imperial Legacy: Ottoman Imprint on the Balkans and the Middle East,* ed. L. Carl Brown. New York: Columbia University Press, 45–77.
Trimillos, Ricardo D. 1995. "More Than Art: The Politics of Performance in International Cultural Exchange." In *Looking Out: Perspectives on Dance and Cricisim in a Multicultural World,* ed. David Gere et al. New York: Schirmer Books, 23–39.
Tsing, Anna Lowenhaupt. 1993. *In the Realm of the Diamond Queen: Marginality in an Out-of-the-Way Place.* Princeton, N.J.: Princeton University Press.
Turkish State Folk Dance Ensemble. n.d. Souvenir program. Ankara: T. C. Kultur Bakanligi.
Urban, Greg, and Joel Sherzer. 1991. "Introduction: Indians, Nation-States, and Culture." *Nation-States and Indians in Latin America.* Austin: University of Texas, 1–18.
Van Nieuwkerk, Karin. 1995. *"A Trade Like Any Other": Female Singers and Dancers in Egypt.* Austin: University of Texas.

Woodhouse, C. M. 1998. *Modern Greece: A Short History*. 6th rev. ed. London: Faber and Faber.
Yugoslav Folk Dances. 1949. Souvenir program. Illustrated by Pedja Milosavljavic and Dusan Ristic. Belgrade: Jugoslavija, 1949-1950.
Younis, Aida. n.d. *Reda Folkloric Troupe*. Cairo: Ministry of Culture.
Zarinkub, Abd-al Husain. 1975. "Arab Conquest and Its Aftermath." In *Cambridge History of Iran*, ed. Richard N. Frye. Vol. 4. Cambridge: Cambridge University Press, 1-56.
Zemtsovsky, Izaly, and Alma Kunanbaeva. 1997. "Communism and Folklore." In *Folklore and Traditional Music in the Former Soviet Union and Eastern Europe*, ed. James Porter. Los Angeles: UCLA, Department of Ethnomusicology, 3-23.
Zurcher, Erik J. 1998. *Turkey: A Modern History*. New rev. ed. London: I. B. Tauris.

Videocassettes

Armenian Popular Dances. Los Angeles: Parsghian Video & Records, 1984.
Armenian State Dance Company. Los Angeles: Parsghian Video & Records, n.d.
Bakhor Ensemble in Concert. Seattle: Uzbek Dance Society, 1989.
Ballet Folklorico De Mexico de Amalia Hernandez. Mexico City: Qualli, 1989.
Les Ballets Africains: Heritage. National Dance Company of the Republic of Guinea. Brisbane: Queensland Performing Arts Trust Production, 1996.
Dances of Khorosan. Tehran, Ministry of Fine Arts, n.d.
Dora Stratou Theatre: Greek Dances—Philopappou Hill. Vols. 1-3. Athens: Dora Stratou Theatre.
Egyptian, Nubian & Sudanese Folkloric Dance. Tape no. 6. Produced by Morocco (Carolina Varga Dinicu), 1984.
Funun Sh'Abiah. Misriyah (Egypt National Group of Folk Dance). Tape no. 1202. Los Angeles: Saut Wa Soora, n.d.
Gharam fi al-karnak (Love in Karnak). Starring Farida Fahmy and Mahmoud Reda. Cairo: Gamal Elleissi Films, 1963.
Hrvatski Narodni Plesovi (Croatian Folk Dances). Zagreb: TVZ (Televizija Zagreb), 1986.
Igazah nisf as-sinah (Mid-term vacation). Starring Farida Fahmy and Mahmoud Reda. Cairo: Gamal Elleissi Films, 1961.
In Concert: The Bakhor Ensemble. Seattle: Uzbek Dance Society, 1989.
Jugoslavija u pesmi i igri (Yugoslavia in song and dance). Beograd: Televizija Beograd, n.d.
Kefalodesimata 1 (Greek Traditional Headdresses). Athens: Dora Stratou Theatre, n.d.
KOLO: Ansambl Narodnih Igara/Yugoslav National Ballet. Beograd: RTB (Radio-Televizija Beograd), 1987.
LADO I, Professional Folk Dance Ensemble of Croatia. Triesen/via, Switzerland: IVS, 1989.
LADO II, Professional Folk Dance Ensemble of Croatia. Triesen/via, Switzerland: IVS, 1989.

Moiseyev Dance Company: A Gala Evening. New York: View Video, 1987.
National Folk Troupe of Egypt: Firqua Kawmiyya in Concert. Tape no. 3. Produced by Morocco (Carolina Varga Dinicu), 1984.
Portrejt Zvonka Ljevakovica. Zagreb: Jugoton Produkcija, n.d.
Rang-a-rang: raqs-ha va avaz-ha-ye mahalli-ye iran (Variety: folk dances and songs of Iran). No. 125. Tarzana, Calif.: Pars Video, n.d.
Raqs-ha-ye mahalli (Folk Dances). No. 124. Tarzana, Calif.: Pars Video, n.d.
Raqs-ha-ye mahalli-ye Iran. New York: CINA, Inc., n.d.
"Reda Troupe" Egyptian Folklore: Firqah Reda. No. 1201. Los Angeles: Saut Wa Soora, 1997.
Russian Folk Song & Dance. West Long Beach, N.J.: Kultur, n.d.
Tanec. Denver: Harold Ryan, 1969.
Turkish State Folk Dance Ensemble (Turk Devlet Halk Danslari Toplugu). Ankara, n.d.
La Vision de una Mujer: Amalia Hernandez y el Ballet Folklorico de Mexico. Un Documental como Testimonio de los 40 anos de Historia de una de las Comapnias de Danza mas Importante del Mundo. Mexico City: Ballet Folklorico, 1992.

Index

Note: Illustrations are indicated by page numbers in **_bold italics_**.

Afghanistan, 2, 24, 139, 234n.9
Ahmad, Feroz, 210
Al-Faruqi, Lois Ibsen, 16, 151, 152, 237n.10
Albanians, 27, 171, 187, 204; in Greece, 165, 172, 173, 205. *See also* Kosovo
Alcedo, Patrick, 46
Amanpour, Christiane, 2
Anatolia, 176, 178, 204, 206, 209, 210, 211, 212
And, Metin, 133, 213
Anderson, Benedict, 29, 161, 197
Angelis, Adiamanta, 166
Ankara, 193, 196, 217, 222
Appadurai, Arjun, 27–28
Appalachia, dances of, 40
Aquino, Frances, 44
Arab World, 137, 139, 141, 152, 162
Arabesk (type of Turkish popular music), 247–248n.10
Arabs, 200, 202, 203, 204, 206
Arkin, Lisa and Marian Smith, 15, 68–70
Armbrust, Walter, 134, 135, 136
Armenia and Armenians, 62, 171, 234n.9; in Iran, 203; in Turkey, 205, 206, 247n.7
Armenian State Dance Ensemble, 24, 55
Assimilation, 31
Astourian, Stephan, 204
Ataturk, Kemal (Mustafa Kemal), 176, 194, 196, 205, 206, 209, 210, 211, 222

Ataturk Cultural Center, 193, 195, 217
Athens, 165, 172, 173, 175, 186, 189, 230
Authenticity, 12, 14, 15, 16, 30, 34–37, 42, 51, 69, 85, 87, 88, 110, 118, 123, 134, 136, 145, 146, 158, 159, 166, 182, 184–185, 208, 216, 226, 248–249n.5
AVAZ International Dance Theatre, 237n.9
Awad, Luis, 136
Azerbaijan and Azerbaijanis, 63, 68, 78, 234n.9; dances of, 76, 77; in Iran, 203
Azerbaijan State Dance Ensemble, 24, 236n.6
Azhar University, Al-, 139–140

Back to the Apes, a Rock 'n' Roll Parody (choreography), 26
Bakhor (State Dance Ensemble of Uzbekistan), 25, 33, 44, 54, 55, 64, 65, 236n.5, 243n.10
Bakka, Egil, 236n.5
Baladi (domestic form of belly dance), 141, 144, 149
Balanchine, George, 38
Balkans, 169, 172, 173, 174; dances of, 117, 163, 178; Ottoman Empire in, 172; Wars (1912–1913), 176, 205
Ballet, 15, 33, 35, 40, 63, 64, 70, 72, 73, 78, 91, 96, 126, 147, 153, 156, 157, 195, 225, 227, 230, 233n.2

Index

Ballet Folklorico de Mexico, 1, 2, 4, 6, 17, 22 (table 1), 23, 24, 25, 26, 28, 36, 40–41, 44, 48, 55, 109, 114, 117, 118, 120, 128, 129, 160, 186, 187, 239n.6, 241nn.1&4, 248n.4; costumes, 82–83, 105–106, 238n.2; dancers, 103–104; finances, 107; history of, 93–94; music of, 85, 104–105; repertoire, 99–103. See also Hernandez, Amalia
Balloon Theatre (Cairo), 156, 158, 245n.13
Baltic Republics, 31, 62, 63, 76; dances of, 14
Bamba, La (dance), 41, 83, 94, 101
Baranjski Plesovi (Dances of Baranja; choreography), 117, **122**
Bartok, Bela, 44, 243n.9
Basanta, Viviana, 94
Baxandall, Michael, 168
Bayanihan (National Dance Company of the Philippines), 2, 3, 9, 22 (table 1), 25, 28, 29, 34, 36, 45, 46, 109, 119, 241n.4; Muslim dances in, 9
Baykurt, Serif, 213, 247n.8
Belarus, 14, 20, 61; dances of, 14, 20, 70, 77
Bellas Artes (theater in Mexico City), 54, 82, 92, 94, 105
Belly dance, 42, 76, 130, 132, 133, 134, 138, 139, 141–142, 148, 149, 153, 155, 156, 160–161, 234n.9, 239nn.3&4, 244n.11, 245n.17. See also *Ciftetelli*
Berger, Morroe, 133, 151, 237n.10
Bernheimer, Martin, 109
Beryozka (dance company), 73
Beza'i, Bahram, 34
Boda en el Istmo de Tehuantepec (Wedding in the Isthmus of Tehauntepec; choreography), 24, 97, 102
Boda en la Huasteca (Wedding in Huasteca; choreography), 102
Bolshoi Ballet, 55, 61, 62, 67, 78
Bosnia, 9, 118, 139, 204
Bottomley, Gillian, 2

Brass, Paul R., 197, 198
Brown, L. Carl, 171
Bulba (choreography), 20, 70
Bulgaria and Bulgarians, 14, 28, 53, 169, 174, 175, 176, 177, 187, 205, 214, 234n.7; dances of, 14, 76, 156
Bulgarian State Folk Ensemble (known in the west as Philip Koutev Ensemble), 9, 22 (table 1), 48–50, 109. See also Koutev, Philip

Cairo, 126, 127, 133–134, 135, 137, 139, 147, 150, 159, 226, 230
Calhoun, Craig, 26, 199
California Folk Dance Federation, 235n.4
Cefkin, Melissa, 218, 220, 247n.9
Character dance, 15, 35, 57, 68–70, 72, 84, 85, 96, 144, 156
Chiapas, 1, 2, 23, 87, 90
Chiapas (choreography), 1, 2, 103
Chicanos. See Mexican-Americans
China, 5, 11, 76, 167, 227
China Poblana (costume type), 82–83, 106, 238n.2
Chinese State Folk Ensemble, 11
Choreographic Institutes *(koreografski instituti)*, 78, 236n.6
Chrisifilopoulou, Angeliki, 166
Ciftetelli (dance type), 141, 195, 209–210. See also Belly dance
Class (social), 25, 89, 93, 119, 127, 131, 134, 135, 136, 137, 138, 145, 147, 154, 232, 242n.7
Clogg, Richard, 174
CNN, 1, 2, 54
Colonialism, 61, 86, 129–135, 162; and British, 130–135, 144, 149, 159, 167, 200; Ottoman, 159, 167, 170, 173
Colonizing Egypt, 131
Communism and the Communist Party, 59, 61, 63; in Croatia, 113, 114, 115, 116, 119, 121, 125, 242n.5; in Greece, 167, 177
Concheros, Los (choreography), 96
Copts, 160
Cossetto, Emil, 115

Costumes, 38, 43, 51–53, 228, 238–239n.2, 239n.8; Ballet Folklorico de Mexico, 82, 105–106; Dora Stratou Greek Dances Theatre, 163, 164, 165, 188; in Egypt, 140; El-Tannoura, 128; LADO, 113, 123; Moiseyev, 14, 57, 79–80; Reda Troupe, 154–155; Turkish State Folk Dance Ensemble, 221–222.
Cotton Dance (choreography), 76
Croatia and Croatians, 2, 5, 9, 14, 17, 26, 39, 41, 47, 108–125, 140, 161, 169, 199, 227, 229, 231, 236n.7, 237n.11; folklore of, 103. See also LADO

Dabka (dance), 110, 156
Dance, pre-Columbian, 96, 100, 105
Dance, pre-Cortesian. *See* Dance, pre-Columbian
Dance, pre-Hispanic. *See* Dance, pre-Columbian
Dancers and Dance Training, 3, 21, 24, 33, 46–48, 227, 233n.2; in Ballet Folklorico, 93, 103–104; Dora Stratou Greek Dances Theatre, 180, 181–182; in Egypt, 128, 137–138, 141, 149, 153, 159; LADO, 120–121; Turkish State Folk Dance Ensemble, 214–215, 217–218
Dances of Baranja (Baranjski Plesovi; choreography), 117, **122**
Dances of Posavina (Posavski Plesovi; choreography), 41, 45, 115, 124
Dances of Prigorje (Prigorski Plesovi; choreography), 41, **111**
Danielson, Virginia, 138
Danza del Venado (Yaqui Deer Dance; choreography), 24, 94, 97, **100**, 102, 105
Dasha, 106
Deer Dance. See *Danza del Venado*
Delgado, Cesar, 97
De Llano, Luis, 92
Demirsipahi, Cemil, 213
Desmond, Jane C., 4
De Warren, Robert, 34, 39, 44, 47. *See also* Mahalli Dancers

Diaz, Profirio, 100
Differentiation, 31
Dioses, Los (choreography), 100
Don Cossacks Dance Company, 23, 61, 73–74
Dora Stratou Greek Dances Theatre, 5, 15, 21, 22 (table 1), 39, 44, 53, 54, 163–167, 168, 173, 230; costumes, 163, 164, 188; dancers, 180, 181–182, 186–187; finances, 188; music, 163, 164, 187; repertoire, 169, 173, 185–186
Douglas, William O., 65
Drmes (dance type), 35, 118

Eickelman, Dale F., 199, 247n.5
Egypt and Egyptians, 5, 10, 28, 32, 42, 68, 86, 126–162, 167, 214, 226, 236n.5; dances of, 76, 141–142
Eley, Geoff and Ronald Grigor Suny, 22
Essentialization (also Essentialism), 14, 29, 30, 34, 35, 69, 74, 93
Ethnicity and ethnic identity, 5–12, 23, 225, 231, 232; in Iran, 202; in Soviet Union, 61–63, 75–77, 78; in Turkey, 198–199, 204, 209

Fahmy, Farida, 137, 138, 144, 146, 148, 149, 150–151, 152, 153, 156–157, 244n.7
Fanon, Frantz, 133
Farabi, Al-: *The Grand Book of Music*, 137
Ferdowsi, 200, 201, 202
Festival of the Nile (El-Nil Folkloric Troup), 144, 158–160
Finances, 38, 47–48, 53–56; Ballet Folklorico, 95, 103, 107; Dora Stratou Greek Dances Theatre, 184, 188; Egypt, 143, 148, 245n.16; LADO, 47–48, 109, 123–124; Turkish State Folk Dance Ensemble, 222
Firqa Qawmiyya (National Folkloric Troup), 129, 144, 152, 153, 154, 155, 159; costumes of, 154, 161
Firqat al-Anwar (former Lebanese Dance Company), 110
Fisher, Jennifer, 96

266 *Index*

Flaubert, Gustave, 141
Flores, Oscar, 93
Folk dance, 2, 4, 6, 7, 10, 13, 20, 22, 27, 31, 34, 38, 43, 68, 69, 78, 82, 96, 102, 149, 157, 165, 185, 224, 225, 226, 227, 228, 231; in Croatia, 113, 115, 119; in Egypt, 134, 136, 138, 140, 142–144, 145, 146, 147, 153; in Greece, 178, 185; in Iran, 202; in Turkey, 194, 211, 213, 214, 215–216, 218, 222
Folk Dance Festival for Greek Youth (FDF; organization), 190
Folk dance "in the field," 14, 15, 16, 17, 19–21, 43, 44, 191, 226; in Croatia, 118; in Egypt, 141–144, 146–147; in Greece, 178; in Greek Diaspora, 189; in Turkey, 211–213, 214
Folklore, 3, 4, 5, 7, 15, 19, 22, 25, 30, 33, 37, 45, 72, 74; Ballet Folklorico, 96; in Egypt, 134–136, 146, 158, 159; LADO, 109, 114; in Turkey, 207, 208, 210, 213, 232, 235n.2
Folklorism and folklorization, 18, 74
Foucault, Michel, 131, 132
Franken, Marjorie A., 137, 138, 145, 162
Furth, Charlotte, 167

Gandy Dancers, 240n.3
Gavazzi, Milovan, 112
Geertz, Clifford, 167
Gellner, Ernest, 27, 197, 200, 204
Gender and sexuality, 23–25, 148, 149–150, 225, 232
Georgia and Georgians, 62, 234n.9, 237–238n.13; dances of, 76, 77
Georgian State Dance Ensemble, 22 (table 1), 24, 55, 61, 109, 156, 234n.10
Germany, Nazi, 4, 215
Gharam fi al-Karnak (film), 152
Gilbert, Paul, 6
Ginniyat al-Bahr, Al- (choreography), 151, 152, 245n.13
Giurchescu, Anca, 3, 7, 18, 235n.2
Gokalp, Ziya, 194, 204

Gopak (Hopak; choreography), 42, 57–59, *58*, 75, 77, 80, 156, 240n.9
Gore, Georgiana and Maria Koutsouba, 13
Graham, Martha, 36, 38, 39, 96
"Great Idea," 176, 177
Great Tenochtitlan (choreography), 100, 106
Greece and Greeks, 5, 10, 54, 140, 163–192, 205, 206, 208, 229, 230; ancient, 161, 169, 170, 174–175, 181; Byzantine, 167, 171, 175, 246n.4; Diaspora, 165, 188–190; history of, 169–178. *See also* Dora Stratou Greek Dances Theatre
Guelaguetza (choreography), 99, 100, 103
Guerrero, Guerrero (choreography), 102, 106
Guinea, 25
Gypsies, 225; in Bulgaria, 49; in Croatia, 112; in Egypt, 159; in Serbia, 8, 9, 225, 233n.4

Hadith, 139
Hafez, 202
Haggalah (choreography), 156
Haq, Jad Al-, 140
Hernandez, Amalia, 4, 16–17, 24, 29, 32, 36, 37, 38, 39, 40, 45, 51, 52, 82–109, 136, 146, 147, 160, 229, 230; choreography of, 92–93, 96–97; life and career of, 90–94. *See also* Ballet Folklorico de Mexico
Hernandez, Norma Lopez, 94
Herzfeld, Michael, 3, 29, 30, 168–169
Hilton, Wendy, 233n.1
Hobsbawm, Eric and Terrence Ranger, 15, 135, 197, 198–199
Hoerberger, Felix, 19
Humphrey, Doris, 39
Hungarian State Folk Ensemble, 109
Hungary, 9, 53
Hutchinson, John and Anthony Smith, 5
Hutzul (Region of the Ukraine), 41

Igazah nisf as–sinah (film), 152

Ilieva, Anna, 28
Imagined Communities, 161
"In the field." *See* Folk dance "in the field"
Ingres, Jean Auguste Domenique, 141
Indians: in Mexico, 88–91, 100–101; dances of, 96, 97, 100
International Encyclopedia of Dance, 66, 178
Invented Tradition, 15, 18, 135, 145, 156, 198–199
Iran and Iranians, 5, 10, 11, 24, 30, 39, 68, 139, 140, 163, 228, 229, 234n.9. *See also* Mahalli Dancers
Isareva, Margarita, 66, 70
Islam, 139–140, 153, 199–200, 229, 243–244n.5
Issa, Mahmoud, 127
Istanbul, 196, 206, 215, 219
Ivancan, Ivan, 12, 43, 44, 117, 125, 234n.10
Ivory Coast, 25

Jalisco (choreography), 40, 82–83, **84**, 97, 102, 106, 238–239n.2, 241n.1
Jamal, 137, 247n.5
Jankovic, Ljubica and Danica, 44
Jarabe Tapatio (Mexican Hat Dance), 41, 83, 84
Jewish Suite (choreography), 66, **67**, 70
Jews, 49; in Croatia, 112; in Iran, 203; in Soviet Union, 66
Jordan, 162, 200
Jozo Vlahovic (Youth organization and dance company), 115–116, 240–241n.8

Kalmuks (Kalmyks), 30, 68
Karras, Athan, 181, 189, 190
Kazakhstan, 52, 65
Kealiinohomoku, Joann, 18–20
Kemalism, 196, 206, 207–209, 210, 211–213, 221, 247n.1
Keyder, Caglar, 208
Khomeini, Ruhollah, 2
Khorumi (choreography), 76, 77, 80
Kirghizia, 52

Kirov Ballet, 55, 61, 78
Kisselgoff, Anna, 70
Kodaly, Zoltan, 44, 243n.9
KOLO (Serbian State Folk Dance Ensemble), 6, 8, 22 (table 1), 23, 27, 39, 113, 180, 225, 233n.4, 240 nn.2&8, 246n.7; and Gypsies, 8, 9, 23; and Slavic Muslims, 8, 9
Koran (Qur'an), 139
Kosovo, 2
Koutev, Philip, 9, 49–50, 112. *See also* Bulgarian State Folk Ensemble
Krauze, Enrique, 88, 100
Kunanbaeva, Alma, 7, 52, 66
Kurds: in Iran, 11, 27, 171, 203, 204, 223; in Turkey, 204, 207, 223

La Argentina, 91
Ladarke (choreography), 108, 109
LADO, Croatian State Ensemble of Folk Songs and Dances, 5, 11, 14, 15, 17, 21, 22 (table 1), 26, 33, 35, 39, 43, 45, 46–48, 50, 51, 53, 54, 103, 108–125, 129, 160, 228, 233n.4, 235n.4, 242n.2, 246n.7; costumes, 113, 123; dancers, 120–121; finances, 123–124, 125; history of, 114–117; music, 50, 109, 121–123; repertoire, 118–119, 124–125. *See also* Ljevakovic, Zvonko
Lane, Edward, 132
Lange, Roderyk, 181
Lebanon, 110, 162
Lewis, Bernard, 203, 210
Life is a Game (La Vida es Juego; choreography), 25, 98, 100, 102
Lincoln, Bruce, 202
Ljevakovic, Zvonko, 14, 15, 26, 33, 35, 36, 37, 39, 45, 50, 51, 110, 112–114, 117, 118, 119, 121, 237n.11, 238n.14, 241n.1. *See also* LADO
Lopez, Salvador Lopez, 94
Louis XIV, 4, 227, 233n.1
Lyceum, 180, 185, 191, 246n.8

Macedonia and Macedonians, 172, 177; dances of, 156, 163; music of, 164
Madcz, Laszlo, 9

268 Index

Mahalli Dancers (former Iranian State Dance Ensemble), 10–11, 22 (table 1), 34–35, 39, 44, 47, 51, 52, 54, 55, 101, 119, 202, 203, 229, 230
Marginalization, 11
Matchette, Vilma, 189, 239n.2, 246n.8
Mavropoulos, George, 166, 181–182, 187
Mayas, Los (choreography), 100
Mazo, Margarita, 21
Mazowse (Polish State Folk Ensemble), 15
Mestizaje, 88–91
Mestizos: dances of, 100; in Mexico, 11, 88, 89, 90, 97
Mevlevi (Mowlawiyah) dervishes. *See* Sufis
Mexican-Americans, 3, 86, 160, 161, 190, 229, 230, 231, 239n.2
Mexico and Mexicans, 1, 2, 10, 28, 30, 32, 39, 40–41, 54, 68, 82–107, 227, 228, 229. *See also* Ballet Folklorico de Mexico
Mexico City, 82, 89, 91, 92, 94, 95, 105, 107
Mitchell, Timothy, 131–135
Modern dance, 33, 35, 91, 92, 93, 96, 97, 98, 225, 227, 230
Modernization, 208, 209, 218
Mohammad Reza Pahlavi (Shah), 201, 230
Moiseyev, Igor, 6, 9, 10, 14–15, 20, 21, 24, 25, 30, 32, 33, 35, 37, 39, 45, 52, 55, 60, 80–81, 83, 92, 96, 99, 100, 118, 136, 146, 147, 148, 181, 182, 226, 229, 230; choreography of, 75–77; life and career of, 66–68. *See also* Moiseyev Dance Company
Moiseyev Dance Company (State Academic Ensemble of Folk Dances of the Peoples of the Soviet Union), 2, 4, 10, 15, 17, 18, 21, 22 (table 1), 24, 28, 29, 33, 35, 39, 40, 42, 44, 48, 49, 51, 52, 53, 54, 55, 57–81, 82, 84, 85, 86, 101, 109, 114, 115, 116, 118, 119, 120, 129, 145, 155, 156, 181, 182, 217, 225, 228, 234n.10, 239n.6, 240nn.9&2, 248n.4; costumes, 79–80; dancers, 77–79;

music, 79, 85; repertoire, 75–77. *See also* Moiseyev, Igor
Moldava and Moldavians, 14, 63, 76; dances of, 14, 76, 77
Moldavian Suite (choreography), 76, 80
Moreska (dance and choreography), 46, 47
Morocco (Carolina Varga Dinicu), 141, 152, 154, 156, 159, 161, 243nn.4&5, 247n.17
Morris, Mark, 38
Mottahedeh, Roy, 201
Moustafa, Tamir, 139–140
Muhammad (Prophet), 139
Music, 38, 48–50, 228, 239n.6, 243n.10; Ballet Folklorico, 85, 104–105; Dora Stratou Greek Dances Theatre, 163–164, 187; in Egypt, 106, 127–128, 159–160, 245n.18; LADO, 50, 109, 121–122; Moiseyev, 79, 85; Turkish State Folk Dance Ensemble, 193–194, 221
Muslims: in Greece, 172; in Iran, 200; in the Philippines, 2, 9, 25; in Serbia, 8, 9; in Soviet Union, 62, 64–65, 68, 85; in Turkey, 170, 171, 200; in Yugoslavia, 199

Na Baniji Bubanj Bije (choreography), 11–12, 125, 234n.10
Nahachewsky, Andriy, 16, 18, 20–21, 35, 41, 235n.3
Nash, Manning, 90
Nasser, Abdel Gamal, 134, 136, 137, 139, 144
Nation-state, 1, 26, 28, 40, 41, 81, 202, 225, 227, 230, 232, 233n.2
National Folk(loric) Troup (Firqa Qawmiyya), 129, 144, 152, 153, 154, 155, 159; costumes, 154, 161
Nationalism, 5–12, 22, 27; in Croatia, 113, 115; in Egypt, 134, 145–146; in Greece, 168–169, 207, 224, 225, 230, 231; in Iran, 198, 200–203; theories of, 197–200, 232n.2, 247n.2; in Turkey, 194, 197, 198, 203–211
Ness, Sally Ann, 233n.2
Night on Bald Mountain (choreography), 76–77, 81

Nil, Folkloric Troup, El- (Festival of the Nile), 144, 158–160
Nureyev, Rudolph, 78

Obregon, Luis Felipe, 91
Old City Quadrille (choreography), 26, 70, **71**, 77, 79, 85
Olmecas, Los (choreography), 100, 106
Omsk Folk Dance Company, 61, 73
Opsaj–diri (choreography), 124
Orientalism, 131, 141, 167, 199, 209, 220
Ottoman Empire, 126, 130, 156, 167, 170–177, 178, 196, 200, 203, 204, 205, 206, 208, 209, 210, 211; Christians in, 171, 172, 173–174; in Greece, 169–177, 246n.5; Greeks in, 176; Muslims in, 171, 219, 220, 223
Ozbudun, Ergun, 140, 206
Ozturkmen, Arzu, 22, 213, 214

Pala, Senasi, 193
Parallel traditions, 17–22, 70, 110, 214, 215–217, 226, 227
Participatory (category of dance), 20–21
Particularization, 14, 21
Partisans (choreography), 76, 77, 80
Partizansko Kolo (choreography), 124
Peasants, 26, 32–34, 35, 99, 110–111, 118, 136, 178, 182, 191, 192, 204, 206, 210, 211, 212, 216, 230, 232, 238n.14, 241n.1
Period Eye, 167–169
Persians, 11, 200–203, 234n.9. *See also* Iran and Iranians
Petrovic, Ankica, 7, 236n.7
Phelan, Peggy, 23, 168–169
Philippines and Filipinos, 2, 10, 28, 30, 32, 41, 45, 68, 86, 228; Muslims in, 2, 25; Tagalog-speakers in, 11, 25, 41
Pirin Ensemble (dance company), 109
Piyatnitsky Chorus, 55, 61, 73
Plaka (district of Athens), 165, 173, 178, 191
Platter Dance (choreography), 76

Poland, 12, 14; dances of, 14. *See also* Mazowse
Poltava (region in the Ukraine), 41–42, 57
Polyanka (choreography), 77
Posavski Plesovi (Dances of Posavina; choreography), 41, 45, 115, 124
Potocnik, Bozidar, 112
Poulton, Hugh, 173, 207
Pratt, Nicola, 135
Preovolis, Peter, 190
Presentational (category of dance), 20
Prevots, Naima, 40, 68, 238n.1
Prigorski Plesovi (Dances of Prigorje; choreography), 41, ***111***
Progonoplexia, 175

Quetzales of Puebla (choreography), 96, 100

Raftis, Alkis, 165, 166–167, 169, 172, 175, 177, 178, 182, 184–185, 186, 187, 188, 190, 191, 192, 246n.8. *See also* Dora Stratrou Greek Dances Theatre
Ramazin, Boris, 155
Raqs Sharqi. *See* Belly dance
Red Army Chorus, 61
Reda, Ali, 147, 152
Reda, Mahmoud, 22, 39, 42, 135, 136, 137, 144–152, 156, 158, 161, 162, 229, 245n.13, 248n.4; choreography of, 150–152; life and career of, 144–148. *See also* Reda Dance Troupe
Reda Dance Troupe, 15, 16, 25, 32, 42, 129, 136, 142, 144, 145, 147–148, 153, 154, 155, 158, 162, 237n.10; costumes, 154–155; dancers, 153; music, 154, 158, 161. *See also* Reda, Mahmoud
Repertoire, 45–46, 228, 230; Ballet Folklorico, 82, 99–103; Bulgarian State Folk Ensemble, 48–50; Dora Stratou Greek Dances Theatre, 169, 173, 185–186; in Egypt, 150–152; LADO, 109, 118–119, 124–125; Moiseyev, 75–77; Turkish State Folk Dance Ensemble, 218–220

Index

Representation, 1, 2, 9, 21–26, 30, 32–37, 40, 80, 85, 93, 168–169, 191, 202, 215, 217, 218, 219, 222, 224–232
Research, 42–44, 66, 92, 97, 212–214, 216, 226, 228
Revolucion, La (The Revolution; choreography), 25, 94, **95**, 97, 103, 105
Road to the Dance (choreography), 66, 78
Rombos-Levides, Marica, 13
Root, Deborah, 157
Rumania and Rumanians, 12, 52, 169, 172, 173, 205. *See also* Vlah
Rumi, 202
Rural populations. *See* Peasants
Russia and Russians, 11, 31, 59, 61–66, 75–76, 78, 160–161, 200, 225. *See also* Soviet Union
Russian Suite (choreography), 75

Said, Edward, 131
Saleh, Magda, 16, 42, 141–142, 159
Sandoval, Gema, 48, 87, 97, 104, 241n.3
Saudi Arabia, 24, 162, 225
Seasons, The (choreography), 77
Segal, Lewis, 34, 93
Senegal, 25
Serbia and Serbians, 11, 12, 112, 169, 172, 174, 175, 205, 208, 233n.6, 234n.10; Gypsies in, 8, 9; Muslims in, 8, 9
Shaffie, Abdul Rahman Al-, 152, 158, 159
Shah of Iran. *See* Mohammad Reza Pahlavi
Shahnameh, 200, 201, 202
Silent Dance of Vrlika (Vrlicko Kolo; choreography), 115, 117, 124
Skovran, Olga, 39, 124. *See also* KOLO
Slavonsko Kolo (Slavonian Reel; choreography), **113**, 115, 124
Slovaks, 27, 231
Smith, Anthony D., 91, 197
Smotra Folklora, 236nn.5&7
Sokcic, Nevenka (Nena), 35, 116, 121, 238n.14

Sokolow, Anna, 91
Solorzano-Foppa, Julio, 92, 93, 95, 104, 106
Sones de Michoacan (choreography), 92, 97, **98**, 99, 101, 103
Soviet Union (former USSR), 2, 4, 11, 12, 27, 31, 39, 51–81, 134, 135, 145, 155, 200, 214, 215, 225, 227, 228; Soviet Bloc, 9, 45, 67, 145, 169, 226, 230; Tatars in, 2, 30, 68, 78. *See also* Moiseyev Dance Company
Spanish Colonial Suite (choreography), 25
Square dance, 40
Stereotypification, 38–41, 70, 228; in Ballet Folklorico, 94–95
Stick Dance (Tahtib; choreography and dance), 142, 244n.11
Stirling, Paul, 205
Stokes, Martin, 194, 247–248n.10
Stratos, Nikolas, 179
Stratou, Dora, 37, 44, 165, 176, 179–184, 192. *See also* Dora Stratou Greek Dance Theatre
Strinati, Dominic, 30
Sufis, 47, 127, 128, 186, 244n.4
Swift, Mary Grace, 23
Sybine, Hypolite (Hipolito Zybine), 91

Tajikistan and Tajiks, 62, 65, 68, 200, 234n.9
Taliban, 2
Tanec (Macedonian State Folk Dance Ensemble), 113, 233n.4, 240n.2
Tannoura Egyptian Heritage Folklore Troupe, El-, 126–129, 144, 160
Tarascos, Los (choreography), 97, 102, 103, 105
Tarima de Tixtla (choreography), 103, 240n.9
Tatars, 2, 30, 68, 78
Tavernas, 37, 165, 178, 189
Terry, Walter, 89
Three Shepherds (choreography), 77
Tinikling (dance), 41
Tito, Josip Broz, 115, 124, 199

Tlacotalpan's Festival (Veracruz; choreography), 24, 41, 83–84, 97, 101, 103, 106, 241n.1
Tlaxcala's Carnival (choreography), 95, 98, 103
Todorova, Maria, 173–174
Traditional dance. *See* Folk dance; Folk dance "in the field"
Trimillos, Ricardo, 11
Tsing, Anna Lowenhaupt, 11
Tudor, Antony, 39
Turan, Mustefa, 52, 215–216, 217, 219, 220, 221. *See also* Turkish State Folk Dance Ensemble
Turganbaeva, Mukarram, 39, 55. *See also* Bakhor
Turino, Thomas, 18, 74
Turkey, 5, 10, 68, 139, 140, 163, 176, 193–223, 227; and Turkish Language, 186, 187, 206, 209
Turk Halk Oyunlari (book by Cemil Demirsipahi), 213
Turkish State Folk Dance Ensemble (Turk Devlet Halk Danslari Toprogu), 5, 44, 52, 101, 168, 186, 193–197, 207, 209, 211, 213, 216–223, 230; costumes, 221–222; dancers, 220–221; finances, 218, 222; music, 221; repertoire, 218–220
Turkishness, 193, 203–207, 209, 210, 218, 222, 223
Turkmenia and Turkomen, 12, 34–35, 65, 234n.9; in Iran, 203
Turks, 170, 171; in Bulgaria, 9, 49, 234n.7; in Greece, 176

Ukraine, The and Ukrainians, 14, 57, 61, 62, 63; in Canada, 41; dances of, 14, 26, 57, 77
Ukrainian State Folk Dance Ensemble, 26, 29, 61, 109
Umm-Kulthum, 137, 138, 154, 159
United States: folk dance in, 19, 40, 68, 215, 225, 235n.4, 238n.1
Unmarked, 167–169, 232
Urban, Greg and Joel Sherzer, 14, 28, 30
Ustasha (Croatian Nazi Party, 1941–1945), 117

Uzbekistan and Uzbeks, 12, 14, 39, 61, 62, 63, 64, 65, 68, 76, 78, 85, 234n.9. *See also* Bakhor

Vargas, Delfina, 94, 106
Veracruz (choreography), 24, 41, 83, 97, 101, 103, 106, 241n.1
Vida es Juego, La (Life is a Game; choreography), 25, 98, 100, 102
Village, villagers. *See* Peasants
Virsky, Pavel, 26. *See also* Ukrainian State Folk Dance Ensemble
Vlah, 172, 173, 187, 190
Voladores ("flying" dancers), 47
Vrlicko Kolo (Silent Dance from Vrlika; choreography), 115, 117, 124

Wahhab, Abdel Al-, 134, 154, 158
Waldeen, 91
Wedding in the Isthmus of Tehantepec (Boda en el Istmo de Tehuantepec; choreography), 24, 97, 102, 106
Wedding in Huasteca (Boda en la Huasteca), 24, 102
Woodhouse, C. M., 172

Yaqui Deer Dance (Danza del Venado; choreography), 24, 94, 97, **100**, 102, 103
Young Turks, 205, 206
Yucatan: Danzon y Jarana (choreography), 103
Yugoslavia (former), 11, 12, 28, 30, 31, 111–112, 119, 199, 228, 231, 233n.4

Zacatecas (choreography), 102
Zafra en Tamaulipas (choreography), 102
Zagreb, 117, 119, 120, 121, 123, 125, 236n.7
Zemlje (Croatian intellectual and artistic movement), 33, 112
Zemotsovsky, Izaly, 7, 66
Zhok (choreography), 77

About the Author

Anthony Shay holds a M.A. in Folklore and Mythology from UCLA and a Ph.D. in Dance History and Theory from the University of California-Riverside. From 1996 to 1999, he was a board member of the Congress on Research in Dance (CORD). In the 1970s and 1980s, he was four times awarded a National Endowment for the Arts Choreographic Fellowship. In 1990, he was honored as an NEA Artist in Residence, La Napoule, France. He was named in 1998 as one of eight outstanding California choreographers by the James Irvine Foundation in Dance, and in 1999 he was awarded by the Dance Resource Center of Greater Los Angeles for outstanding achievement in staging traditional dance. He authored Choreophobia: Solo Improvised Dance in the Iranian World (1999) and has contributed numerous articles and papers on traditional and Middle Eastern dance.